THE YEARS OF PROMISE

By the same author

Novels

SCISSORS
SAILS OF SUNSET
THE LOVE RACK
LITTLE MRS. MANINGTON
SAGUSTO
DAVID AND DIANA
INDIANA JANE
PAMELA'S SPRING SONG
HAVANA BOUND
BARGAIN BASEMENT
SPEARS AGAINST US
PILGRIM COTTAGE
THE GUESTS ARRIVE
VOLCANO
VICTORIA FOUR-THIRTY
THEY WANTED TO LIVE
ONE SMALL CANDLE
SO IMMORTAL A FLOWER
EIGHT FOR ETERNITY
A TERRACE IN THE SUN
THE REMARKABLE YOUNG MAN
LOVE IS LIKE THAT
WIDE IS THE HORIZON
A FLIGHT OF BIRDS
THE PILGRIM COTTAGE OMNIBUS

Miscellaneous

GONE RUSTIC
GONE RAMBLING
GONE AFIELD
GONE SUNWARDS
AND SO TO BATH
AND SO TO AMERICA
AND SO TO ROME
HALF WAY
PORTAL TO PARADISE
ONE YEAR OF LIFE
THE GRAND CRUISE
SELECTED POEMS (1910–1960)
A TALE OF YOUNG LOVERS (POETIC DRAMA)
THE DIARY OF RUSSELL BERESFORD
ALFRED FRIPP: A BIOGRAPHY
A MAN AROSE
THE GROWING BOY: AN AUTOBIOGRAPHY. VOL. I (1892–1908)

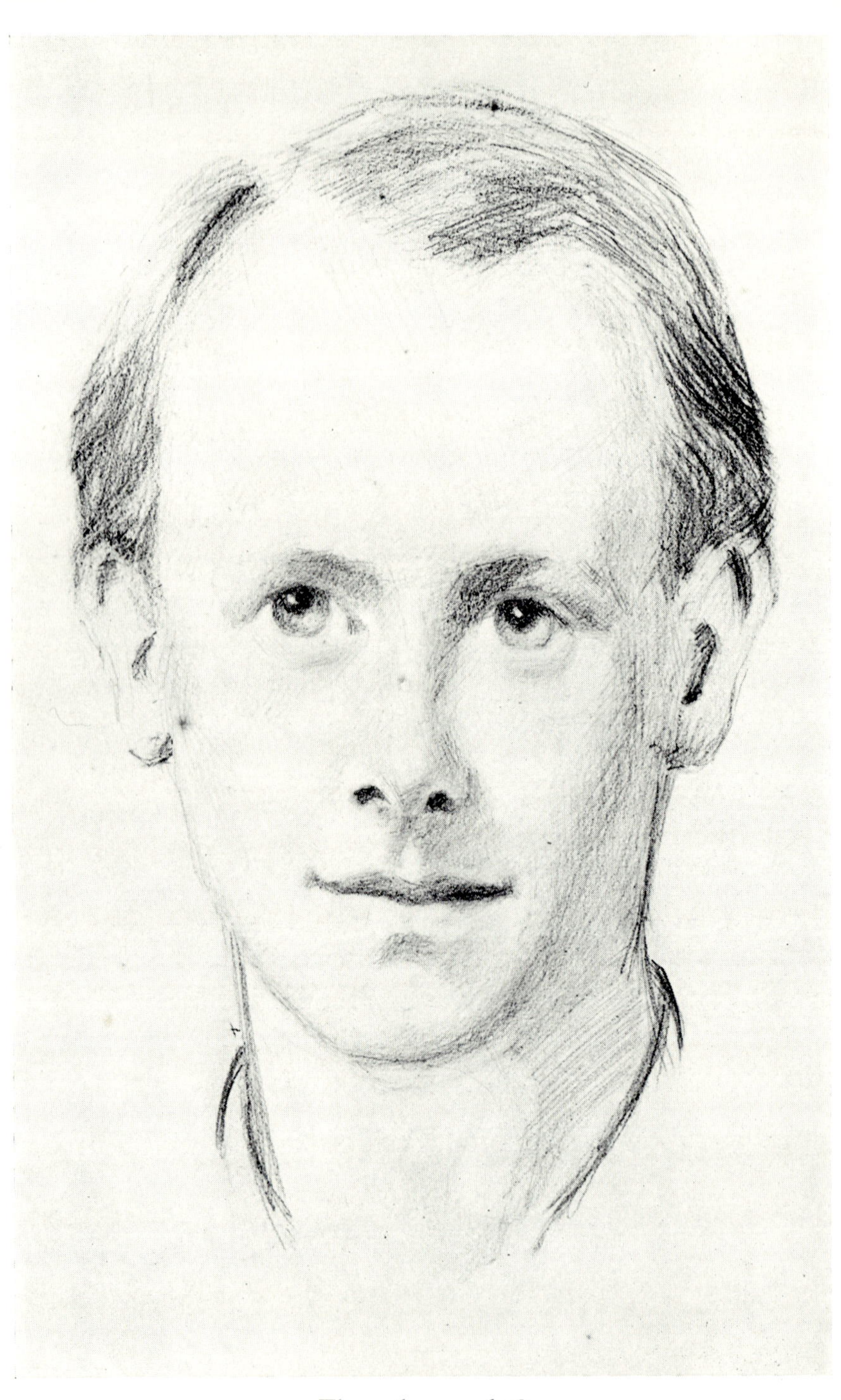

The author, aged 18
(*Portrait by Helen Stiebel*)

THE YEARS OF PROMISE

Being the second book of an Autobiography

1908–1919

by

CECIL ROBERTS

"Reader, loe here is a well-meaning Booke. I desire therein to be delineated in mine own genuine, simple and ordinarie fashion, without contention, art or study; for it is my selfe I pourtray."—Montaigne.

HODDER AND STOUGHTON

First printed 1968

SBN 340 04477 2

Printed in Great Britain for Hodder and Stoughton Limited,
St. Paul's House, Warwick Lane, London, E.C.4,
by The Camelot Press Ltd., London and Southampton

CONTENTS

ILLUSTRATIONS

[1] Duncan Macpherson [2] National Portrait Gallery
[3] Russell and Company [4] Raphael Tuck

PREFACE

In *The Growing Boy*, the first volume of this autobiography, I dealt with the years from my birth in Nottingham in 1892 up to the age of fifteen. My father dominated those formative years of a sensitive and precocious boy. His passionate engagement with his Leicestershire ancestry introduced me to not a little history of my country and my family, reaching back to the fifteenth century and coming down to the nineteenth that pressed so hardly upon my parents.

I take up my story in this second volume when, on the verge of sixteen, suddenly deprived of my delightful father, I faced a bleak future. The next twelve years that engage this narrative were years of struggle but they were also years of promise. A young, caged lion broke the horrid bars and attained a wider world. Looking back, I see that I was endowed with an irrepressible gaiety of spirit, intense ambition and self-confidence. Even so, I could wish for no boy the handicaps with which I had to contend; and yet, possibly because of them, I profited from this discipline of necessity.

A word on the literary technique of this narrative. In the retrospect of seventy-five years I have seen the end as well as the beginning of many things, the mutability that governs our destiny. I have not strictly adhered, therefore, to a chronological sequence in regard to events and persons. Often I have completed the portrait. There is another aspect in which I have tried to enlarge the technique of autobiography. I have experienced much irritation with historians and biographers who are loose or indifferent about dates and economic details. One searches through page after page in order to find in what year a certain event took place; and one is repeatedly surprised by the financial aspect. The person who is the subject of the story suddenly appears in a luxurious limousine, having recently lived in a back street, goes cruising on his yacht, or moves from a drab suburb to fashionable Mayfair. When reading biographies one often comes upon an almost royal secrecy about the financial basis, the sums inherited, received or earned. This reticence is curious in a nation that allows no official to reveal a man's income but blatantly publishes what he dies worth. I do not feel I am exercising an unseemly curiosity when I confess that I would like to know how much money was spent by the admiring Maecenas who financed the lavish holiday tours of the Gladstones, and, recalling how Carlyle insisted that a Civil List pension must be obtained for poor young Alfred Tennyson, what sum in royalty earnings enabled the poet to build his lordly Aldworth. If we are to read about the illness that pulled down our hero why not about the financial success that set him up?

With this in mind I have been frank, and I hope not tiresome, concerning the economic facts of my life, particularly in the years of struggle when the additional pound could effect such a change in one's life and circumstances. Also, in an age of unstable monetary values and social status, I hope the details will prove of interest.

There is one other thing for which I seek the indulgence of the reader. My friends credit me with a phenomenal memory. Even so, I know the curious aberrations that afflict one in the passage of time. Considering the hundreds of names, places and events in my story it would be vain to hope that I have not fallen into error. My task has been made heavier by the loss of diaries and papers in the bombing of London. I have tirelessly sought verification and I wish to express my thanks to numerous persons who have responded so generously to my queries. I shall be grateful for corrections. One of the pleasures of writing this form of narrative is the interest and kindness it evokes in others. I am particularly indebted to the Rt. Hon. Lord Balfour of Inchrye; Dame Laura Knight, R.A.; Capt. Alec Lacy, R.N.; my cousin, Mr. Walter Roberts; Capt. S. W. Roskill, R.N.; the Naval Librarian, Ministry of Defence; Mr. George Madddocks; and the staffs of the London Library, and the British Council Library, Rome.

C. R.

Rome, 1967–8

CHAPTER ONE

The Bright Horizon

I

The tragedy that overtook me in 1908 on my father's early death, making me the responsible head of the household at fifteen, did not overwhelm me. It was a challenge to which I responded. With a mother and a home to support, my ambition was intensified. Not for one moment did I consider defeat. Just how I was going to triumph over these adverse circumstances I could not decide. It might seem presumptuous for an office-boy, his weekly wage compassionately increased from eight shillings to seventeen, to entertain any extravagant dreams but entertain them I did. With a head just above starvation level I looked out on a promising world. Youth is a great legacy. It starts off with illimitable faith, believing that in a just world industry and merit will be rewarded. It carries no memories, no disturbing comparisons. The best is yet to be, the morning glory is about one; these are the years of promise.

I was blessed with a mother who never indulged in retrospect or self-pity. She was destined to face a lonely widowhood for the next eighteen years. The young have no conception of the grey bogy of loneliness. They are too full of ambitious dreams to be able to conceive the burden of the losses imposed by time and by the growing silence of the darkening scene. Only once do I recall my mother commenting on her lonely lot. I fear I brushed it aside with the incomprehension of youth.

At first I, too, knew loneliness. There was no rout of grandparents, brothers and sisters, of uncles and aunts. In any case I had always been an individualist. I could find no companion of my own age in our working-class world, where the only interests were cricket, football and girls, where no house harboured a bookshelf; a world of the cloth cap over the dormant brain. I learned thus early that because of my temperament and tastes my path through life would always be a lonely one, however outwardly gregarious. My father's death left me completely stranded. Our relationship had been very close. Despite his strictness he was a warm companion. He ceaselessly fed my mind from the richness of his own, and the reins upon me, though taut, were adjusted to my nature. Delicate, high-spirited, neurotically sensitive as I was, my father's firm and calm guidance had never failed me. In the coming years I realised increasingly how my boyhood had been blessed by such a companion. His very incompetence in confronting a harsh world only endeared him more to me. His eccentricities were lovable and his gift of tranquil contentment was such as few of us are endowed with. *Who is the happy warrior? Who is he . . . ?* Wordsworth's query always evokes his memory.

I was now the monarch of my domain. Small as it was I knew bright happiness. I loved my attic room, furnished with my few treasures. There, uninterrupted, I planned my campaign. I was to become a great poet, at least a great author. I walked intoxicated with my discoveries in realms of gold. Milton, Shelley, Keats, Tennyson, and above all Wordsworth, sailed into my ken. I was enthralled by Macaulay, by the grand march of his prose, the masterly array of his argument. And then Gibbon's vast survey, *The Decline and Fall of the Roman Empire*, held me entranced. He had been a favourite of my father who had tried to tempt me with excerpts, but without success. I had been too young at fourteen to appreciate the fare he offered. Now in my expanding world I discovered the goldmine in the six volumes on my shelf. Ruskin I found too dogmatic, there was a note of exaggeration in everything he advocated, Carlyle too craggy. Emerson delighted me with his smooth narration, and, picked up for sixpence, doubtfully, a copy of *The Autocrat of the Breakfast Table* by Oliver Wendell Holmes seduced me with its charm. It gave me a new portrait of Americans. I had associated them with Jumbo the Elephant, Colonel Cody, the Red Indians of Fenimore Cooper's Wild West, the assassinated Lincoln of the Gettysburg Speech (memorised at school) and the miracle-man, Thomas Edison, who had given us the phonograph.

Every day I tumbled upon some fresh wonder. There was Hare's *Walks in Rome*. It was in two volumes in the sixpenny tub outside a secondhand bookseller's. They could not be bought separately. A shilling was an enormous outlay but a considerate bookseller let me take away the two volumes on payment of sixpence one week and sixpence the next. It was my first and last experience of the instalment plan, against which I had been warned by my cash-down minded father. In conjunction with Gibbon and guided by Hare, I walked all over the seven hills of Rome. Many years later I was dismayed when Somerset Maugham told me that he had stayed with Hare and that he was a prissy old maid who had ruled out all the words praising God in the Bible. "God is a gentleman, and he would find so much adulation distasteful," said Hare.

My mother, alarmed at my nocturnal hours as I lay in bed reading, seeing the light under my door, often called, "Put out that light and go to sleep!" Rebellious, I cheated her by putting a carpet along the bottom of the door. "You'll ruin your eyesight!" she protested. By Fate's kindness that prophecy was not fulfilled. Sixty years later I could still read a telephone directory without spectacles.

Dismayed at first by its smallness, I came to love the little house to which we had moved, one of five tucked away behind tiny gardens, in the lower part of Nottingham, bordering the Trent. It was a nest that nourished my ambitious spirit. At No. 1 there was a remarkable couple, Mr. and Mrs. Erasmus Horsley. We had a great bond. Mrs. Horsley was a dictionary addict like myself. She would appear with a slip of paper in her hand. "Do you know the word pusillanimous!" she would ask. "Yes." "Spell it!" I spelt it correctly. "What does it mean?" "It means fainthearted." She would go away defeated. But sometimes she caught me out and crowed with delight. In turn I visited her as she sat with her husband in their little garden. "Here he comes!" the crippled Erasmus would shout in his cracked voice. I produced my word, and sometimes I crowed. She swore by *Collins' Dictionary*, I by Dr. Annandale's.

Mrs. Horsley enjoyed some local fame. A tall woman, in her sixties, with a beautiful head and clear blue eyes, her great asset was her speaking voice. It was richly toned. Her English was flawless. Because of her appearance and speech she was regarded as the local Ellen Terry, being the same age as that actress was at the height of her renown. The early years of the century had simple pleasures. The cinema and the phonograph had not yet become sources of popular entertainment. Ladies and gentlemen 'obliged' by singing at the piano. Only the upper classes travelled, having the means. A person who had been to Paris was looked upon with wonder tinged with suspicion of his morals. I regarded with awe an elderly spinster who lived in Geneva and came to visit her brother in Nottingham. Had she come from the North Pole she could not have seemed more adventurous. She stunned me by saying that she could see Mont Blanc, the highest mountain in Europe, from her windows. She spent the summer in a Swiss alpine village rather like the one I had seen for threepence, with its mechanical thunderstorm, in the White City Exhibition at Trent Bridge.

In the winter season the Mechanics Hall was visited by a gentleman who gave travel lectures. He stood in front of a large white screen and talked. He pressed a clicker in his hand and projected coloured slides. We cried in admiration of their beauty. He pointed out the sights with a long stick and described them. One travelogue was called 'Eternal Rome'. Primed by Gibbon and Hare, I sat entranced. I made a vow that one day I would visit Rome. How, I knew not. If someone had told me that a time would come when I should live there, I would have thought he was crazy. Sometimes the picture came on the screen upside down. The lecturer always had a little joke for this mishap. If you sat near the lantern there was a varnishy smell from the hot tin. The slides were hand-coloured. We often surmised they were overdone. It seemed impossible that any sky or sea could be so blue.

A few yards away from us lived a little Wesleyan minister. He sometimes lectured on his travels. He could put the letters F.R.G.S. after his name on the billboard. Once a year he conducted a party for one month to visit the Holy Land. Only the chapel magnates could afford to go. My friend Mr. Lane, the baker, who called me 'Professor', went with his wife, having saved for twenty years. They were never quite the same again. We looked on them as a poor Muslim looks on a pilgrim who has been to Mecca. Whenever anyone spoke of Mr. Lane he added "—who's been to the Holy Land." The Wesleyan minister always contrived to say in his sermon, "When I was in the Holy Land . . ." His congregation smiled. They knew it would come sooner or later.

Mrs. Horsley's personal history was remarkable. She was a woman of courage and resource. Left a widow with three children she became manageress of a small restaurant. Then one day she married again. Her husband, Erasmus Horsley, was a little hunchback with a club foot, a high-pitched voice and a tempestuous disposition. Everyone marvelled at this incongruous pair; she, tall and handsome, he, twisted and irascible. "I married him for his intellect and to give my children a father," she said. It was a completely happy marriage.

Passionate Liberals, they worshipped Mr. Asquith, the new Prime Minister. They canvassed and worked for the local member. It was around the time when Lloyd George's 'People's Budget' with its proposed taxes on land values shook the country. The House of Lords threw out the Bill, which led to the 1910 Election.

In earlier days Mrs. Horsley had possessed a fine voice and was in demand on concert platforms. When her voice began to fail she took up reciting. This was the era of public reciters. Some of them were famous and toured the country reciting from Shakespeare, Dickens, Scott, Longfellow, Kipling and a number of minor poets who produced popular verses for recital. The era closed with the popularity of *Gunga Din* by Kipling, and *The Highwayman* by Alfred Noyes. Bransby Williams toured the music halls with recitals in costume from Dickens. A host of amateurs emulated him. Mrs. Erasmus Horsley was as good as any of the professionals. I once heard her when she was nearly eighty recite *The First Settler's Story* (pathos), *Gone with a Handsomer Man* (humour), *The Prime Minister* (political). She was in demand for some thirty years. Her recitals were given at bazaars, church and chapel mothers' meetings, and political teas. She had an impressive platform presence, and with her aristocratic bearing brought a touch of the great world into the drab lives of her working-class audiences. Her verses usually had a moral. There was a warning to those with sharp tongues, who relented too late—

> Boys flying kites haul in their white-winged birds—
> You can't do that when you're flying words!

Returning triumphant from a recital, she would set the supper table while her adoring hunchback husband would ask—"How many encores, my dear? Three! Bless you, my love!"

She seized me early, noting my precocity. I was worthy to converse with Erasmus, who was well-read, witty—and acid. We debated while she glowed with enjoyment. It was she who had discovered the small house to let in this row of villas when my father's death compelled us to move to more modest quarters. She was delighted to have us as neighbours. I was in and out of their house. They had a good library, freely at my disposal. There were the dictionary debates and, above all, there was Erasmus's intellectual conversation. He was a good Greek and Latin scholar. In the summer he spent much of his time in a wicker chair in the tiny garden. I was often detained by this warm-hearted couple for a 'snack' which had been prepared indoors. I took to them my poems and articles. They were an appreciative audience. It was at this period that I was deep in Wordsworth. I had plodded through *The Excursion*, digging out the jewels in that desert of verse. My own verses took on a Wordsworthian tinge. I read about the little group of which William was the centre at Grasmere and Rydal. I read his sister Dorothy's *Diaries*, noting how her prose became his poetry. "She gave me eyes, she gave me ears." I familiarised myself with the topography of the Lake District.

One day in that summer of 1908 my two friends overwhelmed me with an astonishing proposition. They were going to take a holiday at Ambleside on Lake Windermere. They invited me to become their guest for two weeks. I could not believe what I heard. There was a touch of romance in the foundation of this holiday. Erasmus had a sister who lived in San Francisco. She had married an American millionaire. It was on an allowance she sent them that they now lived in modest retirement. Every year the sister paid a visit to them and entertained them. This year, detained by illness, she sent them a sum of money for a holiday. I knew that they enjoyed 'private means'. In those days 'private means' or 'reduced circumstances' carried prestige in the eyes of the weekly wage-earners. The sister in California was behind their independence. And now, sharing their good fortune, I was to be their guest on a Lakeland holiday.

The great day of departure arrived. They had taken lodgings in a cottage in Ambleside. For two whole weeks I lived in paradise. Sometimes we made excursions together by horse-drawn charabancs that visited the chief glories of mountain, mere and valley. But as Erasmus could not walk, on other days I explored alone. I trod where Southey, Coleridge, De Quincey and Wordsworth had trodden. I even saw Brantwood, in which Ruskin had passed his sad last years, intermittently insane. The poems my mother had taught me became realities for I visited Dungeon Ghyll, where The Idle Shepherd-Boys had played on their 'pipes of sycamore', Gowbarrow Park, of the dancing daffodils that flashed upon 'that inward eye which is the bliss of solitude', and, after visiting the poet's grave at Grasmere, I went to Dove Cottage. This was the most ecstatic moment in all those thrilling days. I found the little garden hut on the mountainside, with its view towards the lake, and there I recited Wordsworth's poem, written in 1802 for Mary Hutchinson, before the poet departed to bring her to Dove Cottage as his wife. It was a poem my father had made me recite to practise the run-over of the lines. "At—'thou rocky' take breath for the turn of the verses until you come to,—'grandeur rare'," he said.

> Farewell, thou little Nook of mountain-ground,
> Thou rocky corner in the lowest stair
> Of that magnificent temple which doth bound
> One side of our whole vale with grandeur rare;
> Sweet garden-orchard, eminently fair,
> The loveliest spot that man hath ever found.

The historic cottage was now open to tourists. You bought a ticket at a small village shop almost opposite, and an old lady, the custodian, let you in. She often left her charges to attend a customer, and I found that at noon she locked up the cottage until three o'clock. This gave me the opportunity to fulfil a desire I nourished. I returned one day about noon and at the closing time hid myself in the garden hut. The visitors gone, the gate locked, I went into the cottage filled with relics of Dorothy and William. Upstairs there was the poet's bed, protected by two cords placed diagonally across it. It was my ambition to sleep there, hoping the divine afflatus might descend on me. I first tried the bed with my hands, for it was ancient and dusty. Then, crawling under the protective cords, I lay down. Certainly the bed was hard, with no mattress and only a cover, but here Wordsworth had lain, and here, one night, being sleepless, he had been inspired to write—

> A flock of sheep that leisurely pass by,
> One after one; the sound of rain and bees
> Murmuring; the fall of rivers, winds and seas,
> Smooth fields, white sheets of water, and pure sky;
> I have thought of all by turns, and yet do lie
> Sleepless! and soon the small birds' melodies
> Must hear, first uttered from my orchard trees;
> And the first cuckoo's melancholy cry.
> Even thus last night, and two nights more, I lay
> And could not win thee, Sleep! by any stealth:
> So do not let me wear to-night away.
> Without Thee what is all the morning's wealth?

Soon after three o'clock the custodian returned with some visitors. I took the occasion to slip out, unseen. I had had no lunch but never was hunger so well compensated. I had lain on Wordsworth's bed!

One day I went farther afield and made the ascent of Helvellyn. On the road, returning, I overtook a tall man dressed in blue shorts, shirt and tie. We greeted each other and soon were quoting Wordsworth. He seemed delighted by my enthusiasm and asked me my age and name. He had a most friendly personality and I seemed to have amused him with my chatter. I noticed that he spoke with a curious accent. I asked him where he came from and he replied, "From the United States. I'm an American." "Oh, how very interesting. I've never seen one before," I exclaimed. "Well, there are quite a lot of us," he said, laughing at my naïvety. Presently he stopped near an hotel in Grasmere, shook me by the hand, thanked me for my company and left me. That evening I told the Horsleys about my American. "Some of them are very uncouth but when they are nice they are very nice—like the one my sister married," commented Mr. Horsley. A few days later Canon Rawnsley called on my landlady. He looked at me keenly and asked me my name. "Are you the boy who talked to my American guest the other day at Grasmere?" I said I was, and remarked that he was the first American I had seen. "Well, he's quite a famous one," said the Canon. "He's Mr. Woodrow Wilson, the President of Princeton University, a great lover of the Lakes."

I little knew then that within sixteen years I should be received at the White House by a President of the United States, Calvin Coolidge, that I should come to know two other Presidents, Roosevelt and Eisenhower, or that my first sight of the Stars and Stripes would be ten years hence, when it floated over the confluence of the Rhine and the Moselle at Coblenz, where the American army stood on guard at the close of the First World War.

My lakeside holiday was productive. It brought me the first money I earned as an author. There was a weekly paper called *Great Thoughts*. It specialised in excerpts from literature and in articles on contemporary writers. It circulated mainly among public speakers and clergymen, being a source of quotations. I was seventeen when I earned three guineas with the first of several contributions on the Lakeland Poets. Three years after my holiday with the Horsleys I took a more ambitious flight and sent an article on 'The Ascendancy of Wordsworth' to *The Contemporary Review*, which accepted it.

After a year's anxious expectancy it appeared, in May, 1912. That overshadowed everything else. I had penetrated into a high-class Review; it was the first real victory in the world of letters. It seemed that fame had touched my brow. It brought me in twelve guineas. I ordered some visiting cards, subscribed to a press-cutting agency and took a five-shilling half-day return ticket to London, where I called upon the editor. My heart thumped when I was shown into the editorial sanctum and was confronted by an elderly bearded gentleman of benign appearance, Sir Percy Bunting. He peered at me, my card in hand, a little puzzled and said, "And how is your father?" "My father?" I echoed. "Didn't your father write 'The Ascendancy of Wordsworth'?" "No, sir, I am the author," I replied, a little dismayed. The old gentleman was silent for a long minute and then said, as though I had practised deception—"Dear me! You wrote it—well, if I'd known that I don't think I could have accepted it." I was dumbfounded. The working of the editorial mind was beyond me. Or was he joking? He did not look like a man who made jokes. I had expected an acclaim of youthful genius. The old gentleman smiled, and became kinder. Perhaps he felt he had given himself away. I left, with a cordial handshake and an encouraging word.

I had another call to make that afternoon. I had been bombarding the editor of *The English Review* with poems, without success. The Review brought Masefield fame by publishing a startling poem, *The Everlasting Mercy*, an innovation, brutal in diction, violent in action, but touched with a radiance that marked the advent of a master poet. It reverberated throughout the land. I longed to appear in this sensational Review, brilliantly edited by Austin Harrison, son of the Positive philosopher, Frederic Harrison. Incensed by continuous rejection, I wrote an audacious protest to the editor. It greatly amused him. "Your letter gave us a bright hour in this office. Come in and see me one day," he wrote. I announced my forthcoming call. The editorial offices were in Covent Garden—strange how publishers and editors haunted the vicinity of a wholesale vegetable market! My welcome at *The English Review* office was most cordial. "Gracious me! Aren't you still at school?" asked Harrison. "No, sir, I'm imprisoned in a Municipal Corporation office." I produced my poems. Alas, he talked of anything but my verses. Somehow we got on to politics. I confessed to addressing political meetings. "I think that's your métier—there's no living for you in poetry," said Austin Harrison. I was dismayed. I had heard this so often. "Look—

I'm due for a tea-party. I'll pass you over to my assistant. And I'll speak to Sir Ellis Griffiths who wants a bright young secretary." I had heard of him. He was a prominent Liberal Minister, a K.C., and Parliamentary Under-Secretary for the Home Department.

I thanked Harrison, somewhat disappointed. It was not what I had come for. A florid-faced sandy-haired man came into the room. "Here's our stern critic, Cecil Roberts," said Harrison. "Now I must go. Goodbye. Thank you for coming." The editor went out. I was offered a seat by his assistant. A girl came in with a tea-tray. It was the tea hour. I was given a cup. It all seemed very promising. I produced four poems from my case. He looked at me sadly as I put them on his desk.

"Of course I'll look at them—but they can't be any good!" he said genially.

"You haven't read them yet!" I protested.

"No, but I know. People who look like poets can never write poetry."

"But that's preposterous!"

"It's true, my child."

"I'm not a child, I'm nearly twenty!"

"Impossible! With that dewy face you're just out of the nursery," he said. "Where do you come from?"

"Nottingham."

"Why do you waste your bright young life in Nottingham—lace curtains and all that?"

"Because I can't get out!" I replied, annoyed by his skittishness. But I liked him.

Our talk was interrupted by the typist who said there was someone who insisted on seeing the editor. "He won't go!"

"Oh, send him in!" As he said this a young man with fierce eyes and a red beard swept in past the typist. Here undoubtedly was The Bard. He carried a silver-topped cane and a large envelope.

"I have brought you my long poem," he said. "I should not let you have it, for I haven't yet decided to release it, but since there has been such a ridiculous clamour over Masefield's—"

"We are unable to take any long poems. We have two of Masefield's in a drawer. If you care to leave your—"

"Since you've not read my poem you cannot possibly know what it is like, but when you have read it you will be ready to discuss the complete Epic that I propose—"

"If there's a stamped envelope we will return it."

"You will not return it," said The Bard, firmly. "You will be glad to have my work. Good day!"

He walked out majestically, closing the door behind him. The assistant editor raised his hands, looked at me, and said, "You see, my boy, what we have let ourselves in for!"

I rose to leave and thanked him for the cup of tea. After that exhibition I did not feel able to leave my poems.

"Come again!" he said, shaking my hand and smiling.

Outside I asked the typist for the name of the assistant editor.

"Mr. Norman Douglas."

It was a name that meant little to anyone then. It was going to mean a lot to many who would be enchanted by *Old Calabria* and *South Wind*, the latter a book destined to create a cult.

Austin Harrison kept his word. I was invited to call at the House of Commons by Sir Ellis Griffiths. He received me rather pompously in his private room. Somehow we did not take to each other. I could not see myself happy with him though I was desperate to get out of my dungeon office into a bigger world.

Later, Lord Henry Bentinck, our local Member, made an effort on my behalf. He invited me to lunch at his London house to meet Sir Arthur Steel-Maitland, M.P. a Fellow of All Souls College. I liked him very much and could see myself as his eager young secretary but there was one great obstacle. He was an eminent Conservative and I was an ardent Liberal, and what would Mr. and Mrs. Erasmus Horsley say to my going over to the enemy camp? We briefly discussed the secretaryship and then had a delightful conversation on literary topics. So Lord Henry's project came to nothing.

But to return to the saga of Mr. and Mrs. Horsley, who were so kind to me and by the gift of a Lakeland holiday contributed to my emergence as an author. Mr. Erasmus died, released from a life of pain courageously borne. Mrs. Erasmus still received the quarterly allowance from her distant sister-in-law. Then her benefactress died but the millionaire husband in San Francisco continued the remittance. Now alone, she carried on as active as ever, giving her public recitals, coming in and out of our house with the dictionary game, and applauding every small success in my own career. When, in later years, I was a Liberal candidate for a Nottingham constituency, her joy overflowed. She was a passionate Liberal, the fallen Asquith still her political god. She was now eighty but whatever the weather she missed no meeting I addressed. Snow on the ground, trouble with bronchitis, a meeting at the opposite end of the town, she would arrive, chilled but enthusiastic and grace my platform.

Her zest for the right word and its pronunciation remained boundless. Often I playfully challenged her. "It's super-fluous," I would say, wilfully mispronouncing the word. Immediately she dived into a pocket of her voluminous skirt—she was memorable in my youth as the first woman I had met who wore a rustling *frou-frou*—to produce the dictionary she always carried. I can see now the sparkle in her eyes as she won her point. She had another passion. Kindness to animals found her an untiring champion. In those days of horse-trams she got out and walked up the slightest hill. Once I saw her hold up the traffic whilst she admonished a carter for thrashing his horse. She would call at a neighbour's house and denounce the occupant guilty of cruelty to or neglect of a cat or dog.

There was a kind touch of Fate at the close of her life. In the last month of her illness she was worried by the non-arrival of the quarterly remittance. We suggested that a mail had been missed, or that the Atlantic liner had been delayed by a storm. The old lady accepted this explanation. She died, like Queen Elizabeth, sitting up on cushions, hourly expecting the letter. When it came, a week later, there was no remittance. An attorney informed her of the death of her millionaire brother-in-law in San Francisco. No provision had been made by him for the pensioner in England.

A few weeks before her timely end she had recited in public, aged eighty-one, wearing a dress she had cut out and sewn. Latterly she had been perturbed because she could not memorise a new poem, and was annoyed by something Mr. Lloyd George had said about Mr. Asquith. Her last gift to me was a dictionary of synonyms. Dear Erasmus had found it useful.

II

I had now discovered another outlet for my ambitious spirit. I had not relinquished the desire to shine as a public speaker, an appetite whetted by my first speech at school the previous year on the occasion of the visit of the Japanese Minister. I discovered that the Y.M.C.A. had a debating class. I joined it and soon became Chancellor of the Exchequer in a mock parliament. It gave me excellent practice. Later, I was chosen as a 'delegate', with travelling expenses paid, to a conference at Blackpool. The Youth section of the Y.M.C.A. was holding a national conference there and I was to represent the Nottingham branch. There were more than a hundred delegates. The conference was presided over by a gentle old man, Sir Matthew Smith. At one of the sessions the Lancashire representative, with a strong local accent, made a forceful but somewhat boastful speech pointing out the great superiority and success of their own efforts. When I came to speak I was witty at his expense, and demolished him. The meeting roared its delight. I had made my mark, quite the youngest delegate there and, elated at my success, walked on air. I took it as a tribute to my prowess when the National Secretary asked me if I would like to have a walk with him. I readily accepted the invitation. We went on the great promenade. He was a man of singular charm and experience. He talked of general things at first and, after paying me a compliment, he steadily deflated me. "It was a brilliant effort but you were very cruel to that poor fellow who hasn't your advantages of education, appearance and fluency. You will probably go a long way, but eloquence can be a very dangerous gift, wrongly employed. Humility and tolerance are Christian virtues. You must guard against mere cleverness."

He put a hand on my shoulder and gave me a warm smile. I was miserable, all the conceit squeezed out of me. "Do you think I should apologise, sir?" I asked. "I think it would be a nice gesture though the damage is publicly done," he replied.

I sought out my victim and said I was sorry if I had hurt him with my remarks. He was unforgiving and churlish. "Ye've got the gift o' the gab, orl reet—I suppose ye'll go into politics and humbug the crowd like Lloyd George," he said dourly. However, we shook hands. Throughout my life I have been grateful for that admonition. Once in a conversation on public speaking with Norman Birkett, a supreme master of the art who never used his gift basely, he said of a celebrated counsel—"He was a brilliant brute. He used to hypnotise his victim with words and then kick the body round the court."

III

In the autumn of 1907 Lieut.-General Robert Baden-Powell took a small group of boys on a camping expedition to Brownsea Island. Here was the birthplace of the Boy Scout movement. He was even then a figure of romance in the eyes of British youngsters. When the war in South Africa broke out he found himself a colonel with one hundred and twenty-five men besieged in the town of Mafeking. A long duel ensued between the Boers and the British shut up in the town. With his small force he defeated every attempt of the enemy to break in. The war was going badly for England. The incompetence of the generals and the failure of the Army organisation were demonstrated by a series of humiliating defeats inflicted on the professional soldiers by the wily Boer commanders. The siege of Mafeking held England breathless. The continuous ingenuity of this unknown colonel captured attention. Here was the dauntless and successful warrior at last. The days, the weeks, the months went by and still Baden-Powell held out. A relief force was sent and England breathlessly watched to see if it would arrive in time. It seemed like Gordon at Khartoum all over again. For two hundred and seventeen days Baden-Powell, exercising infinite resource, held out until the relieving force arrived on May 17th, 1900, and broke the siege. England went mad overnight. Hysterical crowds waved flags, cheered and sang. A wild mob milled round the Eros fountain in Piccadilly Circus. The occasion gave birth to a new word in the language—to 'maffick'—go wild. Baden-Powell's name was now a household word. He emerged from the Boer War with a greater fame than any other general.

It was while locked up in Mafeking that he stumbled on the origin of his idea concerning the training of boys. He had used them as effective assistants during the siege. He was quick to observe that in every boy's nature there is a Red Indian streak. What they had read in Fenimore Cooper's stories of the struggle of a handful of resolute men against hordes of Indians inspired them with the wish to play a similar role. Back in England, experimenting with a handful of boys under canvas, Baden-Powell saw how by a régime of discipline and dedication the eager spirit of boyhood could be directed to its own and the nation's good. The following year, 1908, a series of small handbooks began to appear in *4d.* fortnightly parts entitled *Scouting for Boys*. They were illustrated by the author who evolved a uniform based on the brown sombrero hat, khaki shirt and shorts he had worn in Mafeking. The handbooks had a wildfire sale. So eager was I to get the next issue that I would go down to the railway station to await the train coming in from London that I might buy the new copy the instant it appeared on the bookstall. Boy Scout platoons sprang up throughout England and an improvised headquarters in London struggled to organise the new craze. At just sixteen I was early in the movement. A public-spirited man, C. R. Hemingway, president of the local Y.M.C.A., put funds and a room at the disposal of what was called The Nottingham Boy Scout Movement, which co-ordinated the groups that sprang up in churches, chapels, schools and boys' clubs. Within twelve months we were almost a thousand strong in the city. When boys began to appear in brown shorts, wide-brimmed felt hats, knotted kerchiefs, and gave one another the scout salute with raised forefingers, they met with some derision. It seemed a kid's Wild Indian game, but when these kids showed themselves disciplined and polished-up from head to foot, and made themselves useful in platoons directed by young scoutmasters, the Scouts began to receive admiring attention. In retrospect, how far removed this admirable enthusiasm was from the later Beatle cult, gangsterdom, and filthy attire of longhaired louts demolishing property and assaulting one another with sticks, stones, knuckledusters and cycle chains.

I now had an ambitious idea. I became the honorary secretary and organiser of the local movement. The Corporation office typewriter and duplicating machine which had been used for my poems and articles now took over the Movement's correspondence and literature. Happily, my tolerant chief cast a blind eye on this new enterprise of his office boy.

Baden-Powell was now touring the country. I went to Mr. Hemingway, who regarded me with kindly amusement, and suggested that we should invite Baden-Powell to address a public meeting, asking for support. He considered the suggestion carefully and, agreeing, offered to pay for the hire of a large hall. Further, he thought we might be able to induce the Mayor to take the chair. Hemingway was a J.P., a partner in a large firm of railway contractors, Logan and Hemingway, that had built the Grand Central Railway line across the Midlands. A modest, generous man, a sincere Christian, he was greatly respected. We wrote to Baden-Powell. He accepted the invitation. The Mayor agreed to be present. We hired a hall called The Tabernacle that held an audience of fifteen hundred. I was to appear on the platform with Baden-Powell, the Mayor and Hemingway. The night previous I could not sleep for excitement. I had been working to exhaustion in organising Scout meetings. My mother alarmed by my bursting enthusiasm tried in vain to slow down my activity. I went to see the stationmaster who baulked at my suggestion of a red drugget on the platform. That was only for royalty. But he agreed to a Boy Scout Guard of Honour.

The train arrived promptly. The stationmaster wore his ceremonial top hat, the Guard of Honour, average age fourteen, shone. The carriage door opened and there he was, the Hero in person. He was of medium height, middle-aged, slender, sandy-haired, slightly freckled, friendly and simple. I had read up his history and the Red Indian connection was not wide of the mark. He was a collateral descendant of John Smith of Virginia, who married the Indian Princess Pocahontas! More wonderful, his mother was the great-niece of Nelson! And his great-grandfather was George Stephenson, inventor in 1829 of the pioneer 'Rocket' railway engine. I had informed the stationmaster of this fact and it may have induced the wearing of the top hat. Baden-Powell was the son of a professor of geometry at Oxford. His two brothers went to Balliol College, but the great Jowett did not think Robert 'was up to it', and, unknowingly, did his country a service for, rejected, B-P. went into the Army and made history.

Within one year of founding the Boy Scouts Baden-Powell held a rally of eleven thousand of them at the Crystal Palace. That same year I organised in Nottingham a Scout procession of a thousand Scouts and we marched through the city with a police escort. The movement expanded so fast that the London headquarters and staff were overwhelmed. Later, it was planned to appoint District Commissioners. With other tasks pressing on me, my office, my writing, my Latin and Greek lessons, I retired from the now well-launched movement. After three years, when I had reached the age of nineteen, Sir Robert, as he had become, sent me a special letter of thanks for my services and one of the earliest of Scoutmasters' Certificates. I never saw him again but I carry a vivid memory of this remarkably kindly and simple man, loved and cheered by thousands of his Scouts around the world. All tyrants hated him. Hitler abolished the German Scouts, Mussolini forbade them and dressed the Italian boys in blackshirts and gave them little daggers. But after the war the Scouts came back in Germany and Italy.

IV

I now redoubled my attack on the literary world. My wondering mother was bewildered by the number of letters with editors' rejection slips that came through the letterbox. I could have papered a room with them. *Great Thoughts* continued to be hospitable. In my seventeenth year I earned £22. In my eighteenth year it had risen to £29, with two notable successes. In 1911 had appeared John Masefield's poem *The Everlasting Mercy*. Its language created a sensation. In those days even the word 'bloody' was a forbidden adjective. Masefield wrote, in the quarrel of his two poachers—

"You closhy put!" "You bloody liar."
"This is my field." "This is my wire."

The editor took 'bloody' out of the proofs, and put it in again. Masefield's poem dealing with spiritual conversion found favour with the pulpiteers. Bishops made the poem their text. The public reciters took it up. All the poet's past work, often unnoticed though excellent, was revived. He followed up his poem with two others, equally forceful, *The Widow in the Bye Street* and *The Dauber* in which he drew on his experience as a seaman. Retiring, shy, he caught the limelight and was on his way to the Laureateship. He soon had imitators, having brought poetry back to a public which had forgotten it since the deaths of Tennyson, Browning and Swinburne. Among these was myself. I wrote a long narrative poem called *The Strike*, based on the recent strike of half a million coalminers. To my amazement it was accepted by *The Oxford and Cambridge Review*. The editor asked for two lines to be deleted—

Opening the door, at what he saw he shuddered,
And then in anger shouted—"Well, I'm buggered!"

It was something you could hear every day, particularly when living not far from a mining district, as I was. But, as the editor pointed out, "We have to draw a line between reality in life and reality in print." I agreed, but only a few miles away, also in a Nottinghamshire mining district, there was a miner's son who had just published his first novel. Lawrence by name, he was destined with *Lady Chatterley's Lover* to explode a bomb under verbal reticence. In 1912 the conventions were still strong, and out went my two lines despite Masefield's breach of the ramparts. For this poem of fourteen pages I received fourteen guineas. This again was an occasion for calling on the editor and I expended eight shillings on a day-return excursion to

London. The office of the Review was on the attic floor of a publisher in Henrietta Street, Covent Garden. After mounting two floors I came to a narrow flight of stairs leading up to the editorial premises. I began to mount when the voice of an unseen person called—"Is it your intention to come up, because if so, I can't come down!" I answered, "Oh, please come down!" and retreated. There was a sound of heavy steps and heavy breathing. Presently there came into sight a large fat man in a loose black cape, wearing a wide brimmed black felt hat. A pair of pince-nez bounced against his large stomach. Instantly I knew who he was, G. K. Chesterton, a famous figure of the contemporary literary world, one of a triumvirate dominating the era, all equally agile in debate and all inexhaustible 'copy' for the Press—Chesterton, Belloc and Shaw. The figure arrived at the bottom of the stairs where I stared, wide-eyed, as if a god had descended from Olympus. "I thank you, sir, for your consideration," he said, and with that Johnsonian address, passed on.

I have jumped four years ahead in my story. Let me return to the boy of sixteen, scribbling in his attic, debating in a mock parliament, organising Boy Scouts, imprisoned in a dreary office made tolerable by a considerate chief, living on a pittance that made the purchase of a pair of shoes a problem, pinching himself for postage on rejected articles, with a head full of ambitious dreams, and elated from time to time by the earning of a few pounds from literary work. There was one notable windfall. Batsford, the publisher, had projected a series of short monographs on famous authors. I suggested writing on Oliver Wendell Holmes, my current enthusiasm. They commissioned the book, to be the tenth in their beautifully produced series. Alas, the venture proving unprofitable, they stopped the series with the eighth book. My intense disappointment was mitigated by their honourable behaviour. They sent me the agreed fee of sixteen guineas for my unused contribution.

It will be noted that I had received much kindness from various persons, from our lodger, Mr. Hartley my Latin teacher, the Horsleys who had given me the holiday in Lakeland, and from my office chief. Sometimes in office hours I encountered him in Boots Lending Library, or in a nearby cinema-café, or in a bookshop. He tactfully pretended that he had not seen me. I responded with equal blindness. After all he was playing truant in office hours also.

Around the age of fifteen I had begun to take an interest in lawn tennis. Wimbledon was just coming into fashion. Once a year the private tennis club in the Park held a week's tournament on its beautiful courts in that woodland amphitheatre dotted with Nottingham's exclusive residences. It was a social affair with all the County bringing its house parties, including tennis stars like the famous Doherty Brothers, A. W. Gore and Mrs. Lambert Chambers, for ten years the Wimbledon champion. A covered grandstand was erected. The entrance fee, especially on the final day, was prohibitive for me. I could just peer over the top of the fence and see half of the first three courts staging the chief contests. Then I had an idea. I put on a cricket shirt, shorts and gym shoes and walked in as a ball-boy. To justify my trespass I served on the outer courts but kept aloof from the 'professional' boys. The next year I was promoted to an umpire. I never refused a court except when there was a top display in Court No. 1. I then discreetly tucked myself away at the foot of the grandstand. I had an excellent view not only of the players but also of the star spectators. The County bigwigs, some from the ducal seats, appeared on the final day. There was one lady who arrived with a veritable court. Her attendant gentlemen carried rugs and cushions, and waterproofs—necessary for an English summer. Swathed in tulle, *soignée*, she glittered as she walked, smiling on those who greeted her. I once picked up a programme she had dropped. She thanked me with laughing eyes. It was as if I had looked straight at the sun. She had two daughters with her, one of whom, later, enamoured the youthful Edward, Prince of Wales. But it was the mother who fascinated me. She was Mrs. Charles Birkin, married to one of the local lace-making magnates, Colonel Birkin, who lived six miles out of the city. In the course of time I was to have a more personal view of this radiant beauty, when she called on me in my capacity as editor of the local newspaper, to ask if I could do anything to suppress the gossip concerning her daughter and the enamoured Prince. Forty years farther on in time, at a London cocktail party given by my friend Lady Monckton I was introduced to a Sir Charles Birkin. "Not a Nottingham Birkin?" I asked. "Yes." "Are you in any way related to the beautiful Mrs. Charles Birkin who dazzled my youth?" "She was my mother," he answered. I told him of her 'royal progress' at the tennis tournament. Later, as his dinner guest, he took me into a room looking from Chelsea Embankment across the Thames to Battersea Park, a fairyland of lights between the twinkling suspension bridges. But it was not to show me the view. He handed me a drawing of his mother. Nothing of her arresting beauty had been missed by the artist. I started on seeing the name. It was drawn by my friend Denholm Davis in the very year he had drawn me.

We will return to the tennis court. One day at the Nottingham tournament I was sent to umpire a match. I climbed into the chair feeling immensely important with my promotion. To my amazement at the end of the tournament I was given the Umpire's Prize, a long, leather portmanteau to hold two tennis racquets though I owned none. I think I got the prize because of a certain match I umpired in which the redoubtable Mrs. Lambert Chambers played. In that match the count had gone to three sets with the final set—game 12–10 in her favour. The match was played in the rain, neither lady being willing to quit, though the spectators had all vanished. We ended wet through and Mrs. Chambers bought me coffee and a bun and was concerned whether I had caught a cold, being delicate-looking. Fifty years on, in the lounge of my London hotel, a friend pointed to an old lady. "Do you know who that is—that's the famous Mrs. Lambert Chambers, the Wimbledon champion." I went over to her. "Do you remember a ball-boy at Nottingham some fifty years ago who umpired a game you played, which went to 12–10 in the third set, in a downpour, and for whom you bought coffee and a bun?" I asked. She looked surprised. "Yes, I do." "Well, I'm that boy!" I said. "What, you were that lad, rosy-cheeked, and always so willing! Sit down and tell me what you've been doing all these years." "I've been writing books—I write novels." I answered. "Novels! Give me the name of one, I'd like to read it." "Well," I replied, "there's *Scissors* and *Victoria Four-Thirty*, and—" She looked at me in amazement, interrupting me. "Don't tell me you're *the* Cecil Roberts!" she cried. I said I was. "I've read them all!" she exclaimed. "But what a thing! To think that I could have been telling people all these years that you were once my ball-boy and umpire!" She died soon after our meeting, having turned eighty.

Within two years of umpiring I was playing myself, in a club whose courts pleasantly bordered the Trent. The game proved a social asset and I was invited to play at various houses, some of them several miles distant. This entailed cycling there. Being particular about my appearance I carried my shoes, shirt, and well-pressed white flannel trousers in a cycle-basket so that they should not be soiled en route. Just before I reached my destination, I found a hedge or recess and changed, arriving spick and span. About fifty years later the octogenarian widow of General Sir John Burn-Murdock, sometime A.D.C. to Kitchener in the Soudan, now living in a Scottish mansion, wrote to my hostess on the Italian Riviera, a relation who had told her that I was a guest, "How extraordinary! I remember him as a youth when he came to play tennis at our house near Loughborough. He was always so well-dressed and well-mannered," she replied. So it had been worth the trouble.

V

In my nineteenth year I was able to buy my first evening dress, tails and dinner jacket, with the money earned by my pen. My mother was shocked when she heard the price I paid, at least twice what it would have cost from any local tailor. I went to a good tailor in Savile Row. It required three five-shilling trips to London for fittings. I pointed out that it was an investment, not a luxury, a form of built-in confidence. The result was a masterpiece. I was left with five pounds capital, two of which I expended on a hat for my mother to compensate her for the shock. A week later my salary went up to twenty shillings. 'To him that hath'. Very soon there was an occasion for the dinner jacket. I was invited to speak, responding for the guests, at the annual dinner of the local Society of Chartered Accountants. Someone had heard me in the mock parliament. I surprised them by telling them that the first chartered accountant in history was Noah, who counted the animals he took on a chartered cruise. A dove brought back the first leaf of a new account. This was a fresh experience for me and it widened my aquaintance. The intense pleasure of small things when one is young!

About this time I found a wonderful friend, a man of some genius, with a heart of gold. He was about fifty-five, named William Kiddier. I was familiar with the name. He owned a very prosperous brush-making business, with a shop in the Market Place. It carried a sign in electric lights 'Kiddier Makes Brushes'. This same legend was on all the city's trolley cars that had now supplanted the horse-trams. He was a man with a most striking head and face, the ringed eyes of an eagle, the wavy white mane of a prophet. He led a double life. Downstairs in the shop he was a shrewd tradesman; at the top of his four-story building he led his real life. He had a studio in which he shut himself up to follow his passion for painting. He was a man of great individuality, and sometimes there was a flash of prophetic fire. He founded the local Atelier Society and compelled the Municipal School of Art, in the teeth of bigoted opposition, to create a Life Class. This was no ordinary art school. It made history. With the legend of Richard Parkes Bonington behind it, the son of a Master of the local gaol, it attracted youthful genius. Around 1890 a fatherless little girl of thirteen turned up at the school, one of three sisters living penuriously but with sturdy independence in Nottingham. She was an unusual little girl because she was already an artist. At the age of twelve she had gone to St. Quentin to stay with an uncle who had settled there. The purpose was to ease the pressure at home, and to learn French. While there she revealed an artistic gift, so successfully that she sold portraits of her classmates at three sous a time. The little Laura Johnson hoped that one day she would be able to proceed to one of the famous ateliers in Paris but the next year the death of a sister brought her home to console her struggling mother. So the little artist of thirteen began to study at the Nottingham School of Art. Here she met a pale black-haired boy called Harold Knight, a star student who painted a 'Portrait of Laura, aged 16'. She admired him enormously and put her easel next to his and copied him. One day the students, larking, kissed her foot. Harold in turn implanted his kiss and then, with a smile, went to a shelf and took down a bottle of fixative with which he sprayed her shoe.

At seventeen he was engaged to her, and thus began one of the most famous, long and happy love stories of the world of art. They painted side by side on their individual paths to fame; they both became Royal Academicians. In 1965 Dame Laura Knight, aged eighty-eight, received the unique honour of an exhibition of two hundred of her works in the Royal Academy Diploma Gallery, the only time such a tribute had been paid to a woman. She was an author also and in this same year, thirty-five years after the first volume of her autobiography had appeared, she published a second, fittingly called *The Magic of a Line*. It tells the story of an adventurous love of life. The circus became one of her happy hunting grounds; her horses and acrobats are unforgettable. In everything she revealed zest. She became a familiar figure with the members of the Russian Ballet. Diaghilev gave her *carte-blanche* to make sketches. It was there, seated in the wings during a rehearsal, that I first saw her. She enjoyed the friendship of Pavlova. When she gave studio parties they were rumbustious affairs. The guests came from different spheres of interest; Augustus John and A. J. Munnings, George Bernard Shaw, W. H. Davies, Lawrence of Arabia, Ellen Terry, Pavlova, Karsavina, Lydia Lopokova, Maynard Keynes, and Leonide Massine, many of whom she painted. Kiddier knew Laura and Harold Knight in their early student days. On her ninetieth birthday she said to me, concerning a query I put to her about the Life Class—

"I remember William Kiddier, he was a fine and generous-minded man. When I went there as an artisan-student in 1889 I straightway joined the Life Class for the living head, but was not allowed to study for the nude—this like all the other female students. And when the male students had their nude male model we had to work from the plaster cast. However, after a few years' study when I had left the Nottingham Art School, a nude model was provided for the women."

So Kiddier won the day. He knew also a lad who became Sir Arnesby Brown, R.A., and two sculptors, George and Mary Gillick, another romance, all Nottingham Art School students he had championed in the teeth of opposition. (Illustrations, pp. 64, 65.)

Once a month a small group of enthusiastic amateur artists, and a few professionals, gathered together at the gallery of the local Society of Artists. To this I was taken by my new friend. It was presided over by a portrait painter called Denholm Davis. He had studied at the Art School along with Harold and Laura Knight, then, winning a scholarship he spent five years at the Royal Academy Schools. He studied in turn with Clausen, Sargent, Solomons and Dicksee. After travelling for some years, he came back to Nottingham. One of his sitters, Mrs. Chaworth Musters (shades of Byron's Mary Chaworth!) persuaded him to open a local studio. As a portrait painter he dominated the Midlands and never lacked commissions. He might have won fame farther afield but he made no onslaught on London, content with a smaller domain. In this he was wise, he escaped the acid sediment of fame. He had a large studio in the centre of Nottingham, a country house, a beautiful wife and a pretty daughter. He enjoyed a tranquil life, loving his work, content with a modest success. The local history of the opening of the twentieth century is commemorated by his brush: Jesse Boot (Lord Trent), General William Booth, Captain Ball, V.C., etc. When a new Council House was built in 1927 he painted the Robin Hood frescoes round the central dome. I felt honoured when in 1952 I was invited to open a memorial exhibition of his work, in the Nottingham Art Gallery and Museum. How often I had raced up the seven flights of stairs to burst impetuously into his studio and read what I had just written or published! At seventeen I was as volatile and excitable as he was tranquil and philosophic, a quiet smile playing over his pale face as he stood before his canvas. He drew, when I was twenty-four, a delicate pencil portrait of me, and when I was thirty, and a Parliamentary candidate, a full-length portrait, *à la* young statesman, which now hangs in the Councli Chamber of Nottingham University. (Illustration, p. 240.)

VI

The studio of William Kiddier, high up above the Market Place, became a refuge from my hateful Municipal office in the dark alley, wedged between the Shambles, appropriate name, with its butchers' shops full of hanging carcases, and two public lavatories. A plaque over one of the shops reminded me that Henry Kirke White, the poet, had been born there in 1785 ('Oft in sorrow, oft in woe, Onward, Christians, onward go!'). The poor lad died at twenty-one. There were moments when I felt my own young life near extinction in such dismal, smelly surroundings.

When William Kiddier went upstairs to his studio, leaving the management of his business to his only son, he put on a gabardine painting coat, almost a palette in itself, and went to work in the sky-lighted room stacked with canvases. He was a landscape artist but did all his painting indoors from open-air sketches. He was a splendid colourist. As he did not paint to exhibit or sell but entirely to satisfy his own artistic taste he was a perfectionist. Once as I mounted the high stairs I detected a strong smell. The studio was full of smoke and for a moment I thought it was on fire. The stove was red hot. "I'm burning everything I've painted, forty-five canvases. I'm going to start all over again. You've never seen a Royal Academician do that. Neither his vanity nor his pocket would support it!" said my friend with a chuckle as he stoked the stove.

Invariably when I arrived he put down his palette and brush, swung round an easy chair for me, perched himself on a stool and said—"You've written a new poem. I see it in your face. Sit down and read it!" which of course was exactly what I wanted to do. He was always an enthusiastic listener. "Good, good! That's the stuff!" he exclaimed, as he jumped up, reached for his hat, and added—"Now we'll go and eat. It must have taken it out of you! Growing boys want nourishing!" He led the way downstairs and across the marketplace to a restaurant where they knew him and gave us a table by the window. He was ceaseless in his kindness to me. "You've found a new father," said my mother. He knew the state of mental rebellion I was in, seeking release from that office, my head full of dreams, frustrated, tense, an unbridled colt. I saw ahead those awful examinations that at twenty-two would qualify me to be an Inspector of Weights and Measures and doom my whole life to trapping dishonest shopkeepers. "But it's safe, a Municipal job, with a pension at sixty." Safe. That was the magic word, in an era when to be out of work was a nightmare, since employment was a will-o'-the-wisp. I was counselled to be prudent, to play safe. Never, I vowed. I would rather die young in Rome like Keats, or be drowned like Shelley. My elderly friend was always sympathetic and assuring. "You'll get free somehow. I know you will," he would say, putting a hand on my shoulder when he saw I was near breaking point.

Seventeen. I was driving myself very hard. I must have been difficult and my mother must have suffered. I rose at six-thirty and spent an hour at my writing. Back from the office at six p.m. I read and wrote in my beloved den except on those evenings when I had Latin and Greek lessons. In summer I worked under the laburnum tree in the tiny garden. Then one day I fainted. As usual the doctor felt my pulse, clipped on his stethoscope and went over my chest. Four years earlier I had been lined up in the school gymnasium and told to take off my shirt. One by one we were examined by the school doctor. Breathe in, breathe out, the cold stethoscope over my chest. I knew what was going to happen. He listened, looking like a blackbird hearing the doomed worm. "Stand aside," he said, and took the other boys. I was in the condemned class. Then I was called up again. He listened from the front, he listened from the back.

"It's my idiosyncrasy," I said.

"Where did you get that from?" he snapped.

"Dr. Annandale's Dictionary," I replied. "Our doctor knows all about it."

He looked at me. He may have thought I was mental.

"Have you ever had rheumatic fever?"

"Yes, two years ago."

"Ah!" he said, unclipping the stethoscope, and dictating something to a nurse who wrote it down opposite my name on the sheet. "Put on your shirt."

In doing so I contrived to see what she had written. In the hurried glance I found a strange word. That evening I said to my father, conscious of being unique, "Daddy, the school doctor says I've got a diastole!"

"A what?"

"A diastole, a dilatation alternating with a systole in pulsation," I answered, quoting Dr. Annandale.

"How remarkable!" said my father, almost gaily. "You sound like a faulty metronome."

This time the doctor, called in by my alarmed mother was reassuring. "Nothing serious. He's very highly strung and has been overdoing it. He must take things more quietly."

It is advice I have never been able to take throughout my life. For a month I reduced pressure. I spent a wonderful week at Rempstone Rectory, at Mr. Hartley's invitation. I had Latin lessons, I lay on the lawn and read right through John Addington Symond's *The History of the Renaissance in Italy*. I came home with four new poems to read to my ever encouraging friend, William Kiddier. Later, it was he who was behind a remarkable occasion. Marie Corelli, the novelist, came to the city to give a lecture on Byron and to open a Byron Exhibition in aid of the building fund of the Mechanics Institute. It was arranged that after the lecture I should read a poetic tribute to her that would appear in the programme.

It is difficult now to comprehend the immense fame that Marie Corelli enjoyed in the reading world at the beginning of the twentieth century. She and Hall Caine were the most popular novelists of the late Victorian and Edwardian eras. There were remarkable stories concerning her. It was rumoured that she was an illegitimate child, born of a passionate romance between an Englishwoman and an Italian count, and that she had been adopted by Dr. Charles Mackay. The truth was probably less romantic, but there was a cachet in those days about being illegitimate. It had not become the state-subsidised commonplace of to-day. Illegitimate or not, the Mackays brought her up. She was a child of talent from the beginning. When the Mackays moved from Bayswater to a house on Box Hill, Surrey, they became the neighbours of George Meredith. He encouraged the young Marie in her piano playing for which she revealed a precocious gift. She assumed the name Corelli and gave public concerts, proving a brilliant improviser on the piano. But literature not music was her destiny. At thirty she published her first novel, of which little notice was taken. The next year, on the death of her foster-mother, a friend named Bertha Vyner came to live with her. They were never separated until death took Marie. In 1893 she had her first phenomenal success with her novel *Barabbas*. It thrilled even the Prince of Wales, who rarely read a book. She soared even higher with *The Sorrows of Satan*, two years later. It sold a million copies and had hysterical acclaim. It denounced the sins of Society and had an evangelical, semi-sacred theme. Hailed by the bishops and preached about by the clergy, she became overnight a national figure. Soon she displayed a regrettable flair for publicity, and for quarrelling with people. Hall Caine, with a similar flair, had sited himself on his father's native Isle of Man. He lived in a machicolated castle, grew a Vandyck beard, wore a wide-brimmed black hat and cloak but somehow with his beady eyes looked like a squirrel. He wrote a novel called *The Deemster*, story of a Manx character. From then on he became the uncrowned king of the Isle of Man. He died in 1931 leaving a quarter of a million pounds.

His contemporary, Marie Corelli, chose Stratford-on-Avon as her base. She bought a large house on the town bank of the river and threw off balance the booming tourist cult of William Shakespeare. She cultivated exclusiveness, with Bertha Vyner as the watchdog. She imported a gondola with a Venetian gondolier and was rowed on the swan-haunted Avon, watched from the banks and the bridge by the astonished Shakespeare pilgrims. Nevertheless, she was generous and active in well-doing and she saved Stratford-on-Avon from being exploited and ravaged by promoters of the Shakespeare boom. Equipped with a rapier tongue, she exercised her gift for quarrelling. She quarrelled with the Mayor and banned all local inhabitants from her house. She quarrelled with the critics, being hypersensitive to criticism, regarding herself as the oracle of a moral cause, and would not allow her publishers to send out review copies for the critics to desecrate. Such was the news value of a new novel by her that the Press had to buy it. She refused to allow her photograph to be published. Her showmanship became a fine art. She anticipated her immortality. Although her works would never rank as literature, she was a spellbinder. Like her rival in Manxland she could weave a plot and tell a good story, whose chief ingredient was suspense. She abhorred sex, whereas Hall Caine gave his work a deft seasoning of it.

The great evening arrived. My poem for the occasion was written. The hall was packed. I was invited to the reception before the novelist ascended the platform. Marie Corelli's appearance gave us a shock. She was not a figure of romance, however much the creator of it. She was small and stout, pretty in a fluffy way, somewhat like an ageing chorus girl. Miss Vyner, her companion-secretary, was smaller and fatter. I could understand the novelist's objection to being photographed although her features were pleasant. But what she lacked in stature she compensated in personality and will-power. She held her audience with the subtlest of all platform arts, a diffidence that was coolly accomplished, and she radiated charm. She was clear in her diction and audible. The audience forgot the physical presence in the personality. After the lecture I delivered my poem, with its proper tribute—

Lady, it is most fitting thou
Shouldst bring a token to the dead
And place a laurel on the brow
From which no glory yet hath fled

Having thus coupled Marie and Byron, I went on for ten more quatrains, concluding with—

And maybe he is touched to know
That thou hast honoured here his name,
That Art is gracious still to show
The famous unforgetting fame.

She looked very pleased, autographed my programme, and gave me an invitation for a weekend at Stratford-on-Avon.

Such was the first famous author I encountered. I was destined to meet 'true immortals' in the years to come but none ever gave me the thrill of that first youthful encounter. And perhaps, despite the subsequent slump in her reputation, she had a touch of immortality. In the year 1967 there was a reissue of her novels—more than her illustrious neighbour at Box Hill, the 'immortal' Meredith achieved.

I was still spending money on postage to editors. I worked long evenings in the empty office, not doing overtime but using the typewriter for my articles. There was a duplicating machine. I made ten copies of a twenty-page typed booklet of my verses and presented a copy to my chief. He knew the copy was Corporation-produced but he did not blink and thanked me for the gift. I must have tried him sorely. I was often missing. I could not be all that time at the lavatory. No, I was across the way, up in William Kiddier's studio, reading my latest production. That dear man never failed me as an audience. He was an author in his own right. He had written a book called *The Brushmaker*, which became a classic of the trade, also two small books of painter's essays that Cape published.

Despite the fainting fit I was soon as industrious as ever. I wrote and typed out a book of three hundred pages, in a style too obviously inspired by *The Autocrat of the Breakfast Table*. I sent it off for an opinion, hoping of course for recognition of genius, to A. C. Benson, the son of an Archbishop, brother of two novelists and Master of Trinity College, Cambridge. He was enjoying considerable fame as a prolific essayist. He sent my book back with a four-page letter of criticism and encouragement, and paid the postage! When I think of my audacity in burdening such a busy man with my scribbling, I marvel at his kindness to an unknown youth. It had a lasting effect on me. When, in due time, I, too, was pestered by the unsolicited manuscripts of budding authors, I repressed my impatience and responded as A. C. Benson had responded. I wrote kindly, and paid the postage, if not enclosed.

Financially, for all my labour, I was not having much success. Twenty-two pounds in one year, twenty-nine in another. Our 'reserve', fifty-six pounds at my father's death, was down to thirty-five. My mother had bought herself nothing. Three years after marriage my brother had the first of four duodenal operations that were to make him an invalid for the rest of his life. There was no outside help, no widow's allowance, no health insurance, no medical service, no Welfare State. Mr. Hartley's erratic payments for his lodging took care of the rent. My mother and myself lived on my wages, now twenty shillings a week. Pinched we were, but never depressed by the present, or apprehensive of the future. I never heard my mother complain. There was between us a confidence that sustained us.

How bright the future seemed! Every week there was a new excitement. I received three guineas, and my fare, for a lecture on Francis Thompson, then in great vogue following his tragic life story. I was now twenty and rather astonished the audience by appearing in my Savile Row evening dress, tails and white tie. It must have helped them to feel that they were getting their money's worth. I was asked to repeat the lecture in Leicester. There was soon another occasion for gala attire. A friend came to me with astonishing news. He had been given two stalls for the farewell performance of Sir Johnstone Forbes-Robertson in *Hamlet*, at Drury Lane Theatre, on June 6th, 1913. It would be a great occasion with London Society filling the theatre, we were told. Forbes-Robertson had won fame in this role when he had first appeared in it in 1897. His was an intellectual version and he was regarded as the greatest Hamlet of the contemporary stage. I had already seen him on tour in Jerome K. Jerome's *The Passing of the Third Floor Back* in which a strange lodger occupying a back room had a spiritual effect on the inhabitants of a mean boarding house. With this play he had an immense success. It fitted perfectly his beautiful aesthetic appearance united with a voice of exceptional quality.

His farewell in *Hamlet* marked the retirement from the stage of its foremost actor, at the age of sixty. It was a momentous occasion. I had never been in a London theatre or seen a gala evening. We took half-day return excursion tickets to London. The train left at noon and returned at midnight. We changed at a friend's flat. There was one thing that marred our attire. We had no top hats. It was an era when one could not appear hatless, even on a June night. "That's quite simple," said my companion. "We'll buy a gibus." "A what?" I asked. Somehow the word had eluded me in Dr. Annandale's Dictionary. "It's a squash hat made of black cloth, with a spring inside, that collapses flat—an opera hat," he explained. On arriving in London that afternoon we went to a hatter's, each buying a gibus for £1. When it came to wearing it I felt self-conscious and slightly ridiculous, but I got pleasure in being able to snap it flat, rather like a conjurer.

What a scene that was in the foyer of Drury Lane as the audience entered! The *élite* of London gathered there, lovely women in tiaras and jewels, the men superbly groomed. It was the farewell of a great actor of aristocratic bearing, and also the end of a long partnership with his wife, Gertrude Elliot. For all his sixty years he was still slender and handsome, the beautiful voice undiminished in quality. *The Times* wrote of "the wonderful violoncello tones of that famous voice." I have seen many Hamlets throughout my life but none ever approached the figure that commanded the great stage that night, and I do not think the comparison is weighted in his favour because it was a boy's first experience of a London scene that made theatrical history. Forbes-Robertson had been knighted by King George only three days before. London still retained much of the lavish splendour that had marked the Edwardian era. This was England at the peak of her prestige. London was the capital of the greatest Empire the world had ever known. Her navy ruled the seas, her word was respected across the face of the earth. "Land of Hope and Glory . . . make her mightier yet," sang the multitude, certain that God would grant the request. Yet the seeds of her dissolution were already planted, and a little more than a year ahead lay the first convulsion that would undermine her proud and easy eminence. I could not know on this wonderful night when London took farewell of her favourite actor that we had touched a height in England's peaceful story.

When the final curtain fell with an almost hysterical audience greeting the slim, black figure of The Prince of Denmark, flowers, laurel wreaths and, finally, a Danish flag were handed up over the footlights. Then in a hushed house Forbes-Robertson came forward to take farewell of the audience and the theatre. His speech was perfectly phrased and touched with deep emotion. "But let me say, I am not sad, how can I be when at a great dramatic moment in my life the King has honoured me." The house broke into cheers.

Alas, we could not stay to the end. Our train departed in half an hour. We rushed to the cloakroom, retrieved our dressing-cases and hurried from the brilliantly lit scene. A fleet of Rolls-Royces and a posse of policemen waited outside. My friend had been clever about our exit. He had realised that no taxi would be procurable and had observed the nearby Underground Station from which, in a short journey, we could reach St. Pancras. We pushed our way on to a crowded tube train, conspicuous in our evening dress. I would have flattened and carried my gibus but my friend stuck boldly to his. Near us a black-eyed girl looked at me and then said in a voice audible to all, "Little Lord Fauntleroy!" I felt myself blush and the girls giggled. We raced from King's Cross and up the steps to St. Pancras Station. Breathless, we reached the departure platform with only a few minutes in hand.

In the pre-dawn the streets of Nottingham looked strange and empty. My mother had left a glass of milk and biscuits on the table. I stealthily crept up the stairs. When I was called in the morning and I opened my eyes I could not credit what I had seen the previous night. It had all been sheer Hans Andersen.

CHAPTER TWO

I Burn My Boats

I

THE YEAR 1912 saw the first streaks of dawn in my struggle towards liberty. I had been published in *The Contemporary Review*, and *The Poetry Review*. I was now twenty. At the beginning of this year my friend Kiddier had introduced me to Dr. Frank Granger, who held the chair of professor of classics at the local University College—it had yet to become a university. He was a man of charm and erudition, sympathetic to the young. Through him I encountered other professors, among them Ernest Weekley, the etymologist. One of his former pupils, aged twenty-six, had just published his first novel *The White Peacock*. It attracted little notice. Nine months later the author went off with Weekley's wife. There were those who said it was German-born Mrs. Weekley who had abducted young Lawrence. Once, during the Professor's absence, she had besought Lawrence to go to bed with her, at which he baulked.

Whatever the truth, they had gone to Germany together, and later went to Italy where, in a villa, at Gargnano on Lake Garda, with no money and much rapture, they were now living. Lawrence was engaged on his new novel *Sons and Lovers*, an autobiographical story of his life as a Nottinghamshire miner's son. Almost Freudian in its complexes of father-hate and mother-obsession, it was the first stone in the erotic edifice of his fame, and foretold a new writer of genius.

It was the custom of Professor Granger to hold Sunday morning symposia. At these gatherings in his house Mrs. Granger, a kind, sunny-faced woman, intervened with coffee and biscuits. I was the youngest and the shyest in the company which consisted of various professors, lecturers and college students. The discussions were always lively. It was Granger who suggested that I should enter the annual competition for the Kirke White Prize Poem. I had a theme. I had just suffered the loss of a friend. I wrote a threnody lamenting his untimely end. The banks of the River Trent had been our favourite haunt. I called my poem, six pages long, *The Trent*. It won the prize. Looked at to-day, it has little merit and I find it unbearably crude. The poem was published in the college magazine. William Kiddier had an idea. Why not have it printed and put on sale? He would take care of the printer's bill.

Such was the origin of my first publication. It appeared in blue paper covers price sixpence. Destined though I was in future years to see some forty of my books in booksellers' windows, nothing ever equalled the thrill of that first slim publication. A local bookseller showed it, with a card "By a Local Author". I walked past his window ten times a day. Perhaps, with luck, I should see someone emerging with a copy in his hand. Somehow it sold two hundred and fifty copies, a good sale for poetry. It paid for its printing.

Almost as excited as the author was my Maecenas. One day, after I had read a poem to him as he sat on a stool before his wet canvas, he leapt off it and with a flourish, bringing down his fist on his painting table, exclaimed—"It's time for you to emerge in a real book of poems. Let's have some fun! We'll have a gamble. We'll publish, whatever it costs!"

That was how it began. There was a weekly paper called *The Christian World*. I had contributed three essays to it. The publishers, James Clarke, were a long-established firm with an office at 13 Fleet Street, almost opposite Temple Bar. "Get your poems together and we'll go and see them," said my friend.

On an appointed day we journeyed to London. We were received by a grave, grey-bearded gentleman in a room that looked across Fleet Street to Chancery Lane. He had an old-world courtesy but he demurred at the proposition. "We are publishers of theological works. We have never published poetry. There is always a loss on it," he said.

"That doesn't matter a bit. I'll guarantee you against any loss. This lad must appear with a book!" said Kiddier.

There was a silence. "We have never published a subsidised book," said Greybeard. "There are some unscrupulous publishers who exploit authors willing to pay for publication. They profit by their vanity. We would not like to be confused with them."

He rested his hand on my manuscript which I had sent him. "They are of good moral tone, and I would say, for one so young—

precocious," he said, indulging me with a faint smile. "But I feel I should warn you that there is absolutely no money in poetry, either for the author or the publisher."

"I'm sure you're right," agreed my patron," but that doesn't concern us at all. The appearance is everything. Somewhere near here I surmise there was once a publisher who said the same thing to young William Shakespeare—though my young friend is no Shakespeare! The start is always difficult. I'll lose my money very cheerfully. Would fifty pounds cover any possible loss? He must appear under the imprint of a highly respected house."

The old gentleman was silent for a few moments. "Fifty pounds, or less, would cover any liability," he said quietly.

And so it was arranged. When we had gone out into Fleet Street, Kiddier chuckled. "That 'highly respected house' did it. It went down like an oyster with the old boy." He looked up at the clock by the Law Courts. It was noon. "Let's go and celebrate with a good lunch. A poet is born!" he cried.

I do not know who was the more elated when *Phyllistrata and Other Poems* appeared, price half a crown, in a beautiful blue cloth binding with gilt lettering. My friend reviewed it in a local newspaper. There were half a dozen pleasant reviews and three sniffy ones. I sent author's copies to Rudyard Kipling, President Woodrow Wilson, Alice Meynell, A. C. Benson, and others, all of whom wrote very kindly. I also sent a copy to Professor Knight of Edinburgh University, an eminent Wordsworth scholar to whom I had dedicated my book. He wrote—"What a delightful surprise! I never expected to live long enough to have a book dedicated to me!"

It had taken six months to publish my book. It appeared in July, 1913. I had been counting the days. In a fever of excitement I undid the parcel. I signed copies for my friends sitting at the bookcase-secretaire my father had helped to finish making only a day before his death. In 1962, nearly half a century later, while I was on a world cruise, my publishers had sent to their agent in Hong Kong fifty 'insets' for presentation copies, of a new novel, my twenty-fourth, *Wide Is The Horizon*, that was to be published on my seventieth birthday. As I signed the sheets on the tenth floor of an office building, I looked out over the magnificent harbour thronged with shipping and I recalled that stripling who had autographed his first book with such excitement. What a long and eventful cruise I had made down the years since then!

Phyllistrata appeared just after my twenty-first birthday. I was now six feet tall, slender, highly strung and driving myself at a great pace in my zest for life and achievement. My mother anxiously watched my health but under my frailty there was great resilience. I was writing long after midnight, bombarding editors and elated from time to time by an acceptance and an accompanying cheque. Cheques were then novelties in my life. I read the bank's name with relish. I had not yet a bank account of my own. When, in after years, literary aspirants asked me how one becomes an author, I had one reply. "You write—and you keep on writing." There is no other way.

I sent a copy of my book to another poet, and this was the manner of it. One day in a local café someone had left behind a copy of the weekly *Nation.* In it there was a poem *Brumana* by one James Elroy Flecker, a new name to me. I read, enchanted by its music—

> Oh shall I never be home again!
> Meadows of England shining in the rain
> Spread wide your daisied lawns: your ramparts green
> With briar fortify, with blossoms screen
> Till my far morning—and O streams that slow
> And pure and deep through plains and woodland go,
> For me your love and all your kingcups store . . .

I learned it by heart, as did also my mother, perforce inflicted with my recital of it as I went up and down stairs. Then a year later, in July, 1913, I read a review of a book of poems he had published called *The Golden Journey to Samarkand.* With great extravagance I ordered a copy. It cost two and sixpence. Its contents carried me away. Here was genius. I wrote to Flecker and sent him a copy of my own book. Back came a letter from Switzerland.

Sanatorium Stephani. Montana-sur-Sierre. Aug. 29. 1913.

Dear Sir,

Many thanks for your book and for your enthusiastic letter. Having gained such a power of technique so young you should be able to do anything in time. I am glad to see you admire and respect Middleton. Mr. William Watson on the other hand is by no means an idol of mine. His verse always read to me like the reminiscences of someone else. After all the great thing in all literature is not to be dull. Don't take my Parnassian preface too seriously—unless it inspires you to read Hérédia or de Regnier. But above all you should read a poet not Parnassian—Paul Fort. I think English poets want to get out of England and out of English literature and then to return to discover England like one of Chesterton's heroes by wandering round the world. I am much more interested in modern than in ancient Greece: when I write about Greece I have an advantage—an enormous advantage over other poets—yourself included. I have been there. You talk about the "snow-white porticoes" of the Acropolis. They were rather a lovely golden brown.

Every country in Europe is worth living in but Switzerland. I shall have to stay here all this winter. And people come to holes like this for pleasure! I have a particular horror of fir trees (very different things from pines) and here I am in the middle of a preposterous blackwood of them.

Do write to me again. It is always jolly to be admired in a jolly way . . .

The heading of his letter gave me the key to his fate. He was dying of consumption. "I'm pretty sick of life. I've finished my play (*Hassan*) but I don't suppose it will ever be played," he wrote to a friend.

I am thankful now that in my youthful enthusiasm for his work I offered my own small tribute to his genius. He wrote to Eddie Marsh—"Do you know of a boy or young man vaguely or formerly at Cambridge? Nottingham? He wrote me such a nice letter—all letters of appreciation are nice but his was rather a clever one and it seems he is a poet." His father told me how he had cherished these letters in his exile. The most precious came from George Bernard Shaw to whom he had sent the manuscript of *Hassan*. Back came a letter of criticism and encouragement. "This is the best thing of its kind since Shakespeare," he wrote.

Poor Flecker. When I wrote to him moved by enthusiasm for *The Golden Journey to Samarkand*, I did not know that he was within eighteen months of his death, just turned thirty. The address on his letter had a sinister implication, a sanatorium in Switzerland. I was also unaware of the incessant battle he fought to find a position at home, for despite the beauty and tone of his poems, he hated the Orient and his life as a Consul in Constantinople, Smyrna and

Beirut. During short vacations in England he made desperate efforts to find home employment. In 1912 there was a project, among many, of a lecturership at Nottingham University College. He did not pursue it, afraid of its provincialism after Oxford, Cambridge and the East. "Nottingham is a deadly prospect," he wrote to his father from Beirut. How singular if he had gone to Nottingham. He might have met J. C. Snaith, the novelist, who was living there and of whom he had written, in a review of his work in *The English Review*—"Three of his books are near literature and one is a masterpiece, *William Jordan, Junior*. That work is unique, and it is a masterpiece and it is all but unknown." And in 1912 Flecker would have been an assistant to Professor Weekley, whose wife Frieda eloped with D. H. Lawrence, his former pupil, who was then in Nottingham seeking his recommendation to obtain a lecturership. He and Flecker were the same age. One wonders how they would have regarded each other, both young men of genius, both doomed to die of consumption in exile. They would have met in the year of the elopement and all the scandal it created when Frieda fled, leaving the professor with their three children.

In that year, 1912, the University College had awarded me The Henry Kirke White Prize for my poem *The Trent*, my first publication. We might have met, I, an eager youth of nineteen, he, at twenty-seven, already an established poet with his *Forty-two Poems*. But it was not to be. In December, 1912, from Paris, he wrote to his father—"I am so disheartened. It is my tragedy. I have got to go back to Beirut, alone, possibly to die. No one will do anything for me." Three months later the consumption attacked again and he was in hospital, gravely ill. "This beastly climate with its awful siroccos and days of heat and dust, alternating with blinding rain and hail, has done me no good. All hope of anything, of seeing England again, ever having a home or a happy day again, I have utterly abandoned."

In his play *Hassan*, which he did not live to see triumphantly produced at His Majesty's Theatre in London, with Leon Quartermaine as Ishak, the Poet, an unforgettable performance, he had written a scene, 'The Procession of Protracted Death'. He now began that procession, which was to end fatally in the sanatorium at Davos. So like Keats, young, on the verge of fame, he died in exile.

In 1916 a collected edition of Flecker's poems appeared. It rapidly ran through eighteen impressions but Flecker's parents did not like a part of the preface written by J. C. Squire, and they particularly objected to some extracts from a letter contributed by Frank Savery, a lifelong friend of the poet from Oxford days. Mrs. Flecker wrote to me,

Dean Close School, Cheltenham.
May 13, 1917.

While I think Mr. Squire's review admirable I feel it keenly that such a one-sided picture of our boy should have been given to the world as Mr. Savery's and no other. In his short young life my son was happily married for the last three years and we are much attached to our daughter-in-law and owe her gratitude for her devotion to a sick husband abroad when circumstances kept us very much in England. At the same time I do not feel that such a short acquaintance enables her to be the best biographer of the period before she knew him. Mr. Savery was his friend at Oxford but not his greatest friend nor the one that knew him best . . . Our son is given to the world as more or less delicate and an invalid but till this illness overtook him he was a strong, robust young fellow. He went to Uppingham soon after his 16th birthday and entered Trinity College, Oxford, just before he was eighteen, having won an open scholarship at seventeen and holding also an Exhibition of £60 from Uppingham.

Mr. Savery makes much of his want of development. "He was extraordinarily undeveloped even for an English Public School-boy". In the first place Roy was a year younger than most freshmen at Oxford, but he was just under 6 ft in height, manly in appearance and always passing as some years older than his real age. In thought and conversation also he was in advance of his years. He went straight into the 6th at Uppingham at 16¼. Mr. Savery refers to the purity of his mind and life. I object strongly to the way that is put. It did not appeal to some and they did their best to alter this, with poor results. To our boy with his heredity and Christian environment, both in the house, and in this school, even Uppingham at 16 was a great shock. He had no taste for vulgarity nor impurity and it was partly because he was so unhappy at school that Dr. Flecker sent him to Oxford so young. Early in his Oxford days Roy taxed us with not having told him of all the evil there was in the world and preparing him for it. Some of his friends obtained an increasing influence over our boy, very largely, it seems to us, by the grossest flattery.

We knew he had great gifts but were anxious that his character should become formed in the best and highest way. These friends saw no need for all this and told him frankly he was a remarkable genius and encouraged him to be original at any cost. To say, as Mr. Savery says, that "the sport he afforded was usually excellent" is not a nice reflection on the man who wrote those words.

Besides those mentioned who influenced his work there were certainly some of the masters here to whom, as he acknowledged, even in the last years of his life, he owed much. One had made him translate French poetry as a boy, for instance. He loved France, and increasingly he loved home and England.

The published photographs of Roy are unfortunate and not much like him, especially the one in the book of Poems. It was a snapshot taken by his wife, dear to her because of its association and because he was smiling. His face at rest was grave and even stern. Like Mr. Savery's account it should not stand alone.

I know that you have always been appreciative of our dear son's poetry. Your article and Requiem poem in *The Poetry Review* have given us great pleasure. I hope you will visit us soon. You will have a warm welcome. He had talked to me of your appreciation of his work. In spite of war time the roses will be blooming before very long. Roy loved them and I expect you would find them beautiful too. This Cotswold country has a charm of its own and ought to refresh you in your busy life.

Alas, I was unable to respond to this invitation. And then Mrs. Flecker died, and Dr. Flecker died, and forty-five years later, the poet's wife died. One day, in 1967, walking in the cloister made by Michelangelo out of the Baths of Diocletian in Rome and now part of the National Museum, I saw an English family looking at a long stele on which was carved an announcement of a Roman Festival, for which Horace had written some songs to be sung by Roman boys and maidens. After translating the nigh two-thousand-year-old Latin announcement I asked them where they came from. They said Cheltenham. "Ah, the home of a very good poet, James Elroy Flecker," I commented. The boy's face lit up. "I'm at Dean Close School there," he said. "Do you know Flecker's work?" I asked. Without hesitation he recited—

Oh, well I know sweet Hellas now,
And well I knew it then,

When I with starry lads walked out—
But ah, for home again!
Was I not bred in Gloucestershire,
One of the Englishmen!

That is immortality.

There was a sequel to my requiem on Flecker. One day there came a letter in a very small, neat handwriting, almost printed.

Jan. 8, 1917.

Dear Sir,

I trust you will forgive me for introducing myself to you, but I have just read your poem in *The Poetry Review* on James Elroy Flecker, and I simply had to write and tell you how much I like it. I think it is exactly what Flecker himself would have liked to have had written on him, and that is, I think, the highest praise. It was with great pleasure that I read your *Youth of Beauty* in October, 1915, but there is nothing in that book which I like so much as this poem. The workmanship is perfect, and there is something so inevitable about the lines that make me feel that no other words would be possible . . . But I must not bore you. With my sincere thanks for the very real pleasure your poem has given me,*

I am, yours faithfully,
Alec Waugh.

Later I met my correspondent, a chubby-faced lad of eighteen, who was soon to startle England with his novel *The Loom of Youth*, a pertinent criticism of public schools. It foretold a brilliant writing career too long overshadowed by his ebullient brother, Evelyn. Thus began a friendship that has lasted over half a century. It happened that Alec's father, Arthur Waugh, a distinguished critic and publisher, had already endeared himself to me by reviewing my second book of poems, with others, saying, "We award the laurel crown to Cecil Roberts. His poetry is full of soul, and the soul of man is (inevitably) the life-blood of art."

With a sale of three hundred and fifty copies of my first book of poems, and no loss, my Maecenas said, "Let's have another go!

* See Appendix I.

You've got enough for a second volume." Within a year we had gone to press with a successor, *Through Eyes of Youth*. One day when I read a new poem to him in his studio he took my breath away by saying, "Why not give a public reading of your work. We'll take the Mechanics Hall and enjoy ourselves!" I hesitated. It was a large hall to fill. I had heard on its platform the pianist, de Pachmann, enchantingly dotty, the politician F. E. Smith, in all the insolence of his youth, and others. My patron had no qualms. He booked the hall, and so one evening in March, 1914, I went on to the platform and read some thirty poems. The Sheriff of Nottingham, Lord Henry Bentinck, M.P., and four professors from University College were present. The next morning I went from Parnassus to my office-dungeon under the Mayor's Parlour. The recital had not been ruinous. We were seven pounds in hand.

"And now to fresh woods and pastures new!" exclaimed Kiddier. *De l'audace et toujours de l'audace!* "We'll march on London. This time we'll take the Bechstein Hall!"

The Bechstein Hall was in Wigmore Street, London. After the First World War it changed its name to the Wigmore Hall, following the pattern of the Royal Family that changed from Guelph to Windsor. It was the hall in which musicians, especially pianists, made their London début. Even in the early days when I had dreamed of becoming a concert pianist, I had never aspired to the Bechstein Hall. (Illustration, p. 81.)

A man of action, William Kiddier went ahead. It was all done in an infectious spirit of adventure. An enthusiastic friend undertook to act as press agent, his business taking him frequently to London. The hall was booked for June 12th, 1914. "Let's be original," said my patron. "No tails and a white tie. We'll have a siena-brown velvet jacket, black-braided and well-cut." He took me to his tailor and after much consultation a jacket was made. This time, my father no longer alive to exercise a veto, I grew my hair longish. The whole thing became a spirited adventure with a note of absurdity.

The great evening arrived. I was in a state of nerves such as never assailed me if it was a matter of making a speech or giving a lecture. Would there be anyone in the hall—even twenty? I had looked in at the Bechstein Hall in the afternoon. Its size dismayed me. The tickets were ten and six, five shillings, three shillings and two shillings. Would anyone be silly enough to expend that money listening to an unknown youth reading his poems?

As it turned out the hall was over half-full, better than the fate of many a young pianist making his début. The ever kind Lord Henry Bentinck brought along 'Eddie' Marsh, a figure of immense prestige in the world of poetry. He was private secretary to Winston Churchill but his fame was based on the fact that he had edited an epoch-making volume, *Georgian Poetry*, that presented most of England's eminent living poets, John Masefield, Wilfrid Wilson Gibson, Rupert Brooke, W. H. Davies, Walter de la Mare, D. H. Lawrence, John Drinkwater, James Elroy Flecker, etc. In request as a social figure, intimate with those prominent in the social and political worlds, Eddie Marsh, with a jerky speech, formidable upraised eyebrows and a will of steel encased in an aesthetic physical exterior, was a 'power'. He cultivated the company of gifted young men and nursed them to fame. At this time he had among his disciples one for whom he provided a lodging in his Gray's Inn Chambers whenever he came up from Cambridge. This dazzling young man, Rupert Brooke, was destined soon to make a leap into immortality. After his death Marsh became his editor and biographer.

His ever hospitable roost in Gray's Inn was presided over by a devoted housekeeper from Nottingham, Mrs. Elgy. She was never dismayed by a sudden demand for beds and meals for volatile young guests, budding poets, painters, actors, around whom Eddie fluttered like a hen guarding her chicks. The roost was choked from floor to ceiling with paintings, some there because he liked them, many acquired because he wished to help the painters. Not a wealthy man, he was exceedingly generous. His great-grandfather, the Prime Minister Spencer Perceval, had been assassinated in 1812 in the lobby of the House of Commons. He left a wife and ten surviving children out of a brood of nineteen. The House voted the murdered man's widow £1,000 a year, and £50,000 in trust for the children. One hundred years later Marsh told Rupert Brooke that one-sixth of the trust had come to him on the death of an uncle. He would therefore be willing to guarantee a loss on the publication of *Georgian Poetry* which was then being planned. Through the years Marsh often applied this trust income, 'murder money' as he expressed it, to alleviating the lot of writers and artists in whom he was interested.

Marsh was the perfect, highly-equipped civil servant. Winston Churchill had been quick in recognising his merit and a lifelong association ensued. His loyalty never failed though it had many severe tests. He was equipped with a prodigious memory. At the age of twelve he committed to memory the first four books of *Paradise Lost*. He had a tin-whistle voice, an air of precision. Perhaps to correct the impression of being an aesthete, something that enrages the British Philistine, Marsh wore a monocle, the Galloping Major badge* that, together with his Mephistophilean upturned eyebrows, gave him a fierce look. But his smile was bland, his movements feline.

His presence in the audience at the Bechstein Hall made me nervous. The High Priest of English verse was surveying the acolyte. He came round to the artistes' room afterwards and was politely complimentary. Little did I know of the very changed circumstances in which we were to meet again.

The recital finished, an artist friend of Kiddier's took us off to the Café Royal in Piccadilly, a bohemian haunt that tried to produce an air of Montparnasse. There was a great smoky room with caryatids, long gilt mirrors and red plush benches. It was packed with a singular crowd of patrons, some famous, some notorious, many hoping to become one or the other. The women looked bedraggled, the men raffish. Most of them affected a shabby untidiness in their attire. A tough, stocky little man, obviously Jewish, wearing a jersey, with uncombed hair, was pointed out to me. He was the sculptor, Jacob Epstein, who had created a controversy with his nude males on the façade of a Strand building. He was to shock many down the years with his aggressive neo-Assyrian-Judaic figures. But he was always 'news'. Near him sat Augustus John, amid what seemed a group of gypsy women, a sharp-eyed, lean figure with wild hair. He already enjoyed much prestige as a superb draughtsman. A young Jew sat near him, Mark Gertler, an artist of promise who would die young, one of Eddie Marsh's protégés.

It was after midnight. The great salon buzzed with conversation under a thick haze of tobacco smoke. Well, I had seen Bohemia. The chief impression left on me was that most of its members wanted a bath and their clothes pressing.

The next morning Kiddier took me to visit Ernest and Mary Gillick who had studied at the Nottingham School of Art. They had now made a reputation as sculptors. Gillick produced, later, memorials for Emmanuel and Trinity Colleges, Cambridge, and figures for the Cardiff Town Hall and the Glasgow War Memorial. Mary Gillick had concentrated on medal and portrait bas-relief.

* About this time there was a famous music-hall song that ran—*Hi! Hi! clear the way! Here comes the Galloping Major!*

They lived in a large enclosed meadow, tree encircled, at World's End, a sharp turn at the bottom of the King's Road, Chelsea. You rang a bell at a gate in a high wall and then stepped into an astonishing green oasis. It might have been a hundred miles from Piccadilly, so quiet was it with its great lawn. Once upon a time it had been a Moravian Burial Ground, and since that sect did not favour memorials, the long lawn was devoid of tombstones. The old Regency chapel had been converted into a house and studio, and here the Gillicks lived and worked, a happy pair. They gave us a great welcome. I intended to return there one day, but, alas, I delayed too long. When fifty-two years later I went back, Mary Gillick, a widow, had just died, aged eighty-four, after a distinguished career. In 1952 she had designed the uncrowned head of Queen Elizabeth for the coinage of the United Kingdom and Commonwealth and also used for official medals. In 1953 she made the joint portraits of the Queen and the Duke of Edinburgh, used on medals to commemorate royal visits. For these works she was given an O.B.E. Thus ended another romance of a young couple from the Nottingham Art School.

I had already had experience of 'Bohemia in London', with which the Café Royal sample compared badly. The Poetry Society, recently founded, organized a dinner in the wine cellar of the renowned Cheshire Cheese in Fleet Street, where it was alleged Dr. Johnson had once been an habitué. At the high table, with a background of wine bins, sat Sir Beerbohm Tree, robust and benign, the master wizard of His Majesty's Theatre. Stephen Phillips, then editing *The Poetry Review*, which had printed a poem of mine eight pages long, took the chair. Near him was Israel Zangwill and other well-known authors. I looked at Phillips with deep interest. He had risen like a rocket that blazed and then spluttered out. Related to Wordsworth, educated at Stratford-on-Avon, the muse seemed to smile on him when he privately published, at twenty, a book of verse. He first thought of becoming an actor, being six feet tall, athletic, with a handsome Roman head, and endowed with a gift for speaking verse. At twenty-one he joined the famous Shakespearean company of his cousin (Sir) Frank Benson, but seven years later he left the stage, feeling that poetry was his métier. With *Poems* published in 1898, he had a resounding success. *The Oxford Dictionary of Quotations* gives him only two poor one-line quotations but in his day, as in Swinburne's, young men went about declaiming lines from *Marpessa*. "I read it on a June evening when young", wrote John Drinkwater. "I can never forget the exultation with which I read his poem. It was an experience never to be forgotten."

Wounded with beauty in the summer night
Young Idas tossed upon his couch, and cried
"Marpessa, O Marpessa!" From the dark
The floating smell of flowers invisible,
The mystic yearning of the garden wet,
The moonless-passing night—into his brain
Wandered, until he rose and outward leaned
In the dim summer: 'twas the moment deep
When we are conscious of the secret dawn,
Amid the darkness that we feel is green . . .

He deserves better than the *O.D.Q.*'s mean treatment. In 1900 Beerbohm Tree produced at His Majesty's Theatre Phillips' verse drama *Herod.* It proved a triumph. The critics were ecstatic. George Alexander commissioned a play, *Paolo and Francesca.* When it was produced in 1902 Phillips was hailed as in the same rank as Sophocles and Shakespeare. Tree followed up his success with *Ulysses* and *Nero.* Both were resounding triumphs. But the praise had been too extravagant. From that time on, the descent of Phillips' reputation was swift. The critics, feeling they had overpraised him, now savaged him. The cruelty of it broke him. He became feckless, indolent and took to drink. Soon he was penniless. Martin Harvey, who had produced one of his plays, gave him a walk-on role. Later he was glad to earn a few pounds editing *The Poetry Review.*

Such was the poet now taking the chair. He had a noble head and a commanding manner. He stood up and recited a chorus from *Atalanta in Calydon.* I can still hear that resonant voice—

He weaves, and is clothed with derision;
Sows, and he shall not reap;
His life is a watch or a vision
Between a sleep and a sleep.

Within two years of his recital Swinburne's lines had a prophetic note. Harassed by poverty, bitter, Phillips was dead, aged forty-seven. He left seven pounds.

He was followed at this dinner by Beerbohm Tree with a witty speech, but the contribution of the evening was made by Israel Zangwill, the chronicler and champion of Jewry, who had invented the term 'The Melting-Pot' for America. He had a striking Semitic head covered with black curls, and I thought that Disraeli once might have looked like that. His impromptu speech was graced with wit, pathos and scholarship. It held the company spellbound. I was destined to have personal contact with him four years later in my capacity of dramatic critic, when I found to my pleasure that he was my neighbour at a Sutro première. We got into conversation and I recalled his speech at the Cheshire Cheese. We promenaded between the acts. I think he was not beyond taking pleasure in the admiration of an eager young man. He talked of his experience in the theatre and said he had once read a play to George Alexander in his dressing-room at the St. James' Theatre. Half-way through the reading Sir George halted in putting on his trousers to listen to the engrossing curtain of the drama. "Alas, though he put on his trousers, he did not put on my play," said Zangwill sadly. We parted at the close of the performance with much cordiality. A few days later I was surprised to receive a letter from him, beginning—"I am ashamed to say that before meeting you at the Sutro première I had never read your works," and went on to say that he had bought a book of mine, *Twenty-Six Poems*, and read it with very great pleasure. "I have rejoiced to make the acquaintance of so sane a singer, so free from the follies of Futurism, which have invaded even literature. There is so much versatility shown in these poems that I think you have it in you to do work still finer. If there were others of your calibre at that Cheshire Cheese supper, I must hasten to make their acquaintance."

I felt like a private who had been complimented by a Field-Marshal. Then, five years later, there came a letter from him on the publication in 1923 of my novel *Scissors*. In that book I had drawn a portrait of him under the pseudonym of Luboff.

"While I am touched by your kind reference to myself, my critical instinct wonders what I am doing in that galère, and why there is the mixed technique of presenting Wells under his real name and me under an invented. I did not like the title when I saw it advertised, as it suggested a flippancy which did not seem characteristic of you . . . But of course one gets accustomed to the name and its attractive owner, one of the nicest boys in fiction."

All this was in the future. As usual, after that exciting evening in 1913 at The Cheshire Cheese, almost Parnassus itself to me with those 'immortals' in the flesh, I had to rush to the station to catch the midnight train to Nottingham. Surely there was never such a five-shilling's worth as that half-day excursion, that brief penetration into the heart of London where the laurels of fame awaited the acolyte. I woke in my attic bedroom scarcely able to credit what I had experienced a few hours earlier. There must have been a glow about me the next morning when I walked into the dismal Weights and Measures office where sundry shopkeepers were waiting to retrieve their weights plugged with little bits of lead, and stamped with a crown to guarantee correct weight. "And what have you been doing now?" asked a fellow clerk. "Last night I dined with the gods on Olympus!" I replied; which was about as crazy an answer as they expected from that mad young Roberts.

On my twenty-first birthday there was no coming-of-age celebration for me. No 'loyal address from the tenants', no Grand Tour. I received two presents, a leather attaché case from William Kiddier, a fancy waistcoat from my mother. The former present went with me round the world for over fifty years. This coming-of-age aroused in me a mood of sheer desperation. Time was on the wing. I felt I must get out of that office with its drab life-long security, its pension at sixty. There was a vast exciting world to be explored. I would try every door until I found a way out. I offered myself to the two local newspapers as a cub reporter. They turned me down, unimpressed by the work I had had printed. I well knew there was no money in poetry but I was sure I would break through somehow, sometime, like the chrysalis in the cocoon, and find wings in a free world. I was torn between adventurous ambition and the caution entailed by my position as the home-provider. I had one friend who believed in me. "Don't worry yourself too much. I know you'll find a way out one day," said William Kiddier.

II

It was about this time that I had a bad attack of calf-love. It came on me as quickly as that other scourge of the young, measles. I ran a fever at once. There had come into the city a remarkable woman of about forty. She had been appointed as the manageress of a café that had opened above a new cinema in the marketplace. This cinema was a frequent refuge from my dungeon under the Mayor's Parlour. For the sum of sixpence you were transported into fairyland. The seats were wonderfully upholstered. You walked in on thick carpets. There was a long dark room with a silver screen. Sometimes they put on 'travelogues' and while appropriate music pervaded the cinema you sailed down the Nile, walked in Florence, went on safari through the African jungle or visited the birthplaces, with opera extracts, of Verdi, Puccini, Wagner, etc. One day there was an excursion along Lake Garda in peach-blossom time, with snow-crowned mountains rising from the blue lake. Lago di Garda. The very name was an incantation. Outside awaited reality—a damp, fog-laden November afternoon of the dour Midlands. When the lights slowly went up one came back to earth.

Over the cinema, up an oak staircase, with thick pile carpets and flowers on the landing, you came to the café. It had soft divans and easy chairs. The lights were gold-shaded, the waitresses were dressed in neat blue uniforms. There were flowers beautifully arranged and massed in vases. Someone of singularly good taste had done the designing and made the setting. For threepence, the price of a cup of coffee, you could sit there in luxury for an hour and read *The Tatler* or *The Illustrated London News*. Once a week I indulged myself in this warm luxury. One afternoon on leaving I saw a lady at a desk giving instructions to a waitress. I was stricken like Paris first seeing Helen. It was difficult to believe that she belonged to this earth. The loveliness of her face, voice, figure, overwhelmed me. She had about her an aura drawn from another world. Who was she, and what was she doing here, managing a café in a provincial town? I made enquiries. It appeared that I was not the only one to be dazzled. In a short time she had become the most talked-of woman in the city. It was an artist friend who answered my queries. She kindly arranged for us to meet in her studio. I learned that my *donna* was married! Somewhere in South Africa there was a husband of fifty, of a distinguished family, who had been left behind after a hopeless marriage. It chanced that his name was Cecil! The report was that he was handsome, full of charm, but a spendthrift. He must have been a dolt to let a woman like this escape him, was my verdict. Her beauty, her charm, the gaiety of her manner, the quickness of her mind, enriched by wide reading, her ravishing smile, and a pair of mocking blue eyes, long-lashed, combined to hold me in thrall. Was she *la belle dame sans merci*? I hoped not. She had soon invaded the inner circles of the stuffy county set. Without money, in a town whose only criterion was wealth, she established her leadership. Young squires arrived in their sports cars and begged to take her out. Elderly tycoons found pretexts for talking to her. She held them all adroitly in competition. The two reigning beauties of the county, the Duchess of Portland and Mrs. Charles Birkin, had a rival.

I fell deeply in love, although this lady was my senior by some twenty years, an experienced woman of the world. I learned that she was one of three beautiful sisters, of South African-Irish extraction. How fate had brought her here, to manage a café, was a mystery. "Something wrong somewhere, old boy!" said one suitor. "Another Paula Tanqueray," snorted a Master of Foxhounds. They had been well snubbed for presumption. I, an insignificant stranger, with only an office boy's salary, had little hope, well down in the queue. To my amazement she noticed me and took me in hand. "You're very intelligent," she conceded, "but too precocious." I showered verses on her, about which she was encouraging. Somehow she seemed always informed on current literature although she worked twelve hours a day. Her waitresses, whom she kept in strict order, adored her. She was one of those rare women whom women like.

Her tiny flat reflected her personality. It had a distinction that made the homes of the local magnates seem heavy. I believe she lived on some five pounds a week, yet she was always chic and fashionably dressed. "It's her eyes and her voice, my boy. When she laughs you can't see anything around you!" exclaimed a county buck, accustomed to commanding whatever he wanted. She played bridge well, she was stylish when taken to a Meet. She graced At Homes of women with ten thousand a year. Anyone who secured her for a dinner party was assured of its success. My mother was the only one who did not succumb to her allure. She feared for me. "She's a head-turner. And where's her husband?" she asked after I had produced her for tea. It was a mistake. I should have known that mothers with sons in the nest are suspicious of strange birds.

Of course I had rivals with whom I could not compete, young men with fine homes and cars, and money in their pockets, but I could make rings round them conversationally. They stared at me. What insolence for a nobody! So a queen let me join her court, Penelope and the suitors, with the mysterious Ulysses, her husband, far away. "Sometimes I wonder if you aren't the only real Cecil, and the other a phantom!" observed Helen Stiebel one day while drawing my portrait.

It pleased my *donna* to treat me like a schoolboy, despite my protests. In a year she wrought a change in me through moments of humiliation and resentment. My hypersensitive nature, with its aestheticism and alternating shyness and audacity, was shaped by her to a more balanced control. When I vowed I loved her she laughed and patted my cheek, "*Cher enfant*, you mustn't be so serious. I could be your mother!" she said. Preposterous! When I wrote poems to her she accepted them like a *donna* at a Renaissance Court. Her smile was sunshine and her voice music. Some praised her hair, her eyes, her mouth, others her grace, her wit, her style. We all agreed that she was the kind of woman who should be the chatelaine of a great house, that it was a crime for her to be wasted on a provincial town.

Some years later, returning to Nottingham with a friend, both of us now sophisticated travellers, I took him to call on her. The fervour of adolescence had long subsided. Should I be disillusioned? No, the old magic was there. Coming away, my friend exclaimed, "What a lovely creature! What an extraordinary woman to meet here. Unbelievable!"

"She enchanted me fifteen years ago, and I was not the only one. So you don't think I was wrong?"

"Wrong? Wrong?" he exclaimed with some excitement. "Why, she's, she's—but fancy here! Here in this place!" he cried.

In due time I learned that her husband had died and that she had married a Yorkshire squire, a widower, with a lovely home. Forty years after that early infatuation, returning from my villa in Italy, I heard that she was now a widow, living in a small London flat. She had just recovered from a serious operation. I had a desire to see her again after so many years. I called her on the telephone. "It's a ghost from the past speaking," I said, inviting her to lunch with me. "It's a wreck you're inviting," she replied. But her voice had the old enchantment.

On the day of our lunch I wondered if it was not an act of folly. I calculated that she must now be about eighty, and I was on my way to being an elderly gentleman. Returns are often perilous.

She was announced and I went to the reception room in my club. She rose from a chair and I saw in a moment that whatever Time had taken from her she was still a woman of great beauty, dressed with the old allure. Though the hair had silvered she commanded notice. Our lunch was a great success. We talked of old days, we laughed a lot. Her eyes and voice had lost so little in the passage of time.

A few days later I went to tea in her little Kensington Garden apartment. The touch of her hand had graced everything in it. She had invited a few friends. I lingered after they had gone and I insisted on helping her to wash up in the little kitchen. "I live quite alone and look after myself. Do you see what a lovely tree I look out on?" she asked, opening the kitchen window and revealing a lime tree in all its June glory.

I left. I had a feeling that her circumstances required economy, masked by the books and flowers around. There had been a costly fight with cancer. At the door I told her that I would be back in England next year. "Then next year be sure to call me, darling Cecil," she replied. I kissed her goodbye and went to the lift.

But there was no next year. Before the spring came she had gone.

A boy's love is a fragile thing but it is a flower whose scent remains down the years; it is part of the miracle of being twenty.

III

At that time of my youth we had no foreknowledge of the disaster that was to overwhelm the world and start the decline of the British Empire. Our Navy triumphantly ruled the seas. The gold sovereign was paramount among currencies. To be born British was to be born of a race that had achieved a supremacy unknown to the Roman Empire at the height of its power. The great Viceroys of India, never so magnificent as when the omniscient Lord Curzon held office like a god, were the representatives of a King-Emperor. Our ships sailed throughout the world putting into ports where the Union Jack proclaimed the British sovereignty, and, in Kipling's words 'Dominion over palm and pine' (this line quoted with a suspicion that it was too good to last and we had better make sure the Almighty was still our backer). Governors with gold-laced uniforms and white-plumed hats ruled from Residences, held their Councils and dictated to the 'lesser breeds without the Law' (again Kipling). Cecil Rhodes had placed South Africa in our lap and a Boer War, magnanimously settled, gave us precedence in a land rich with mines of diamonds and gold. Exclusive Park Lane was lined with the palatial homes of South African millionaires. They sometimes came to the help of the harassed King Edward. The Bank of England was independent

William Kiddier. "I remember William Kiddier, he was a fine and generous-minded man." Dame Laura Knight, R.A.

Laura Knight at 16, painted by Harold Knight. When Dame Laura Knight (Laura Johnson) was 13 she studied at the Nottingham School of Art. Harold Knight, aged 17, was a student there. They married in 1902, painted together for nearly sixty years and both became Royal Academicians and not a tool of the Treasury. The crisp five pound note, beautifully engraved, meant something. The pound was a solid gold coin, not a constantly devalued piece of paper. The City controlled the credit of the world. Soldiers and sailors were cheap to buy and ready to perish in far places for something they did not possess. "Give me enough of that article and I'll win battles," said the Iron Duke. Servants, the semi-helots of the upper and middle-classes, could be hired for ten shillings a week, to work in basements and sleep in attics; a million men, unemployed, rotted, standing in queues for jobs, while another queue in the Mall lined up in Rolls Royces and Daimlers, each automobile with the two prescribed chauffeurs, containing jewelled peeresses, dowagers and debutantes with three ostrich feathers in their hair, and wearing long white kid gloves. The crowd peered in on the Court guests. Good-natured, enjoying the free pageant, it cheered and waved to them. It was all part of the London show. Later with their trains trodden on, half fainting, they were lined up and shuffled like cards past the King and Queen, with the bored family royalties grouped about them. Elegant gentlemen of high birth, carrying wands, walked backwards, a thing never designed by Nature but a feat that contributed to the *mystique* of the throne. All this was my England, though an unattainable part of it. It was impossible to imagine that fifty years later a young Queen would fly to Africa to give a coloured colony its 'independence' and open a State ball with a black President's arm round her waist: a political autocrat chased out of his country a few years later and charged with tyranny and embezzlement.

Northwards in England, over a countryside blackened by chimneys and scabrous with coal mines, thousands of miners toiled in the bowels of the earth, at twenty shillings a week, to produce the coal that went outwards across the sea as ballast, and enabled the world's greatest shipping nation to extract a vast revenue from coal-less countries. The ships returned filled with cheap imports. In 1912 100,000 miners went on strike. When a vociferous little miner named Cook dared to challenge a young Duke who drew £100,000 a year from coal revenues, he was called 'a dangerous revolutionary'. It was these same miners, regarded as semi-savages, without one bath to a hundred hovels, who, when the challenge came to the British Empire, readily went forth and died in the mud trenches and on the wire of the bloody battlefields of the Western Front. For on June 28th, 1914, a crazy student shot a stuffy Austrian Archduke and his wife by a bridge in Sarajevo. The little Bosnian town caught the headlines. No one knew then that the fatal shots had fired a train of powder that would blow up the world.

I was not well that summer of 1914. I had exhausted myself with the excitement of publishing, with the recital in the Bechstein Hall, with night work, and most of all by my rebellion against the fate that threatened me in my office; and there was also the constant financial strain of my home life. With a wage of twenty-two shillings a week, to which was added eight shillings a week paid by Mr. Hartley, my gentle Latin teacher, for his lodgings, our total budget of thirty shillings a week was inadequate. I wanted new clothes, shirts and shoes. The dandy inherent in me was thwarted. In six years my uncomplaining mother had not had one new costume. I had earned in the last twelve months, with my pen, twenty-seven pounds, the result of incessant labour beyond midnight. The cost of paper, postage, and visits to editors in London, strained my resources. But such is the resilience of youth that nothing of this dismayed my spirit. I had not the slightest doubt that somehow I would throw off my shackles and one day be prosperous and famous. My mother shared that faith. Nevertheless there were some black hours of frustration.

Neglecting my mother's warning against burning the midnight oil, one day I collapsed. My two-weeks' office holiday was due. The doctor ordered me to the seaside. Two whole weeks was beyond my means. I spent one of them at Rempstone Rectory, gardening and reading in that paradise, and the second week at Skegness, on the East Coast, always, as the posters declared, so bracing. I went there in the first week of August. For two weeks there had been somewhat alarming headlines in the newspapers. Austria had plunged into war with Serbia, determined to crush her. The armies of the stiffnecked Emperor Franz Josef and of the sabre-rattling German Kaiser, whose forked moustache the British public found comic, were tramping across the frontiers. At home men in the reserve services were warned, but we thought that somehow we should contrive to keep out of the mess. The situation was being handled by the calm Mr. Asquith and the handsome Sir Edward Grey. Suddenly Germany invaded Belgium. On the morning of August 5th the newspapers had flaring headings—*England Declares War!*

Seated at breakfast in the little seaside boarding house, belligerently named Balaclava House, there was something unreal about the whole thing. Through the windows we looked out on the tranquil waters of the North Sea. Right across that expanse lay Germany. An old gentleman stood in the porch surveying the sea with a pair of binoculars. "They won't dare to come out. We'd pulverise them!" he declared, alluding to the German Navy.

"You'll see, it'll be all over in a month," said a pale little man to his wife.

"But they've millions and millions of soldiers!"

"Goose-stepping blockheads!" he retorted.

What was I to do? Go home? I had been there only four days of my week and the landlady would expect payment. I decided to stay. The next morning there was no milk for breakfast. The young milkman had vanished, called up. A girl brought the milk an hour late.

The following day at lunch a liver-spotted woman with big glasses and a rusty voice, exclaimed, "I always said Lord Roberts was quite right. We should have had conscription long ago. Every young man should be in the army fighting for his King and country."

She looked straight across at me, the only young man in the house.

It gave me a shock. I had not realised I was to be involved. The whole situation in that calm seaside resort seemed unreal. I had no desire to fight anyone, anywhere, least of all for a woman like that. I had only seen one German in my life, a pianist called Wilhelm Backhaus, who looked like the young Beethoven. I had paid a shilling to hear him play divinely.

The following day there was alarm among the boarding-house keepers. The visitors had gone overnight. Crowds packed the trains. "Who knows, they might land on the beach here!" exclaimed a mother with three children in tow at the station, the only place that had any life. I walked in deserted streets. The shopkeepers stood at their doorways, depressed and silent. The long wide beach formerly crowded with happy families was empty. I took a long walk that morning, out to Gibraltar Point, a spit of sand running out at the corner of the Wash. There was not a soul in sight. And this was August, at the height of the season. Every morning, with wild extravagance, I had hired a horse and galloped along the firm sands. I had had the same horse for half-a-crown an hour and became attached to it. I was a Leicestershire lad again. I wondered what had happened to that groom at Market Harborough who seven years ago had given me my first riding lessons. Had he emigrated to Kentucky as he said he hoped to, or would he, like all the other young men in England, soon be marching away? That morning as I walked along the beach there were no donkeys and ponies for hire—and the sands were splendidly empty, with no menace of riding down any straying children.

There was a somewhat battered piano in the sitting-room at Balaclava. I sometimes played on it after removing a jingling glass dome full of stuffed birds. I had an appreciative audience. That evening as I was playing Beethoven's Moonlight Sonata, the rusty-voice woman sitting in the bay window rose, advanced on us and addressed me, her face distorted by rage.

"How dare you play that filthy German's music! It is an outrage! Why don't you go home and enlist!" she cried.

There were murmurs of protest from my audience. I got up from the piano. "Madam, if you don't like what I'm playing no one will compel you to stay in the room," I said.

There was a knobbly little man from the North. He was always begging me to play. He swung round in his chair and looked at the irate woman.

"Hey, I'll tell ye summat! Why should a bonny lad go and sacrifice hisself for a withered old geezer like you?" he demanded.

Her mouth opened but no words came. She walked out of the room. He turned to me. "If that's Beethoven, German or no German, I like it. You go on, lad!"

I resumed my playing but I was disturbed in my mind. I began to comprehend that a pleasant world was going to pieces. Things would never be the same again.

At the end of the week I left the deserted little town. As I came down the stairs with my bag the landlady was in the hall. She was a fresh complexioned woman, a widow, who ran the boarding house with her two daughters. We shook hands. Then she said quietly—"Can I kiss you goodbye?" I stooped, put my arms round her and kissed her. "Good luck, and God keep you!" she said fervently.

IV

The next six months were a mental nightmare. There was no general call-up. Recruiting was on a voluntary basis. I had no desire to be a soldier. The newspapers printed pictures of joyous recruits at drill, sticking bayonets into bags of straw. I felt revolted by the debasement of the human race. I had no strong urge to lay down my life for King and Country. Neither of them had raised a finger to help me and my mother in our struggle for a decent existence. We owned only the worn clothes we stood up in. One Sunday in church the vicar embarked on a fiery diatribe against the wicked Germans. In Belgium they had cut off the hands of children. They had crucified a Canadian soldier. On the noble British army rested the survival of our Christian civilisation. They were the warriors of our Lord Jesus Christ, etc. I felt my mother stiffen in our pew. Suddenly she got up and walked out, with me following, stared at by all the congregation. Outside she said, "I suppose thousands of German, French and Belgian mothers are listening to the same blasphemy."

Little by little the mass hysteria eroded my resistance. My friends were vanishing. One, very dear to me, died of pneumonia, as hundreds of others who had to sleep on ground sheets in crowded training camps. Then one day with two friends I joined the University College Officers' Training Corps. We drilled three nights a week in a yard behind the Guildhall, where the Fire Brigade was housed. We put on belts with bayonets, sloped arms, marched, formed fours. I had no idea how to handle a rifle. The beastly thing defeated me. "This is your most precious possession," said the sergeant, slapping the butt of the rifle as he lectured us. I felt like giving him the thing as a keepsake. Once ordered to draw and fix bayonets, I clumsily stuck a youth in front of me in the buttock. He gave a great yell. He was a son of the Birkin brood. I had drawn millionaire blood, the only blood I was destined to draw in the Great War. Poor lad! He never became third baronet of his line. He was killed in 1917.

One evening one of my O.T.C. friends said, "I've had enough of this marching about. Let's go and join up and get the real thing." In the wayward exuberance of youth three of us went to the recruiting office. There had been long queues but now the rush was over and they were thirsting for recruits. We were given forms to fill in and then told to go into another room and take off our shirts. Here we waited with other youths. In about half an hour a sergeant appeared. Three at a time we were taken into a room with a doctor and an army clerk. Just then the doctor was called to the telephone and we waited, half-naked and shivering. He came back and began to examine us. Like a woman buying a roasting fowl, he felt the first plump youth. He ordered him to lower his trousers, cough, bend, jump. He told the clerk what to enter on the card. One of my friends came next. I was the last of the three. I felt humiliated. We were just cattle being vetted for the slaughterhouse. The doctor put his stethoscope on my chest. Here we go again, I thought. "Breathe in, Breathe out. Turn round." He applied it to my back. "Turn round." He put it on my chest again. He unclipped his stethoscope. "Have you ever had rheumatic fever?" he asked. "Yes, but a long time ago." He said nothing to me and spoke to the clerk who gave me back my card. As I went out three more youths came in. I joined my friends. I went up to the sergeant at the desk. He looked at my card and said brusquely, "You're out, you can buzz off home." I stared at him. "Out—rejected?" I asked. He nodded. My two friends were accepted. One was killed at Vimy. The other became a major and marched with Allenby into Jerusalem. When we met again twenty years later he was hardly recognisable, with a paunch and a beefy face. He was the father of four children, a director of a prosperous engineering company. "Ah, those were the days! I enjoyed every minute of the war. Would like it all over again. Nothing touched me! You see, I've got gappy teeth. That means luck!" he exclaimed.

On reaching home I said nothing to my mother. I did not want to agitate her, feeling rather ashamed of my thoughtlessness. I was her sole support and what would have become of her? Little by little it became a less pleasant world. People began to show the strain. There was an air of hostility. Restrictions began to grow. The politicians and generals were bitterly assailed. Everything seemed to be going wrong on the Western Front. The casualty lists swelled. Day after day some neighbour's son was killed. Mrs. Horsley's beloved Mr. Asquith was harshly criticised. A witch hunt began. Sir Edgar Speyer, a former friend of King Edward, a Privy Councillor, was accused of German collusion, and hounded out of the country. The war had now been transformed into a Christian Crusade against the barbarian Huns. And those Americans—'too proud to fight'—were making fortunes in armaments.

I sometimes went to play on the piano at a friend's house. We had lost our piano in the family disaster, and she had most kindly let me use hers. One day I noticed that she had pasted a strip of black velvet over the name Bechstein. I took the hint and played no German music. A neighbour's dachshund had been so brutally kicked in the street that it had to be destroyed. How debased could the human race become? We were told this was The War To End War. The hoardings carried the glowering face of Field Marshal Lord Kitchener who pointed an accusing finger above the legend *Your Country Needs YOU*. A great soldier, he was an unsympathetic character, domineering, with a rigid mentality. He had degraded himself with the desecration of the Mahdi's tomb in the Sudan campaign, denounced by Churchill as 'A wicked act'. Before the war's end he became something of a problem with his opposition to all innovations. His tragic death, after unstinting service, when H.M.S. *Hampshire* was mined off the Orkneys on a mission to Russia, had solved this. There were monstrous rumours that the Government had sent the ship through mined waters to be rid of him. Nothing was too crazy in these days to be believed. People vowed they had seen thousands of Russian soldiers transported from the north of Scotland to the south of England for embarkation to the Western Front. They had seen the snow on their uniforms when the trains halted in stations en route! There was also the legend that angels had appeared to the British soldiers at Mons to assist them in the battle. It was an old, old myth that had been used to explain the victory of the Christian Emperor Constantine over the pagan Roman Emperor Maxentius at the battle of Sax Ruba in A.D. 312. The angels at Mons did not carry banners with I.H.S. (*In Hoc Signo* we will conquer) as on the former occasion. Four soldiers, who swore they had seen the angels, were interviewed and then sent off round the country to assist recruiting.

At the beginning of 1915, in an atmosphere of general malaise I faced a personal crisis. Despite my industry I had failed to liberate myself from my dungeon-office. My very tolerant young chief called me in one day and said that I could delay no longer preparing for the examination to qualify as an inspector of weights and measures. Before the examination it was customary to spend two weeks at a crammer's who specialised in this Board of Trade examination. The cost was £20 for board, lodging and fees. I had desperately accumulated £25. I was determined not to spend this in achieving something I was so opposed to. A long humdrum career with a pension at sixty seemed to me like a 'life sentence'.

"I don't think you will have trouble with the examination. The war has created a dearth of inspectors and I believe the Board of Trade won't be exacting," said my chief, encouragingly.

I told him that I would think it over. He peered at me over his gold rimmed glasses. He had shown a great deal of patience with me.

"It is not a matter of thinking it over. This is the next step and the time has come when you really must make up your mind," he said with a peremptory tone. He must have felt like a father whose preposterous son is determined to go on the stage instead of entering the family business. I asked him for a week in which to decide. He agreed but looked hurt.

I passed a week tortured by irresolution. My mother saw I was anxious and preoccupied but she was one of those women who refrain from cross-questioning. Finally I went to my trustworthy friend Kiddier. I told him that I had decided to burn my boats. I just would not go on. He listened carefully and then said, "You'll never be happy there, I know that, and if you jump off the bridge I don't believe you'll drown—you'll swim somehow!"

The next morning I went into my chief's office. "I wish to give you a week's notice, sir. I've decided to go," I said.

"You have found another position?" he asked.

"No, sir."

"No!" he repeated, amazed. "But you're not going to throw up a safe position—"

"It's because it's so safe and deadly that I'm giving it up."

"How much money have you got?"

"Twenty-five pounds."

"Twenty-five pounds, with yourself and a mother to keep! Roberts, are you mad?" he asked. "Now think it over again. I won't take your notice. Think it over for a week. You have a safe profession in your hands, and you propose to commit suicide. What does your mother think?"

"I've not consulted her. I don't think it fair to put the burden of my decision on her. If I am going to starve because of twenty-two shillings a week then I'll starve."

"But there's the prospect of a career with—"

"The prospect horrifies me, sir. I want to be an author. I'm determined to be an author. If I don't jump off the bridge now I'll never have the nerve to do it later. I wish you to accept my notice, sir. And I want to thank you for all you've put up with. I know I've been a nuisance."

"I would not agree to that but you've certainly been somewhat of a problem—a most unusual boy. You are firm in your decision?"

"Yes, sir."

"Very well, I accept your notice. I wish you Good Luck."

So I had done it. It left me a little breathless. Twenty-five pounds could be spun out to last four months. A lot could happen in four months. It never occurred to me that I might starve.

When I told my mother what I had done she showed no sign of dismay. "I expect we'll manage somehow," she said quietly. "And if you feel happier that is something. I don't like seeing you worried as I have lately."

Grand old warrior! I took her in my arms and hugged her.

It was wonderful to get up in the morning and not have to go to that dismal office. I was free! I sat at my desk and reviewed my assets; a few pounds, some articles taken by Reviews, and two books of poems. The last could not rank as assets of any value. They had brought me no money and little renown. I had sold several articles to *Great Thoughts* and been well paid for two lectures. I was in some request as a speaker but this was not remunerative. My true assets were a bright irrepressibility and boundless faith in my star. Some people of course regarded me as an audacious pup and wanted to kick me but I had some firm friends. I had been blessed with good looks, a tall figure, a quick mind and a vivid sense of humour. I was delicate and nervously taut though I never let anyone detect how diffident I was under my bravado. I had done my best to repair a defective education. My down-to-earth brother thought I was 'balloony', he, poor fellow, being bound to earth with a family and dogged with bad health. He had had two operations, preceding three more that he faced with invincible courage and fortitude.

On my first free morning of May, when I was on the verge of twenty-three, having been over seven years office-bound, I opened an exercise book and began writing. I was so intent on my work that I did not see that my mother had come upstairs with a glass of milk and biscuits until she spoke to me.

"What are you writing now?" she asked.

"I've begun a novel!" I replied, almost triumphantly.

She smiled and left me. *Incipit vita nova.*

V

After two months I began to grow apprehensive. My manuscripts came back with depressing regularity. My small reserves steadily dwindled. I had earned exactly seven pounds. I put the proposed novel aside. Then a door opened. A friend knew someone who ran a preparatory school for boys. The war had drawn away his assistant masters. I went to see him and liked him at once. His name was

B. O. Corbett. He was famous as a Corinthian footballer and a Double Blue. With his wife he ran a school of some forty boys. It was established in a delightful old Georgian House, Shardlow Hall, in a large park, near Castle Donington. This meant I should not be very distant from my home. There was the added attraction of long vacations, good country food and air. So I joined one of the oldest professions in the world. I was *paidagogos*, schoolmaster. In that role I experienced some of the happiest and most miserable hours of my youth.

There was one other assistant master at the school, an Oxford graduate. He was a huge fellow, two years my senior but he was not as robust as he looked for he had suffered a nervous breakdown, in a form of religious hysteria, while at Oxford. He took a gloomy view of life and regarded schoolmastering as the lowest form of servitude. He warned me against any sentimental weakness and regarded small boys as merciless enemies. I loved them all, with their merry vitality, and, as he had warned me, reaped trouble, boys being quick to trade upon affection.

We shared a sitting-room with a nice view upon the lawns and lake but unfortunately it was next to the boys' changing room. There were bangs and yells; worse, there was a piano on which the smaller boys did their practice. Silence only came after they had gone to bed, when we marked their exercise books. The noises and the piano brought me to a point of hysteria. My colleague had brooding fits when he would not speak a word for hours. I began to worry over my inefficiency. I sometimes lost control of the classes. At times I forgot the task in hand and the boys sat spellbound as I entertained them with a dramatic reconstruction of history.

Do parents who forward their cheques at the beginning of term realise how much they get for their money? Corbett and his wife worked prodigiously. Being conscientious, they did not relax for a moment. There were outbreaks of measles and mumps to be identified and isolated. Coughs, colds, toothaches, heartaches, bedwetting, malingering and incipient criminality had to be dealt with sternly or sympathetically. The situation of the Hall was delightful. The River Trent, shining, wound through lush meadows. There was a park of tall elms and a lake on which we could boat. There were smooth lawns and flower beds. In the evening when the boys had gone to bed there came a delightful twilight silence broken only by the last mellow fluting of birds and the cawing of homing rooks. But I was not happy. I had changed one cul-de-sac for another. The gloom of my colleague oppressed me. I found no time to write, no privacy. I was away from everyone I knew. One evening I had an episode with a difficult boy. I had to detain him for disobedience. Suddenly he flung himself on me and burst into tears. Poor child, he was homesick like me and I held him to me in our mutual desperation. "Quite the wrong way to tackle that nonsense! You should have given him a clip over the ear!" declared my colleague. Yet for all his brusqueness he was patient and gentle with the boys.

One night I, too, reached breaking point. At two in the morning I burst into my colleague's bedroom. He sat up in astonishment while I declaimed against the injustice of life. Loneliness, overwork, starved nerves, thwarted ambition, had brought me to utter despair. Suddenly I threw myself down on his sofa and cried like a schoolgirl. When I got up, apologising for making an ass of myself, he went with me to my bedroom and tucked me up as he would a child. Poor fellow. Under a sham façade he had a kind heart. After surviving the Western Front and the Palestine campaign he was drowned bathing at his seaside home. He was the only son of a widowed mother who had deprived herself of much to send him to Oxford.

After the Easter vacation, during which I pressed on with my discarded novel, I returned to the school for a second term only. Once more I had decided to burn my boats. I do not think the headmaster saw me go with much regret. I was not of the stuff of which pedagogues are made. What did surprise me was a demonstration of affection by the boys. I had introduced them to some of the work of Francis Thompson, then enjoying a post-mortem vogue. I drilled them in the declamation of *The Hound of Heaven*. They subscribed for a four-volume de-luxe edition of Thompson's *Life and Poems*. I departed, feeling somewhat like Daudet's *Le Petit Chose*.

I often wondered what happened to those boys. They were too young to be sacrified to Moloch. There was a velvet-eyed and apple-cheeked boy with a gift for mimicry and engagingly fractious in class. Six years later, when a poetic drama of mine was produced, a young member of the cast came up to me during rehearsal and asked if I remembered him. His eyes and smile gave me the clue.

To this episode of my life I can now add, fifty years later, a singular footnote. In November, 1965, in the lounge of the Grand Hotel at Rome, while waiting for a dinner guest, I picked up a copy of the

London *Daily Express*. It had a photo of a football team on the sports page, with the caption—"Here are the new Corinthians". Since I had known a Corinthian, my chief at Shardlow Hall, I read on, and then found a photograph of 'the oldest living Corinthian'.

> Bertie Oswald Corbett, last of the legendary Corinthians, won't be at the Corinthian Casuals *v.* Watford Cup Tie. He is 91, and although he still drives a car, the strain of travelling to London and back from his Dorset home would be too much. He is living Soccer history and very lively. In 1904, with giants like C. B. Fry and G. O. Smith, he popped over to the Continent, on the nightboat to Flushing, for a seven-match tour of Hungary, Austria, Bohemia and Germany. They polished off Hungary's best men 6–0, 9–0 and 12–0 one weekend, sauntered off to win 7–1 in Vienna, won 7–4 and 4–1 in Prague, and finished the tour, 4–1 winners, in Leipzig. The Corinthians, who attracted crowds of 100,000 by their footballing magic, were the darlings of the Edwardian age of strong silent amateur Sportsmen.
>
> —Harry Langton.

I wrote to Corbett across the fifty years since I had been his assistant master. Back came a letter in a bold handwriting:

> It is a long beat back to Shardlow days. We retired in 1929 and came to live in this delectable part of Dorset where we still are. My wife is alive and has a wonderful garden and reads as much as ever. When war came in 1940, in order to justify my existence, I started farming my estate. I found it so interesting that I only gave up when I was 86 since it had become too big an undertaking for one of my years.

VI

For a second time I had burned my boats. It became clear to me that I must not get into another cul-de-sac. I wanted to be an author. I was certain I could write. I was still of the opinion that journalism offered the best training and the best opportunity. I had wooed the two local newspapers in vain. I now attacked again but this time from a different basis. I went to my trusted friend William Kiddier and asked his aid in my plan of campaign. He had a persuasive manner.

There are few who can resist something for nothing. On these lines I asked him to approach the acting editor of *The Nottingham Journal* with the suggestion that I should join its staff as 'a gentleman pupil'. The 'gentleman' implied that I was willing to work without remuneration. Such a category carried the prestige of 'independant means', a term of economic snobbery then current. I laughed inwardly at my independent means. They were precisely a capital of thirty pounds. I could hold out for six months. I had chosen *The Journal* rather than its more flourishing rival in the city because of its remarkable literary tradition. It was one of the oldest newspapers in the Kingdom, having been founded in 1710. When young James Barrie had finished his education at Edinburgh University he decided to enter journalism. *The Liverpool Post*, unaware of genius knocking at its door, rejected him. He then applied to *The Nottingham Journal* for the post of assistant editor-leader-writer and was appointed at three pounds three shillings a week. He was not quite sure what a leader was.

> The chance had come at last, with what we all regarded as a prodigious salary, but I was wanted at the beginning of the week, and it suddenly struck me that the leaders were the one thing I had always skipped! Leaders! How were they written? What were they about? My mother was already sitting triumphant among my socks, and I durst not let her see me quaking. I retired to ponder and presently she came to me with the daily paper. Which were the leaders, she wanted to know, so evidently I could not get help from her. Had she any more newspapers, I asked, and after rummaging she produced a few with which her boxes had been lined. Others, very dusty, came from beneath the carpets, and lastly a sooty bundle was dragged down the chimney. Surrounded by these, I sat down and studied how to become a journalist.

He wrote his first article in the train to Nottingham, in February, 1883. He was a lonely young man. He made no friends. He wrote the leaders and every Monday contributed a special article under the name of 'Hippomenes'. None of these contributions revealed any genius, nor did his novel *When a Man's Single*, which he began to plan there, and in which *The Journal* figures as *The Daily Mirror* and Nottingham as Silchester.

After handing in his first article on arrival at the office he went off to seek lodgings. The rest of his career belongs to literary history. Other distinguished writers on the *Journal* staff had been Philip James Bailey, author of *Festus*, Sir Dodds Shaw, a famous parliamentary reporter, and Sir John Foster Frazer, who won fame by going round the world on a bicycle, then coming into use as a means of transport.

Kiddier's overture succeeded. I was to join the paper as 'a gentleman pupil'. Ten years later *The Journal* was to have another 'gentleman pupil', aged twenty-one, who came there to start a writing career. His name was Graham Greene.

At first I was attached to the reporting staff, received with some suspicion, but soon enfolded in the camaraderie of journalism. I was lucky. I did very little reporting. The editor found another use for me. He was a tired, battered fellow who had been washed out of London journalism and was now decaying in a provincial backwater. Any writing seemed a great effort for him. He found that I was a rapid producer of copy. He took me into his room and gave me a desk. Within two weeks I was writing most of the leaders. I started also a series of sketches entitled 'Men of the Hour' which attracted attention. The editor was delighted. He sat back, drank and smoked. Towards midnight he went up to the linotype room and composed the lay-out and headings. He kept me until about one o'clock in case any special news came in. The deadline for going to press was 2 a.m. for the local morning edition. If a news titbit came in he would hand it to me. "Half a column," he would say. As I wrote, he read the sheets and sent them up to the composing room. "Good boy!" he would say, sitting back and lighting his pipe.

I was in heaven. At last I was doing what I wanted to do. I walked home through the dark streets with the new morning paper in my pocket. But I did not go to bed when I reached home after 2 a.m. A flask of hot cocoa awaited me in my den. I sat down and now wrote for myself. I was not going to be swallowed up in the quicksands of journalism. At 4 a.m. I went to bed and slept until noon.

My editor said very little and often looked at me quizzically. Sometimes he rejected my copy. "Too audacious, my boy. You have a bright prose style, but too much stiletto. We don't want to get into trouble." I learned later that he had once got into serious trouble, a costly libel action. It had led to his downfall and banishment to the provinces.

I heard that I was proving satisfactory in a roundabout fashion.

The editor met William Kiddier. "That boy's a worker. I've never seen copy produced with such speed and gusto in my life, and a crystal clear style. But too much imagination, he goes off into poetical flights. He has to be watched and brought down to earth." I laughed on hearing this. There was now no watching, editorially. He just sat back, smoked and hardly ever picked up a pen, happy to see me working in my corner. Soon I made a claim for signed articles. I could not see why he should get all the credit. He demurred. "The best journalism is anonymous—look at *The Times*," he said. "This isn't *The Times*," I replied. I won my point. I was in a strong position. I could walk out—or so he thought. The strong position was an illusion, of course, the financial aspect could not be ignored. The nightmare that had held me since that tragic hour of my father's death still hovered. My capital was being slowly depleted. The day was approaching when I should have to reveal the false colours under which I was sailing. The 'gentleman pupil' would have to ask for a salary. I knew that the paper was financially frail. The linotype machines were ancient, the advertising revenue poor, the transport under strain. The paper was being kept alive by the local Maecenas, Sir Jesse Boot, to give the Liberal party, of which he was a staunch supporter, a press in the city, and to challenge the rival Conservative newspaper.

One day at the close of the seventh week Fate directed my eyes to an advertisement for a literary and dramatic critic. The war was draining men away and replacements were difficult. I applied, with small faith in the anonymity of a box number. I was able to send a dozen clippings of leaders and signed articles. I said nothing about three published books of poems. Poets are always under suspicion. Drink, drugs, immorality and bohemianism are often their failings in the public eye, and if not these, they are slightly mad. "Did you know old Wordsworth had a mistress and an illegitimate daughter?" asked a solicitor to whom I had presented a copy of my Wordsworth article in *The Contemporary Review*. "Yes," I replied. "And do you know that solicitors sometimes embezzle their clients' money?"

I therefore made no mention of my books in my application. I waited a week and then received a reply. *The Liverpool Post* was considering my application. Henry James was very seriously ill. They would like me to write a critical obituary notice of twelve hundred words. Henry James. The choice was most unfortunate for me. I had heard of him as an American novelist of much prestige but small sales, who had settled in England. Alas, I had not read anything he had written. There was no time to be lost. I fervently hoped that he might be spared for a few more hours while I wrote his obituary.

I hurried off to the Public Library. They had the works of Henry James in ten volumes. I asked to see the librarian and explained my plight. I had to digest those volumes in a few hours. A man of sense, he gave me permission to take the volumes away for twenty-four hours. I invested half-a-crown in a cab, stacked them up and drove home. It was 10 a.m. The *Journal* did not see me that day. By 6 p.m. the next day I had digested the volumes and written my twelve hundred word critique. I hurried with the manuscript to the station and tipped the guard of the Liverpool night express to post the envelope on arrival there. I telegraphed the editor to say that the article would arrive the next morning. Thank God, Henry James did not die that day, nor for many days.

A week later I was offered the post of literary and dramatic critic at a salary of £156 a year. When I told my editor of my appointment he looked at me a little dismayed. "My God, you're a lucky fellow, it's a first-class paper!" he said, and then added, "Well, you deserve it." When I shook hands with him on leaving I had an awful feeling that it must seem to the poor fellow like Youth on the way up and Age on the way down. I would have been sadder had I known that within two months he was to be dropped for economy.

Henry James did not die until February 28th, 1916, soon after receiving the Order of Merit from the country with which he had chosen to throw in his lot, taking British nationality. The public wondered who he was. His books had never had any considerable sale, he had failed miserably as a dramatist. But he was known among the small influential set, to-day satirically called 'The Establishment', that gets rewards for its protégés, whether in politics, diplomacy or the arts.

I now had a problem arising from my appointment. My capital was down to fifteen pounds. I should have to send my mother a pound a week to keep the house going, and live in lodgings on the other two pounds of my salary. It would be a squeeze. And there was a menace over me as I set foot on the first rung of the professional ladder, the Government was combing all possible recruits. Under pressure from the mounting massacre on the Western Front the medical standards were being lowered. There was therefore no

The author, aged 21, the year of his first book *Phyllistrata and Other Poems*

BECHSTEIN HALL,

WIGMORE STREET, W.

CECIL ROBERTS

(Author of "Phyllistrata and Other Poems," "Through Eyes of Youth," Etc.)

IN

Recital

OF HIS OWN POEMS

FRIDAY EVENING

JUNE 12th, 1914,

At 8.30.

TICKETS—

10/6, 5/-, 3/-, & 2/- (Balcony).

At the Hall (Telephone No. 1282 Mayfair)
and of the Poetry Society,
16 Featherstone Buildings, Holborn, W.C.
(Telephone No. 2188 Holborn).

In the anti-German wave following the First World War, the royal family changed its name from Guelph to Windsor, the Battenbergs to Mountbatten. The Bechstein Hall became the Wigmore Hall, but the Bechstein piano retained its name certainty as to how long I should remain a civilian. Even in a low category I might find myself clerking in a barracks or washing up in a canteen.

I began to prepare for my departure to Liverpool, a city I had never seen. I should be parted from my mother and should lose my friends, in a circle which had grown recently and opened a new world to me, that of the prosperous middle class. There had appeared in Nottingham about a year earlier a young man just down from Oxford named Bridges Adams. He had married a girl with local connections, Muriel Pratt, a professional actress. His ambition was to be a theatrical producer, lameness having prevented his being an actor. Subsequently he became renowned as a brilliant manager-producer at the Shakespeare Memorial Theatre at Stratford-on-Avon. Now in Nottingham he staged a performance of the Towneley Miracle Plays with his wife in the lead and an amateur cast of which I was a member. There I encountered two young men who became my friends until their deaths nearly forty years later. The younger, Duncan MacPherson, my junior by two years, had recently left Oundle School. I was welcomed into his delightful family. He had two brothers, the youngest, the Adonis of a good-looking family, was still at school. They lived in a large house with a long garden on a steep hillside above the city. Duncan's father was an architect. Tall, handsome, well-read, he was some twenty years older than his little sparkling wife. Their house was always full of young people and had an air of prosperity. When the war came, Jack, the eldest, engaged, went into the army and within twelve months was killed. My friend joined the Royal Flying Corps and after a bad crash was invalided out. He was a fine draughtsman and photographer and later drew a map of the Venetian lagoons for the endpapers of my second novel, *Sails of Sunset*.

My other friend, met in the cast, was John Grosvenor Laing. He was locally renowned as an amateur actor. Tall, endowed with a beautiful speaking voice and with a commanding appearance, he was often likened to a young Forbes-Robertson. At twenty-four he had already made a notable Hamlet. He might have chosen the stage for a career but for a parental veto. He was destined to inherit the family business, which he detested. His father, a prosperous wine and spirits merchant, was an elderly granite-like man. He was not of Scottish descent as his name implied but of Flemish stock, of the family of the Counts de la Laing of Hoogstraeten on the Dutch frontier. He had the dour Flemish temperament. The Laings had a luxurious home in The Park but it was not a happy one. It was obvious that Mr. Laing had suppressed his gay-spirited little wife. As for Jack, the only child, with his love of art and the theatre, he seemed incomprehensible; father and son were often near the flashpoint. I thought how different was the fate of that other wine merchant's son, John Ruskin, encouraged and pampered in his obsessive passion for the arts. When a domestic explosion threatened, Mrs. Laing would rush in and damp it down. Dear little woman, she complained of her son's obstinacy, 'the Flemish blood', and of her husband's hostility towards everything that his son liked. "I lead the life of a zoo keeper, trying to preserve peace between a panther and a bear," she once said to me. Jack adored his mother. When I was brought home Mr. Laing looked at me dourly. I was under suspicion. Who was I? (he looks well-born). Where did I live? (a bad point there). What did I do? (a poor Corporation clerk, another bad point). Where had I been educated? At a local school (another bad point). He thought I was too sharp-witted, too self-confident for my station, too full of life. I refused to be intimidated and set out to tame the bear. Mother and son watched anxiously. I talked and, miracle of miracles! I made him laugh despite himself. Basically he was a sound, grave man but had no warmth of nature and only a feeble sense of humour. I thought of my own father, and the love and comradeship I had enjoyed with him, a scholar in comparison, and full of fun.

In the evening the Laings dined in state, two beribboned parlourmaids standing solemnly behind the master's chair. Once there was a frightful mishap. A maid, holding a dish with a creamy sweet before my host, was convulsed by a sally of mine. She suppressed a squeak but the dish fell out of her hand and the contents slithered over the table. It seemed as if the ceiling would come down. There was an awful silence but Jove did not thunder. His long grave face thawed into a wan smile as he said solemnly to me—"You're irrepressible! Quite irrepressible!" without any tone of censure. We were becoming good friends.

I was often invited to stay for supper on Sunday evenings. After the meal there was a solemn procession to the drawing-room. The great crystal chandelier had had its muslin cover taken off, all the tiers blazing with light. The walls were covered with watercolours and oil paintings. They were part of the Wadmore Collection. My hostess's father had been a great collector and had built himself an art gallery at his Tonbridge house. He had also been a Master of the Worshipful Company of Skinners. In token of this, once a year Jack, a young Skinner, was allowed to go to the annual banquet. It was a great occasion; he stayed a night in London and came back carrying a large box of chocolates, flamboyant with the Skinners' arms on the lid. For weeks afterwards this was opened solemnly and passed round.

On these evenings, the brass firescreen having been removed, an enormous coal fire blazed in the grate. It made the yellow eyeballs glint in the head of the tiger whose skin was a rug. The carpets were spongy. The whole room reflected an unassailable bourgeois prosperity. A maid served coffee. Mr. Laing put on spectacles and barricaded himself behind the Sunday newspapers. At half-past nine there was a singular procession into the drawing-room. An elderly stout cook led the way, followed by two maids. They each carried a tin alarm clock. They stood quietly in line while Mrs. Laing checked the setting and then wound up the clocks, which she returned to each maid. There was to be no mishap about rising at six in the morning! The cook and the maids said goodnight and then withdrew. Jack and I escaped upstairs where he had a bedroom and sitting-room. He was a precisionist, everything was tabulated and neatly placed. There was every kind of reference book. He was delighted if I set him off on a search for obscure information. He had a small printing press, and night after night we laboured late, setting up and printing a private edition of my war poems, later repressed by me.

In summer there was croquet on the lawn, slow and dull. There was a time, after the war, when Miss Laing, my host's sister, paid her annual visit. She had a considerable presence, tall, slim and by no means dour. In her sixties she had gone afield and now lived in Geneva. She had been the cause of Jack's education there. It gave her a little glamour, for she moved in the best Geneva society. Often she relapsed into French. She treated her brother with a patronising playfulness. I believe he thought her rather a light woman. Why should she wish to live abroad?

Sometimes Jack, his mother, and I made excursions in an old limousine with brass lamps. It was driven by an ancient coachman who hated and feared the horrid new contraption. He drove very cautiously on roads still empty so there were no accidents. It was in this car that Mrs. Laing made visits to me at Shardlow Hall, Jack being away in the army. She knew that I was lonely and brought me large cakes made by the cook. The shining limousine with its uniformed chauffeur and crest-emblazoned door raised my prestige.

There were occasions in later years when I was an overnight guest at the Laings. This was something of an ordeal because of morning prayers. Immediately after an elaborate breakfast with always a row of silver covers on the sideboard, a parlourmaid placed a Bible in front of my host. The door opened and in came the cook and the other parlourmaid. The three servants occupied chairs on the opposite side of the table. Mr. Laing, at the head, put on spectacles and began to read the appointed Lesson. He had no idea how to read, making pauses in the wrong places and running out of breath. It was agony for me. We all sat like solemn owls. I tried not to catch the eyes of the servants, all very demure. The Lesson read, Mr. Laing said, "Let us pray." We all got up, reversed and went down on our knees, burying our faces in our hands while we chorused the prayers. This ended, we got up, all of us self-conscious in the strained air of piety. The servants then shuffled out. I always wondered what they said about us in the kitchen. How strange it all seems to-day! That disciplined breed of maids with 'good characters' has gone forever.

Such were the backgrounds of my two friends, Duncan and Jack. I must add a brief history of another who was to play a fateful part in this story of my early days. In Denholm Davis's studio I had encountered a remarkable character, George Burrows, some five years my senior, although he looked not a day older than twenty. Small, sturdy, with apple-rosy cheeks and a fine head crowned with wavy blond hair, he had an irresistibly infectious personality. Already he had won some fame. Possessed of a beautiful voice, he had appeared as the Clown, singing 'With hey, ho, the wind and the rain' in Granville Barker's production of *Twelfth Night* at the Savoy Theatre. When a youth he had been organist at Chirk, and was taken up by Mrs. William Cornwallis West, King Edward's beautiful friend, and the mother of Daisy, Princess of Pless, who dazzled the Kaiser Wilhelm. Her son married in 1900 Winston Churchill's mother, Jennie, and a year after a divorce, in 1914, Mrs. Patrick Campbell.

Under the patronage of Mrs. Cornwallis West, young George met with immediate success. A fine pianist, he sang to his own accompaniment. He was at his best in drawing-rooms for his exquisite voice had not a great volume. The purity of his tone and his artistry were superb. I had seen him reduce a company to tears by his singing. He was much in demand. Unfortunately women fell in love with him, captivated by his unsophisticated youthful exuberance as well as by his voice. Adulation turned his head and led him to disaster. He had tremendous energy but was unpredictable in his conduct. In after years he forswore singing, ran a seaside concert party, failed as an impresario, and opened a kiosk opposite the pier at Skegness, selling imitation jewellery. In this huckstering he ruined his voice but made a lot of money, which he lost on concert enterprises, engaging Gracie Fields and other top artists. Later he became one of Billy Butlin's early assistants when he was founding his Holiday Camps. His father dying at a great age, George was left some small shops in the High Street of Beeston, on the fringe of Nottingham. When the Second World War broke out and the munition workers and profiteers had money to squander, George opened a cheap jewellery shop in one of his properties and above it ran a Lucullan restaurant. Sumptuously furnished, with a kitchen that produced most things out of the black market, regardless of cost, his restaurant was booked for private parties at a high fee. As a special concession George would sit down at a baby grand piano and sing for his clients, some of the old allure still in his voice at fifty.

By judicious conversion of the little shops on the main street of the booming satellite town, he made a fortune. But money was something to play with. He bought for a song a large villa nearby with a beautiful garden. The servant problem had put it out of the market. George furnished the house luxuriously. There were great chandeliers in the rooms, often three Turkish carpets on top of one another so that one walked as on air, magnificent curtains, corridors lined with fine pieces of furniture, drawers full of Chinese silks, Indian shawls and costly embroideries. He had a passion for precious stones. There were cabinets laden with them. We used to tease him by saying he must have Jewish blood in his veins, which he had not, being vividly Anglo-Saxon in his fresh colouring, which he retained until his death. Most of these furnishings he had bought at auctions, sometimes held in ducal houses. The chandeliers came from Welbeck Abbey (Duke of Portland), the library furnishings from Clumber House (Duke of Newcastle), the curtains from Bestwood (Duke of St. Albans). There was a dining-room with Gothic alcoves and windows, and a long table for sixteen guests. The vitrines gleamed with fine china; all this, and not a servant in the house! He employed by the hour a series of myrmidons, male and female. One of them was a young lorry driver who liked to make 'a bit extra'. "I just love being among all this!" he exclaimed, carrying Sèvres and Limoges china from the cupboards to the dining-room.

George slept alone in his Aladdin's Cave. "Aren't you afraid of burglars?" I asked, seeing all the silver and trays of gems. He laughed. When George laughed it was a fountain of music. It was so rich, so intoxicating that I had seen people in a restaurant turn in amazement and then, infected by its gaiety, find themselves swept into a supporting chorus. At sixty he still had his beautiful hair, his rosy complexion, his gusto for life.

When he planned a dinner party for twelve, cooked and served by himself, the long table shining with silver and fine glass, a shopping expedition was necessary. He could not drive a car and would not have one. He rode everywhere in taxis. From a taxi he raided the grocery and wine shops in Nottingham. All the shopkeepers knew him. He was a lavish though discriminating buyer. He would buy ten pounds of out-of-season Muscat grapes, a large jar of caviare, a dozen pineapples, a leg of cooked Prague ham, a turkey, six dozen oysters, four chickens, a large tongue in aspic and six bottles of champagne, etc. The pile in the taxi grew and I often wondered how we should get into it and go home. He began this preparation two days before the event. On the day of the dinner he was up at six. He was assisted by two of the myrmidons. He said to one, who was late, "I see by your eyes you've been out all night with a girl—just a tomcat!" "Oh no, Mr. George!" cried the accused. "Oh, yes Mr. Tomcat! Now get on with those potatoes!"

The dinner finished, which had been marvellously cooked, we all went upstairs to the drawing-room, stopping to admire a Byzantine ikon en route. After coffee, liqueurs and cigars, he would sometimes open the Bluthner grand piano and there would be an expectant pause in the conversation. What we hoped for, came. There were a few preliminary runs over the keyboard and then he would sing. His songs were carefully chosen these latter days in order not to exceed his diminished range, but some of the old magic was there. Usually he ended with *The Moon Cradle* by Herbert Hughes, and with Sinding's Swedish cradle song *Sylvelin*, sung very pianissimo, and fading away into its final phrase—'. . . because your heart is pure'. It left us with a lump in our throats and we couldn't applaud, lifted out of our surroundings. He shut down the lid, sat for a few moments in silence, and then said, "I've made an awful mess of it—I might have been a great artist." He got up, lit a cigar. We had all demurred politely but sadly, knowing that the self-accusation was true.

Forty years earlier, when he was about twenty-five, he had sung for a party at Denholm Davis's country house on a hill. I had written for him some lines, marking the occasion. He cherished them and had them framed. The last verse need not be changed after half-a-century.

> Ah, the triumphs of years and the laurels of years
> Shall fade, but the little things
> Will all come back with a grace of tears
> On soft inaudible wings;
> And the wind shall wail o'er a phantom hill,
> The music come to an end,
> And we shall mourn the voice grown still,
> The songs of a vanished friend.

When George was seventy-two I persuaded him to visit me in Rome. He had never been to Italy. He flew out. Through every hour of that fortnight he was in ecstasy. "But why didn't I come before! What a fool I am! I'll shut down the house and come here every winter!" he exclaimed. On his last evening, towards midnight, we went down to the Fontana di Trevi, and threw in a coin to ensure his return. Outside the Grand Hotel he went behind the balustrade of the Moses fountain, and caressed the marble paw of one of the four amiable lions spouting water. "See you next Christmas, old boy!" he said, patting its back.

The following summer I found it difficult to fit in a visit to Aladdin's Cave, feeling that I should be with my invalid octogenarian brother, but I visited him after all, since he made such an outcry over the telephone, and sang to me Albert Chevalier's famous lines—"We've been together now for forty years an' it don't seem a day too much". So I cancelled my next engagement and stayed with him for a week, in luxury. Just before my departure for Italy he gave a dinner party for me at the Dorchester Hotel. He was to visit me in Alassio and Rome next winter. But it was not to be. Two months later his heart gave out under an emergency operation. He was seventy-three. A failure? I don't think so. He had lived with tremendous gusto and given to many much pleasure. And he had a last surprise for us. Our prophecy that he would ruin himself, as he had done from time to time, was not fulfilled. He left £68,000.

When in October, 1915, I set out for Liverpool, to enter a strange world, George had accompanied me. Once a week he went there to give singing lessons to private pupils. Thereby he was destined to effect a momentous change in my life, as will be seen.

CHAPTER THREE

Beatty, Jellicoe and Jutland

I

MY DEPARTURE FOR Liverpool meant the loss of friends, such as my kindly Latin tutor lodging with us, Richard Hartley, and William Kiddier. How often I had rushed up the stairs to Kiddier's attic studio, hot with a new idea, always to find an enthusiastic backing. It was he who had been the architect of the new life about to open for me. But saddest of all was the separation from my mother. She faced my departure with characteristic restraint, aware that just now all over the world mothers were suffering the departure of their sons in more hazardous circumstances.

On my arrival at my new post the acting editor, a taciturn middle-aged Scot, gave me a desk in his room. He wrote the first leaders, I the second. I also reviewed books and did the theatrical criticism. All this work was anonymous at first. Later I was allowed to append my initials to articles and reviews. I found that I was a Sassenach in a world of Scots. There was a golf bag in most of the editorial rooms. This very prosperous and influential paper was run by the Jeans family, father and son. Its most famous editor, Lord Russell, one of Lloyd George's earliest backers, had retired. The whole place vibrated with energy and a sense of influence. It dominated a vast area, contesting part of it with the celebrated *Manchester Guardian.*

At first I worked under some constraint. The newspaper that had rejected young James Barrie, who then went to the *Nottingham Journal*, had accepted me, who came from it. I was on trial for three months. My very capable editor made me aware of my drawbacks. I was not a Scot, not a university man. The ghost of a brilliant young critic, killed in the war, Dixon Scott, was raised from time to time, the suggestion being that he had gifts I could not aspire to. The editor was a friend and admirer of Lascelles Abercrombie, one of the

Georgian poets. I read his poetry and found it contrived and sadistic, getting nowhere. I said so. The editorial eyebrows were raised.

I was a rapid writer. I came from the theatre and wrote my thousand-word notice within the hour. It should have been a virtue in a career where one must beat the clock in getting to press. My editor was a cautious slow writer. He had time, for he would begin his leader about nine o'clock. My facility irritated him. Sometimes skimming my proof copy, he would say, over the top of his desk, "Don't you think it would be better to write . . . ?" Tactfully I always agreed, if it did not alter the sense. I was a writer who needed encouragement and worked better for it. He never gave me a word of praise. I began to grow more and more nervous. Was I a failure? Secret things were gnawing at me. I was alone as I never had been before, in a vast grim city. I had made a mistake in my lodgings. Delighted with the great Mersey River and its liners and ferry boats, like fireflies at night, I had taken a room across the water at Seacombe. Each afternoon I walked along the riverside promenade to Egremont pier and took the ferry over to Liverpool, landing in the shadow of the towering Royal Liver building. My office hours were from six to midnight but if there had been a theatre notice to get to press it was often 1 a.m. before I got away.

The weather grew colder, the winds were icy. My widowed landlady kindly let me use her sitting-room, living herself in the kitchen. To occupy myself I began to write a poetic drama set in the Renaissance period. I had no idea what I would do with it but it assuaged my loneliness. I also wrote some poems. I sadly missed William Kiddier and Denholm Davis, Jack, Duncan and George, the studio teas and the use of a friend's piano, but most of all my mother. I had never before been separated from her and my home. When I was at Shardlow Hall I had had the company of a colleague and those vivacious boys, and my home was only a few miles distant. Here the wintry nights chilled me, the foghorns moaned along the river. I touched the depths of depression.

And oft the siren's wail is heard,
Borne inland, like a cry of pain
Of a lost soul, to darkness lured,
That has no hope of light again.
The sound of wind and moving seas,
The unknown, silent ships that pass,

Symbols are these of mysteries
Discerned but dimly in the glass
That mirrors life behind our sight,
Contracting to the eyes' domain
The reaches of a vaster night,
Unmeasured worlds that still remain.
O friend, there is a time when speech
Is frozen with the breath of awe,
When all the little truths we preach
Seem fragments of a vaster law;
And in these days of lengthened view
How I have longed that you were here,
To walk with me, debate, construe,
And differ—as in days of yore.

There was death these days over the Mersey Bar. The *Lusitania* had been torpedoed off Kinsale Head with 1,198 victims, of which 100 were Americans. Not even this moved President Wilson to action despite a wave of American anger. "There is such a thing as being too proud to fight," he said, an unfortunate phrase, torn out of its context, that hung around his neck like an albatross for the rest of his life. The toll of sailors with homes along the Mersey grew steadily.

I found great pleasure in my theatrical criticism. Liverpool possessed a very good Repertory Theatre. My initials footing my notices became known. One night a much boosted London Revue produced by the great Cochran, with lovely Mlle. Delysia in the star role, arrived at another theatre. I thought it very poor, and said so. My editor read my copy. "Do you really want to say this?" he asked. "Yes—why not?" I replied. "Well, it's on your own head," he said, grimly. I was at breaking point. For two months I had done my best but had not received a word of approval. I turned on him. "I suppose you'll be glad to have my head off!" I retorted. I let myself go, exasperated, near to tears. When I had exploded he said, very calmly, "Laddie, you've got it all wrong. We're very pleased with you but you're a young horse in the ring." For the first time he gave me a difficult smile, then went out of the room with my copy.

Two days later he said, "My wife's having a little party on Saturday night—at eight, with a bite to eat. She'd be very glad to see you." I went. She was a beautiful woman, with two children. "Oh, but you're an infant!" she said when I was introduced. "I'm twenty-three!" I protested. "Impostor! Let me take you to one of your victims." She introduced me to a tall, pale young man with a mop of sandy hair. He looked frail. He had given a fine performance as Sir Andrew Aguecheek in *Twelfth Night*. He was one of the Repertory Theatre players. Thus I came to find another remarkable friend, William Armstrong. He often moaned, shuffled a hand through his long hair and cried, "Oh God!" finding life a trial. But his despair was always rich comedy. He was a born raconteur. "That's Arthur Pusey," he said, pointing to a junior lead. "He's only one kidney, so he's out of the Army. He's a good actor but he's no heart. He likes to bite the lobes of girls' ears!"

"And why are you out?" I asked. It was the question these days of repeated combings of men for the Army.

"I? Oh, I'm mentally unstable. They're afraid I'd shoot the General, but they kindly say it's a hernia."

In later years after touring with Mrs. Patrick Campbell he returned to The Playhouse, as it was now known, as manager and producer. He made history there. It became the finest dramatic school in England. Young actors and actresses queued up to get into the company, certain they were on the way to stardom. The London theatres grabbed his graduates. Twenty-four years later he was destined to produce a play of mine in what proved to be tragic circumstances.

Little by little I began to be asked out and to go about socially. I had not spent a lonely first Christmas in Liverpool. The leading bookseller of the city, Mr. T. N. Philip, radiating goodwill, invited me to spend Christmas Day at his home in Birkenhead. It was an experience wholly new to me. I found myself in the midst of a boisterous family, parents, sons, daughters, aunts, uncles, nephews, nieces and grandchildren, over a score in a large warm house that exuded prosperity. There was an immense Christmas tree loaded with presents, there were roaring coal fires in all the rooms, plenty of servants and a huge dining-table, candle-lit, shining with silver, a present on each plate, and such a feast that we sat at the table for hours. Accustomed to a lonely childhood and boyhood, I had never experienced anything like this. There was something Dickensian in its gusto and kindness. My apple-cheeked host beamed above it all. There was a day to come when he would fill his window with my books, but this early kindness to an obscure stranger at the gate was never forgotten by me.

II

Soon after my arrival in Liverpool I found among the new books that had come in for review one by Richard Le Gallienne. In the famous Eighteen Nineties, the era of *The Yellow Book*, young Richard Le Gallienne was the brightest and most noticeable figure among a galaxy of writers. He had come down from Liverpool, a provincial lad of twenty-five, whose appearance was so striking that he was immediately a prominent figure on the scene. He had a sensitive, beautiful face crowned by a mane of hair, grown provocatively long to declare the poet, a declaration emphasised by an artist's wide bow. Something of the sensation he created can be surmised from a portrait drawn by Wilson Steer. The great mass of his black hair provoked one of Max Beerbohm's best caricatures. The descent on London had followed a battle against home ties and parental plans. The Gallienne family came from Guernsey stock. His father was the manager of the Birkenhead Brewery Company. Richard, destined for a chartered accountant, revolted and at the age of twenty fled the parental nest, crossed the Mersey and took an attic room in Liverpool. He romanticised his name by adding Le to Gallienne, and declared himself an independent man of letters, with little to sustain him except ambition. It was the old story of youth in collision with a dismayed father. When he arrived in London his flamboyant personality attracted some attention, and criticism. He seemed too full of what Byron had called, referring to an enthusiastic American youth who had called on him offering incense, 'entusymusy'. Le Gallienne was the schoolgirl's dream of the handsome young poet, the head as Byronic. Presently, with the prestige of the Bodley Head imprint, a book of poems appeared. It met with success and rapidly passed through three impressions. He followed this success with *The Book Bills of Narcissus* and proved himself to be a fanciful essayist with a gossamer style and wit. Two collections of essays called *Prose Fancies* added to his reputation. He had appeared on the London scene just in time to join the brilliant young writers that John Lane had gathered around him at the Bodley Head. They created the era known as 'The Eighteen Nineties' which had a spicy touch of decadence, and was dubbed 'The Naughty Nineties'. In April, 1894, the first number of the epoch-making *Yellow Book* appeared. Among the contributors were Max Beerbohm, Arthur Symons, George Moore, Henry James, Arthur Waugh and Edmund

Gosse. The startling cover was by Aubrey Beardsley; the frontispiece, to add a note of Victorian respectability to its provocative contents, was by Sir Frederick Leighton, P.R.A. The other artists presented were Wilson Steer, Walter Sickert, Joseph Pennell, Will Rothenstein and J. S. Sargent. Among the contributors was Richard Le Gallienne.

In the second volume of his *Prose Fancies* I had found an autobiographical essay 'A Seventh Story Heaven'. It told how he had broken out of his prison, determined to become an author—

> At the one end of the city I love there is a tall dingy pile of offices that has evidently seen more prosperous fortunes . . . It is the end where the cotton that everybody sells and nobody buys is seen, piled in great white stacks, or swinging in the air from the necks of mighty cranes that could nip up an elephant with little to do, and set him down on the wharf, with a box on his ugly ears for his cowardly trumpeting. Here are the shops that sell nothing but oilskins, sextants and parrots, and here the taverns do a mighty trade in rum.
>
> It was in this quarter, for a brief sweet time, that Love and Beauty made their strange home, as though a pair of halcyons should choose to rest in the masthead of a cattleship. Love and Beauty chose this quarter for its cheapness. Love was a poor poet in need of a room for his bed and his rhymes. and Beauty was a little blue-eyed girl who loved him. It was a shabby, forbidding place, gloomy and comfortless as a warehouse on the banks of the Styx. That seventh-story heaven once more leads a dull life as the office of a ship-chandler, and harsh voices grate in the air where Beauty sang. The books and the flowers and the lovers' faces are gone forever.
>
> I suppose the stars are the same and perhaps they sometimes look down through that roof window and wonder what has become of those two lovers who used to look up at them so fearlessly long ago.

There was a tragedy in Le Gallienne's life, for this girl he loved and married, died young. He wrote of her—

> She's somewhere in the sunlight strong,
> Her tears are in the falling rain,
> She calls me in the wind's soft song,
> And with the flowers she comes again.

Arriving in Liverpool, I recalled this essay of his youth. I, too, had broken out of an office, out of 'safety', to establish myself as a man of letters. Standing among the review copies, with one of Le Gallienne's books in my hand, I thought of him, and sent him my review. He was now a man of fifty. He had emigrated to the United States. There was a long silence after I had sent my letter. Then, at last, came a reply in his own beautiful handwriting—

Rowayton, Conn.,
U.S.A. Dec. 10, 1916.

What can you have been thinking of me all this time since you wrote me that beautiful letter—like a draught of pure crystal from the magic fount of youth? I must tell you of the flood of sympathy that warmed my heart as I read of your Liverpool adventure—so like my old dream days, and my gratitude to you for associating me with it. And oh, how well I know those thrills of which you speak, of having that wonderful shelf of review books all your own to pick and choose from. Oh, don't I know it all!—it was just the same when I got that 'Books and Bookmen' column on *The Star*, please don't remember how many years ago! And to think as you did of my (so long lost) 'Seventh Story Heaven'—ah, dear Cecil Roberts, such affectionate sympathy—particularly coming from one whose face I have never seen makes the heart and eyes overflow. God bless you for so cherishing another man's sanctities.

As you were kind enough to speak of that 'Seventh Story Heaven', I wonder if you would care to know exactly where it was? When I was last in Liverpool I was foolhardy enough to steal up those stairs and look in through the glass windows in the door. Tailors were sitting cross-legged, in a murky light and girls were bending over sewing-machines—the place where Beauty sang was now a sweat shop. It seemed as though I saw noisome snakes gliding in a foul twilight about the stones of a forgotten altar . . . but perhaps romance was still there in the heart of one of those girls and possibly one of the Jew tailors was an embryo Spinoza! The place, should you care to pilgrimage there for my sake, and leave a votive sigh, is Trafford Chambers, South John Street—the topmost floor. I wonder if the tavern is still there at the foot.

If you and I are ever in Liverpool together we must make votive libations there. As you reach the top landing take the corridor to the left, and it is the last door on the right. I only tell you this because you have been kind enough to care about another man's romance.

When I came to write about Le Gallienne's early life in his Seventh Story Heaven I began to wonder what was the subsequent history of that youthful nest of dreams down the twenty-eight years since he had climbed its stairs. I asked my friend Frederick Davies, living in Birkenhead, who specialises more in Goldoni than Gallienne, if he could supply a few facts out of his local knowledge. He wrote—

I am afraid that I found as I had expected I would Le Gallienne's Seventh Story Heaven is now up in space. Trafford Chambers and all South John St. were all wiped out during the 1941 blitz on Merseyside. Where Trafford Chambers once stood is now a vast car-park. Richard's home in Birkenhead is still standing. He left Liverpool in 1889 to go as secretary to Wilson Barrett, the dramatist-actor-producer. Barrett went on tour to America and Richard had to remain behind on account of his asthmatic chest. Too proud to return to his father's house, he found 'a literary loft' at the top of a tall block of offices near the Customs House in Liverpool. Here he lived for nearly two years supported by his mother, his sisters and his aunts. At night he would often return to his home; his younger brother would let him in when his father had gone to bed and take him up to sleep in his room in the attic. Next morning when his father had left for the office Richard would descend, eat a huge breakfast, and return laden with food to continue his writing in his room at Trafford Chambers. He appears to have romanticized this period a little in his story, possibly because it was one of the few happy times in his long, tragic but courageous life. His father was not at all a 'Barrett of Wimpole Street' figure. His appears to have been the genuine but sympathetic bewilderment of a steady hard-working thrush at finding a rebellious cuckoo in the nest.

Twenty-three, amorous, handsome, within two years Le Gallienne got to London as a book critic for *The Star*. Through Wilson Barrett he had been invited to Tite Street by Oscar Wilde who showed him much kindness and encouragement. He visited Meredith at Box Hill, he was kindly received at The Pines, Putney, by Swinburne and found that 'the lower part of his face was disastrously unfinished'.

Le Gallienne was now a figure in London but his ill-luck dogged him as it would all his long life. He married the girl of 'the literary loft' but she died within two years leaving him with a baby daughter, Hesper. The next year he paid his first visit to America, and married a Danish girl, Julie, who gave him a daughter, Eva, born in London. He now knew everybody in the literary firmament. He met Marie Corelli and Sarah Bernhardt when he went to Stratford-on-Avon to report the appearance of the Divine Sarah in *Hamlet.*

> You will laugh when I tell you in whose carriage she was driven to the station—O the bathos attendant on great things!—you would have thought Sarah might have been spared—Marie Corelli's! Quite true! That terror had a house there. However, owing to the terror's knowledge of my face I owe a beautiful moment... With good luck the carriage came round the corner and as I stood on the sidewalk Sarah caught my eyes. I raised my hat and she smiled and bowed. Marie recognised me and I saw her tell Sarah something, probably my name.

Doubtless that head of hair on the handsome young man did the trick. Le Gallienne immediately rushed off to the station. Entraining, Sarah saw him and held out her hand. They could neither speak the other's language but he gave her a book of his and she gave him a flower. Was there a photograph of him with the book? He was overjoyed to learn later from a friend that she kept his photograph on her bedroom mantelpiece.

He was soon back in America on a lecture tour. He had written his first novel *The Quest of the Golden Girl,* which had attracted attention. In Minneapolis he found a fellow countryman, Winston Churchill, a guest in the same house. Obviously there was a clash between the two egotists. Richard was scathing about the other young man, also on a lecture tour. "He's the very pink of British insolence—an aristocratic bounder of the first water. It was hard for us all to be civil to him. I was, as little as possible, for to me he was one of the rudest, most arrogant young pups I've ever encountered." It would be interesting to have had Winston's opinion of the flamboyant poet.

A persistent philanderer, it was not long before Le Gallienne's second marriage came unstuck. Following his divorce, Irma, with a young daughter, came on the scene. The marriage began inauspiciously. An intermittent alcoholic, the bridegroom arrived at the altar in a state of elation. When the clergyman asked—"Do you take this woman . . ." he replied, "You bet I do!" and fell flat on his back. Revived, he wanted to fight the best man. Yet this marriage lasted thirty-six years in unbroken devotion until he died aged eighty-one. Asthma, the bottle and women plagued his first forty-five years, and asthma was with him to the end, a heroic martyr. Always harassed by debt, dunning his old father and others, he never reached security but never lost hope. He wrote some fifty books of which only one, *Pieces of Eight*, might be considered a masterpiece but Stevenson's *Treasure Island* took the wind from its sails. He was always an exquisite poet.

In 1927 Le Gallienne settled in Paris. He met the expatriate colony—Ernest Hemingway whom he thought a rumbustious college boy, Scott Fitzgerald, a genius, Ezra Pound, an affected showman, and James Joyce, a pleasant fellow whose *Ulysses* he found unreadable. He was respected by the colony as a 'has been' of the nineties, and managed to eke out a livelihood with a 'Paris Letter' for *The New York Evening Sun*, but this raft, as so many others, sank under him. He and his devoted wife struggled on through the First World War at Menton, where he died, still handsome, and respected. He was buried in Menton in September, 1947. Grant Richards came over from Monte Carlo and read one of Le Gallienne's poems *What of the Darkness—is it very fair?* at a memorial service in the almost empty Anglican church. The poet was worried about the fate of his old wife for whom he had been unable to make provision. But he need not have worried. The British Government gave her a Civil List Pension of £225, on which she contrived to live until her death eight years later.

Walking down Broadway in 1946, I saw in flaring letters the name 'Eva Le Gallienne'. Richard's daughter was one of the most famous actresses in America. She had founded the Civic Repertory Theatre. I went round and called on her after the play. For some reason I had thought her father was long dead and was astonished to learn he was living in Menton. "Go and see him, he's as full of life and charm as ever," she said. Alas I never found the opportunity. He died within a year.

Forgotten, a ghost of the vanished Eighteen Nineties, it might be thought that that was the end of Richard Le Gallienne. But Fate plays curious tricks. Richard Whittington-Egon, rummaging in a bookseller's attic in 1947, discovered one of Le Gallienne's books and became interested in him. A week later he read of his death. It occurred to him to ask a question. Why had Le Gallienne as a writer 'died' at thirty-five? He had been the golden boy of the nineties —and then followed a dwindling away into comparative obscurity. Mr. Whittington-Egon began a laborious enquiry that lasted seven years and was just about to begin a *Life* when he got a letter from Geoffrey Smerdon who had decided, when he was a schoolboy of sixteen, to write that *Life*. The two authors, born in Le Gallienne's Liverpool, joined forces. They produced in 1960 *The Quest of The Golden Boy*. It is an astonishing work, an elephantine life of a mouse. It runs to 600 pages and 300,000 words. Detail by detail, it marches down the eighty-one years of its subject's life. Proustian in its scrutiny, its microscopic dissection, it is nearer to life than Proust's circus of artificial people revolving in a narrow radius that, for all the *réclame*, makes one exclaim—'*Il y a des longueurs dans cet ouvrage.*' Le Gallienne is dissected but the golden boy is not a puppet, a snob's creation of socialites with no real blood in their veins. It is a mirror held up to a very long and very varied life. From that Seventh Story Heaven in Liverpool to the quiet burial in Menton one follows a pilgrimage encompassing the wonder and mystery of man's mortal journey. Like the pyramid of Caius Cestius by the walls of ancient Rome, the book enshrines, as noticeably, Le Gallienne, but tells us far more about him and his times than we shall ever know about Caius Cestius. And there, in this monumental work, we will leave him.

III

Finding my nightly journey from Seacombe to the office too rigorous, I moved into Liverpool. I found a large back bedroom in a house in stately Rodney Street, favoured by doctors, and where Gladstone had been born. My landlord was mysterious, a foreigner who had very little furniture in his house. My large room had a double bed, one tiny carpet on the big bare floor and a wardrobe with a cracked mirror. But it was cheap, convenient for the office, and had a good address. The address-snobs when I said 'Rodney Street' accepted me. The room was perishingly cold and the tiny electric fire too expensive and impotent. I wrote with my feet on a hot water bottle in a box of straw.

I was overjoyed to have a visit from my friend Duncan, on leave.

We huddled together in the big bed like the Babes in the Wood. Then one day I was called up for yet another medical examination. I was glad of this, tired of living in uncertainty and unable to make future plans. Disasters in France were eating up the youth of the country. The medical standards were lowered and lowered. Men of forty with hammer toes or defective eyesight were being taken, inferior cannon fodder. Employers struggled to hold their workmen. I stripped and shivered. A doctor got busy on me. After a few minutes he said, "Go over there," giving me my card. With about a dozen other shivering men I waited. Then a pair of doctors looked us over and held a conference. One of them marked my card. "Wait there," he said. We waited. Presently a sergeant came in with a list and checked us. "Go!" he said. "Where?" one of us asked. "Home! You're out!" We dressed. My card was marked C III. It was the lowest category next to total rejection. One could still be called but only from the bottom of the barrel. I felt rather indignant. I certainly was not of the stuff of which heroes were made but surely I wasn't as bad as all that! Was I doomed? In a pub I bought a whisky and soda. It warmed me. The landscape began to clear. I could now make plans. I wanted to bring my mother to Liverpool.

Fate smiled on me four days later. I had written some special articles on the Mersey defences, under the auspices of the Navy. A bad sailor, I had been frightfully sick over the Mersey Bar but I got all my facts. It seems the authorities were very complimentary. This adventure was to bear fruit.

IV

In May, 1916, I was sent on a special naval mission. The Admiralty was conducting a selected group of journalists to see the Navy in its various activities, and to lift the veil of secrecy somewhat. We were to visit battleships, battle-cruisers, destroyers, submarines, and the shipbuilding yards all round the coasts of Great Britain. We assembled in London. I was the baby of the party. After visiting the arsenals and the shipyards of the Tyne and Clyde we went to the East Coast. At Yarmouth I boarded a minesweeper. It was a grim experience but I was fortified by the fact that Joseph Conrad had experienced a similar adventure. I arrived back on shore like a human icicle. From Yarmouth I went to the submarine base at Harwich. The heat, the oily smell, and the claustrophobia of those submarines!

This was the era of white mice in a cage to detect deadly fumes. It is singular how the human being can adapt himself to any conditions. I should have thought a period in Dartmoor Prison preferable, but nothing seemed to dim the robust gaiety of the submerged ratings. Miraculously, I was not sick under the waves though abject on them. The worst was the condensed water dropping down one's neck from the hundreds of pipes, like intestines, and the disadvantage of being six feet tall. Submarines are craft for pigmies.

Following this adventure I was transported overnight to visit the Battle Cruiser Squadrons at Rosyth and Cromarty Firth. The next morning at Rosyth we boarded H.M.S. *Lion* which lay behind the Forth Bridge, flying the flag of the Commander-in-Chief of the Squadrons. There we met the now legendary figure, Vice-Admiral Sir David Beatty. He was to be the last spectacular figure in British Naval history. Never again would the Service touch such a height of power and glory. It was fitting that Beatty should fly his flag in the *Lion*. He was a lion of a man with his handsome strong-jawed face, his bulldog air and his habit of wearing his peaked Admiral's cap at a rakish angle. He was the perfect image of the public's idea of a daring sea-dog in the Drake tradition. His postcard photo was in every newsagent's window. The Press built him up. He came of horsey Irish stock, hence his hunting box in Leicestershire and constant riding to hounds. He had married a Chicago store tycoon's daughter, a divorcée. They lived in some state with a house in Grosvenor Square, a castle in Scotland, a yacht, and a hunting box, Brooksby Hall, the ancestral Leicestershire home of the Villiers for five hundred years, and where the famous Duke of Buckingham was born. Beatty had something in common, a panache, with that Leicestershire lad in whose home he now lived. Like Villiers, he was *persona grata* at Court. Behind this spectacular façade was a man of very solid achievement and some sensational episodes in his march to fame. At twenty-five he had shown singular daring in the Nile expedition for the recovery of the Sudan, reaching Dongola, which he occupied. He went on to the Fourth Cataract, winning Kitchener's praise and the D.S.O. In September, 1897, he reached Omdurman. Another enterprising young officer there was named Winston Churchill. Beatty at twenty-seven was now a Commander. At twenty-nine he was a Captain, adding to a growing legend with service in the Boxer Rebellion. He was under thirty-nine when he was promoted Rear-Admiral, a record almost matching Nelson's. When Churchill went to the Admiralty as First Lord they met again, Beatty now the youngest admiral in the Navy. Soon, by Churchill's longsight, he was appointed to the command of the First Battle Cruiser Squadron over the heads of senior officers. When, three years later, I stepped on board H.M.S. *Lion* at Rosyth, I looked upon a national figure. A glance showed him to be no postcard hero. Though short in stature, the fighting head was superb, the personality of this man of forty-five dynamic.

He was very affable with us, talked freely to everyone. He was fretting for action. "I wish we could get at 'em. If only they'd come out!" How little any of us there that morning knew what was ahead within a week. Yet he had not been inactive. He had drawn blood in the Battle of the Bight, and his men were the envy of all those who so far had been denied action.

From the *Lion* we went on board H.M.S. *New Zealand* for lunch. How very remote the war seemed as we sat at the Captain's table, the ship's silver shining along the white cloth, the band playing on the deck flat. A very agreeable and good-looking young lieutenant, who had seen action at Heligoland and the Dogger Bank, was one of my neighbours. I discovered that he collected rare editions. After coffee I went down to his cabin and he showed me with pride some special bindings. Since I received many books as a reviewer I asked him if he would like an occasional parcel. He said he would be delighted. I asked him his name. George Battenberg. So he was the son of Prince Louis of Battenberg, former First Sea Lord, and elder brother of young Prince Louis. He had just become engaged and showed me a photograph of his fiancée, Nadejda, daughter of the Grand Duke Michael of Russia. Some years later, when I lunched with them, they had become the Mountbattens, he having succeeded his father as the second Marquess of Milford Haven, and I held their baby son, David, Earl of Medina, on my knee. This infant was destined to be the Duke of Edinburgh's best man when he married Princess Elizabeth, our future Queen. (Illustration, p. 192.)

There was one thing on board H.M.S. *New Zealand* that I was not shown. When, after being commissioned, the ship visited New Zealand there were welcoming ceremonies. One of these was the presentation to her captain by a Maori chief of a *piu-piu*, the natives' grass skirt. The chief foretold that if the captain wore it in battle the ship would never suffer harm. At Jutland Captain Green, commanding the *New Zealand*, went up on the bridge wearing the grass skirt, thus conforming to the superstition. The battle cruiser was hotly engaged and saw the *Queen Mary* blow up, with 1,000 officers and men, within 150 yards of her, but she emerged unscathed.

V

The eve of the war had revealed a singular fact. There was no place on the north-east coast of Great Britain in which to keep the Grand Fleet at anchor. On this Fleet Britain depended for its existence, since the aeroplane had not yet become the menace to our island security, for only one German naval victory could paralyse us and involve the collapse of the Western Front. The massive weight of this responsibility lay on the shoulders of an Admiral almost unknown to the British public. On August 1st, 1914, the Commander-in-Chief of the Home Fleet was the 62-year-old Sir George Callaghan. He was due to retire on October 1st and was now considered to be too old to face a long war. Churchill decided to appoint Sir John Jellicoe.

The situation at the Admiralty was curious and difficult. In 1911, conscious of his high merit and great record, Churchill had appointed Prince Louis of Battenberg his First Sea Lord. It was Battenberg who, after a telephone talk with Churchill, week-ending at Cromer, on July 27th, 1914, had given the order for the Fleet to remain mobilised after the naval manœuvres. What Churchill had failed to foresee was that Battenberg's name and German origin would make it impossible for him to remain in office. Immediately on the outbreak of war, despite his long service, he was subjected to all kinds of rumours and attacks in the Press. On October 21st, as a final act of patriotism, he resigned as First Sea Lord, and went out of public life until his death ten years later. In 1917 under pressure of opinion both the Royal family and the Battenbergs dropped their German names; the Guelphs became Windsors, the Battenbergs Mountbattens.

On the fateful July 27th Churchill hurried to London. Jellicoe was called in to see him and Battenberg. He was told that in certain circumstances he would replace Callaghan in command of the Home Fleet. This intimation filled Jellicoe with dismay. He thought such a sudden change in the command would be disastrous. Despite his protest he was despatched to Scapa Flow, bearing a sealed envelope, to be opened on further instructions. Jellicoe knew its contents. He spent the next three days at Thurso despatching telegrams of protest to Churchill and Battenberg, alarmed at what he was commissioned to do. On August 4th he received instructions to open his sealed envelope. Dated July 31st, 1914, it ran:

> I am commanded by my Lords Commissioners of the Admiralty to inform you that, in the circumstances that will have arisen when the present letter will have been opened, they have been pleased to select you to be Commander-in-Chief of the Grand or First Fleet in succession to Admiral Sir George Callaghan. You are therefore forthwith, on receipt of orders to open this letter, to repair with it on board H.M.S. *Iron Duke*, show it to Sir George Callaghan as your authority for so doing and arrange with him for whatever immediate steps may be necessary to make your succession to his command effective. Thereafter Sir George Callaghan will come on shore.

This ranks as one of the most momentous letters ever written. The signature at the bottom was "Your obedient servant, W. Graham Greene," then Permanent Secretary of the Admiralty. We are to see that name again, fifteen years later, on the back of a novel with which his nephew was to open a distinguished career. When three years later Churchill went to the Ministry of Munitions, Greene followed him as Permanent Secretary.

Never was a man more dismayed by his task than Jellicoe. A kind man, loyal, and popular with his colleagues, he was now deputed to deal a deadly blow at a senior officer he greatly revered. Sir John's protests by telegram were all ignored. "I hope never to live again through such a time as I had from Friday to Monday. My position was horrible. I did my best but could not stop what I felt was a great error," he wrote. It was a bitter moment for Callaghan who had expected that his period of service would be extended at such a great moment of history. He had had his command of the Home Fleet extended a year, to October 1st: the interm arrangement was that, in the event of war, Jellicoe should be his second-in-command. Now his command was abruptly ended. He left his flagship very early on the morning of August 8th. Jellicoe took up his command in the *Iron Duke*, and at 8.30 a.m. proceeded to sea as instructed by the Admiralty.

"Who is this Jellicoe?" asked the public. His reputation lay out of sight, known only to the Admiralty and the Service. A great gunnery specialist, a martinet for efficiency, affectionately called The Old Man, everyone from the bridge to the stokehold was soon aware of 'the spies of the *Iron Duke*' as the Admiral and his staff came to be called. His was wholly a Service reputation. There were no photographs of him in the shop windows. He was not photogenic, or a favourite of the Press. He commanded the largest naval fleet the world had ever seen, or would ever see, since naval power was to suffer an eclipse and a great Empire would go voluntarily into dissolution.

Before the Great War Jellicoe had had in view a safe anchorage for the Fleet but it had to be created. No natural harbour existed. Good harbours are a gift of God. Somewhere on the long east coast bordering the North Sea the Fleet must be stationed. It happened that Germany was also unfortunate, for Great Britain lay like a watchdog on the threshold of her exit to the high seas. There was no safe exit via the Dover Straits since it was blocked. The only way out was up the North Sea and round by the Orkney Islands. It was a long corridor and whoever commanded it was master of the seas. Fortunately for Britain, Nature had provided the means of creating a harbour of great size and security at Scapa Flow, at the northern extremity of Scotland, across the Pentland Firth and in the heart of the Orkney Islands. It had advantages and drawbacks. When the various islands had been linked together by barrages an interior sheet of water was created that provided space for gunnery exercises of a ten-thousand-yard range. It had several deep entrances and strong tides that menaced submarines, making their attack difficult.

Here the Fleet under Sir John Jellicoe kept its war station. One dire disadvantage was soon demonstrated. It was too far north to prevent the hit-and-run tactics of the Germans on the lower east coast. Yarmouth and Scarborough were bombarded. The hope of the enemy was to create an outcry that would force the Admiralty to bring the Fleet down from its northern base, scattering it in smaller harbours and thus easing the northern sea passage. The German hope proved vain. A Battle Cruiser Force was stationed at Rosyth and Cromarty Firth under Beatty. Destroyers were also based at Harwich. The North Sea corridor remained hazardous for the German Fleet. It must either risk all on a breakthrough or remain bottled up.

Scapa Flow was a ghastly place, situated at the maximum distance from London. In summer it had very long days that merged into continuous twilight. In winter it knew hardly six hours of daylight.

It was a place of howling winds, freezing sleet and snow. Beatty called it "A damnable place. Even the midshipmen are depressed." Access to it was miserable. It involved a long tedious journey in a train crawling amid Scottish moors and hills. When it was our base again in the Second World War one's journey there was made more wretched by being cooped up in suffocating carriages, blue-lit and curtained against air attack.

It was there I arrived by train overnight. On a bright May morning in 1916 I stood on the bridge of H.M.S. *Oak*, keeping well in cover of the canvas screen as we tore through the water at some thirty knots. It was early and cold, and this T.B.D., the messenger-boy of the Commander-in-Chief, was taking me from Thurso, where civilisation ended, out to Scapa Flow.

Monotony is often the mother of amusement and wherever the English are gathered together there is a certainty that there will be a cricket pitch, a football ground, and a golf course. It was so at Scapa Flow. Bleak, exposed to gales and barren of trees, human life was absent on these islands except for a few farmers. The desolate Flotta Island in the south-west corner of the harbour became the sports stadium of the whole Fleet. Here with much ingenuity, as well as a cricket pitch and football ground, an 18-hole golf course had been made, each hole created by a ship's labour. One of these ships distinguished itself by having turf transplanted for its green from a famous Scottish course.

There were other diversions while grimly awaiting a cautious foe. Perhaps the most popular ships amid a crowd of minor craft were two old hulks, the *Borodino* and the *Gourko*, the servants attending the pleasures of the mighty. I never discovered the origin of their Russian names. The former represented the Army and Navy Stores and was run with all the efficiency of a London store, in which almost everything was procurable. The *Gourko* represented the lighter side of life. She was the theatre ship capable of seating an audience of six hundred. There was a constantly changing repertory, with well-known plays and London scenery. One day, forty years later, in the home of a French marquis, I saw a photograph of a theatrical company in costume, flanked by British naval ratings. It looked oddly out of place in a French château. I asked about it. "Yes, it is on board a British ship, the *Gourko* at Scapa Flow during the First World War," said my host. "That's me!" He pointed to an alluring girl in black tights with a feathered headdress and fan, à la Gaby Delys, who dethroned the young King of Portugal. "You!" I exclaimed. He laughed. "Yes, me! Being hard up in my young days I played in a French cabaret as a female impersonator. I was in a show in London. I volunteered to join a company sent around Britain to entertain the troops. And that's how I got to Scapa Flow. Mon Dieu! It was the greatest fun. I sang in French. *Oh la la! Oui oui!* How those boys whistled! *Formidable!*"

When I arrived at the Grand Fleet on that cold May morning I was told that the great enemy was boredom. Nothing ever happened. The Germans seemed reluctant to fight, save for an odd hit-and-run exploit. The Fleet was thoroughly sick of firing at targets, or of being galvanised into sudden expectant activity by false alarms. "We're off! Jerry's out!" they shouted gleefully as the Fleet sailed out of Scapa Flow. But he wasn't. He had succeeded in getting a submarine through the screen and the Fleet had to put out to sea to avoid being a sitting duck until the intruder was disposed of. It was one of the weaknesses of this improvised harbour.

A ceaseless punctilious routine was demanded by The Old Man. But to what purpose? Would that German Fleet ever come out? There was every reason why it should not. Strategically it was in a bad position, numerically it was inferior. The hope these dull days was that the pressure of public opinion in Germany, the necessity of fulfilling the Kaiser's boast of invincibility, would compel the German Fleet to take a chance. It must not rot in harbour. The risk was not total for them if defeated. On board H.M.S. *Lion* Beatty had said, "If the German Fleet gets wiped out it really loses little. If we get wiped out we lose everything." He thought submarine warfare was their best chance, to menace our merchant shipping, our supplies to the Army, and to starve us. As it turned out they came near to achieving this.

As H.M.S. *Oak* ploughed through the choppy waters on that cold windy May morning,* two naval planes roared overhead. An officer followed them through his glasses. He turned to me as they went down the sky. "How old are you?" he asked abruptly. He was a man of about fifty, called out of retirement. "Twenty-three," I said.

* No one on board H.M.S. *Oak* that May morning in 1916 could foresee that within two and a half years this same ship would transport, on November 16th, 1918, a German admiral from his ship in the North Sea to H.M.S. *Queen Elizabeth* at Rosyth, to sign, before Admiral Beatty, the surrender of the German Fleet.

He looked at me oddly. "My lad, I'll venture a prophecy. If you live to be a grandfather you'll see those bloody things put 'paid' to our mighty navy. No one believes me and I'm glad I shan't live to see it."

I have often wondered whether he was alive on December 7th, 1941, when, in an hour, at Pearl Harbor, the Japanese dive-bombers wiped out the American Pacific Fleet, and again, three days later, off Malaya, sank two of our capital ships, the battlecruiser H.M.S. *Renown* and the new battleship H.M.S. *Prince of Wales*, with a loss of one thousand men, including Admiral Phillips, who ventured forth without adequate air cover. "With these two air disasters England had lost command of every ocean except the Atlantic," observed Churchill.

Presently we drew alongside H.M.S. *Iron Duke*. We mounted the gangway and were conducted by a staff officer to the Admiral's cabin. It seemed almost a social call rather than a naval occasion. We found ourselves in what might have been a drawing-room except for a large chart on the wall by the fireplace. On this chart the tracks of German submarines were plotted every few minutes from wireless reports. Could this be a battleship? It was so peaceful and homelike. There were easy chairs, and a divan covered in flowered chintz. French windows opened on to a stern walk bright with potted geraniums. Seagulls whirled in the bright morning. I was astonished to see in one corner a baby grand piano with open keyboard and loose sheets of music on its rack. A silver-framed photograph of Lady Jellicoe stood on the flat top. Near a divan chair there was a revolving bookcase. A large carpet, curtained windows and a log fire burning in the open grate, with a terrier dog asleep on the hearthrug, completed the domestic scene. Was it possible that the whole thing could be obliterated, together with a thousand lives, in a few minutes?

Admiral Jellicoe himself, apart from the heavy gold lace on his sleeves and his ribbon decorations, contributed to the illusion. Sturdy, medium in height, with a smiling round face and twinkling eyes, in other garb he might have been a country vicar like his brother. He had nothing of Beatty's leonine appearance, but we knew of an incisiveness that belied his amiable appearance. He had the reputation of being a quick worker and a man who never showed any temper. The admiration of his officers, the devotion of the whole Fleet and the facts of his career were impressive indications of his worth. Alfred Noyes aptly described him:

The weatherwise face that showed no ageing sign
But only grew in kindness year by year,
The shrewd brown twinkling eyes, the gentle heart,
The resolute truth in judgement and in act . . .

Jellicoe was aware of the criticism of the Fleet's apparent inactivity. He smiled at us, the representatives of the Press, as he addressed us, knowing its penchant for 'copy'. "Gentlemen," he said, "I will be frank with you—the less said the better. The main danger which we have to guard against is that of the Fleet being forced to make false strategic moves owing to some outcry being caused by people who think that unless guns are being fired, or the Fleet is constantly in the vicinity of the enemy coast, the Navy is not doing its work to win the war. Were a naval policy of this nature developed, it is quite conceivable that a few hours of bad luck in a minefield or in a submarine-infested area might see the Fleet brought into a position of inferiority compared to the German Battle Fleet. The moment they oblige me by coming out we shall be there to give them a warm welcome." He smiled and added—"And that's all I have to say, gentlemen."

It was very little after a long journey north to see him but we swallowed our disappointment. One of us asked a question. "Do you think the German Fleet will ever come out?"

"Now you mustn't depress us! We always hope it will be to-day or to-morrow or the day after. I pray the German public will be less patient than the British and give them a push!" he commented.

Stewards appeared with trays of drink. The Admiral went round amongst us. Presently I found an opportunity to ask a question that wasn't naval.

"May I ask, sir, if you play that piano?"

"Very badly. But I've a young officer who's almost a professional. And we're lucky to have a piano-tuner among the ship's company. We are in every sense a complete ship, and always in tune!" he replied, with twinkling eyes.

I have often wondered about that piano. On the shore of Scapa Bay there was a great dump of furniture, chairs, tables, bookcases, pictures, carpets and pianos. When the Fleet hurriedly sailed out of Scapa Flow, stripped for action, it jettisoned all inflammable and extraneous articles from the wardrooms and gunrooms. Pianos were among this hastily ejected furniture. Was Admiral Jellicoe's piano dumped, or did it come safely through the Battle of Jutland? Or, surviving Jutland, was it a casualty in the Second World War? On October 17th, 1939, four days after a German submarine sank the battleship *Royal Oak*, with a loss of eight hundred men, the Luftwaffe raided the harbour and so badly straddled the *Iron Duke* with bombs that she had to be beached to prevent her sinking. I never learned what was the fate of the piano I saw in Jellicoe's salon.

In retrospect, Jellicoe's words stressing caution had great significance. Behind that serene face there may have been gnawing worry, for he knew something the world did not know. It transpired later that he was not happy about the relative strength of the opposing fleets. In numbers the British navy was superior, but in quality, in gunnery and armour some disconcerting facts exerted a cautionary influence on Jellicoe's strategy. We lived confidently in a great tradition, but we had fought no major naval action since Trafalgar. Behind Jellicoe was the knowledge that he had striven for reforms not carried out. As late as July, 1914, while Second Sea Lord, he had directed the attention of the First Lord to the comparative quality of the British and German battleships. "The inferiority of the protection of the British ships of the 1909–11 classes against guns and torpedoes is very striking. This undoubtedly is a weak point in the design of our ships. It is highly dangerous to consider that our ships, as a whole, are superior or even equal fighting machines compared with the German."

Jellicoe knew also that, though the Grand Fleet was numerically superior, the German destroyers outnumbered the British. They were faster and carried more and better torpedo tubes. Their battleships had thicker armour plate. Our shells were inferior in armour-piercing power. The magazine chambers had dangerous defects. The ship design was often faulty. It was found that the *Iron Duke*'s six-inch batteries had restricted elevation and were too near the water line. There was something worse than all this; the standard of British gunnery suffered from inadequate practise and shorter drill. But the real thing that hampered our gunnery was the inferior quality of our range-finders and other optical instruments. The German instruments were far superior.* And above all there was a menace unknown to Nelson, the deadly submarine and the mine.

* Our cordite was also defective, being unstable at high temperatures. In July, 1917, the *Vanguard*, with a thousand men on board, blew up. Only two men survived this terrible explosion. During the war the battleship *Bulwark*, the cruiser *Natal*, the *Princess Irene* and the monitor *Glatton* all met the same end.

Jellicoe, when he addressed us, knew all this. The British public did not. No wonder he stressed caution. There would be a large element of risk in any total conflict with the German Fleet.

After our visit to H.M.S. *Iron Duke* the *Oak* took us to lunch in the battlecruiser *Invincible*. Each of these great vessels was like a floating town. The ship's wardroom bulkhead had a panoramic painting by one of her officers recording the Battle of the Falkland Islands, in which she had taken part.

We were a merry party at lunch, and afterwards three bright lads, having asked me for news of the world so remote from them, took me to their mess. They were Sub-Lieutenants Raymond Portal, Lionel Johnstone—the latter looking even younger than his nineteen years—and Midshipman Edward Hodgson, who had been in the Falkland Battle. These boys showed me over the ship, a vast departmentalised organisation with sections in which the work went on co-ordinated with other sections; there seemed to be somewhere a hidden brain at work, a master-mind. The men in the revolving turret, loading a twelve-inch gun, saw nothing of the outside world, and were unaware of the direction in which they were shooting. They told me that the noise was so deafening that they were scarcely able to distinguish between their own fire and being hit. They were controlled solely by an officer watching an indicator on a dial, himself under control of those above who constituted the eyes of the ship. A huge shell in its case came screaming up in the hoist; the great gun moved into life like a waking animal, there was a roar of compressed air as the breech flew open. A powerful rammer drove in the smooth shell, the breech closed, an indicator finger moved over the dial, a button was pressed, the great gun fired, then recoiled, having hurled a shell that might sink a battleship worth four million pounds. Yet in that revolving turret the intricate mechanism seemed utterly remote from its mission of slaughter. I was lost in fascination of the scene; the loaders became figures on a Greek frieze, half-naked and perspiring, automatic in their wordless task. The muscles of their lithe young bodies slid rhythmically under the satin flesh. Locked up in this blind turret men had been known to go on serving the gun while the ship was sinking to a watery grave. I came out into daylight on to the long deck. It was all like a dream as I emerged into the living day. Could this clean shining ship populated by its young, dedicated crew really be an instrument of death?

My three young guides, Raymond, Lionel and Teddy, finally escorted me to the gangway, and waved as I went down it. We were all going to meet again, somehow, somewhere. "It must be London!" cried Raymond. "Piccadilly Circus, the Savoy!" added Lionel. Their figures, high on deck, diminished as the *Oak* bore us away across the harbour. The great grey ship fading over the water was a moving sight.

VI

Six days later when I arrived at my office on the evening of June 2nd, the editor had some galley proofs in his hand. There had been a great battle in the North Sea. The Admiralty had made a news release for the morrow. My editor looked very grave and said—"Well, you were only just in time to see the Grand Fleet. It's been in action and it looks as if we've been badly mauled." He passed the galleys to me; I read and reread the Admiralty release. It was quite incredible. A heavy gloom fell over us all. Our losses were terrible while the German losses seemed neglible. We were all stunned. That this could happen to the great British Navy!

My editor wrote the display bills four times. He revised the news headings again and again. When it came to writing the leader he sat motionless at his desk. "What on earth can we say?" he asked. Every newspaper in the land faced the same task. *The Times* the next morning appeared with a poster—*Great Naval Battle. Heavy Losses. 6 British Cruisers and 8 Destroyers Lost.*

Surely there were German losses? The Admiralty communiqué said laconically—"The enemies losses were serious." Nothing more. We read the long list of our ships sunk and disabled. The battle-cruisers, *Queen Mary*, *Indefatigable* and *Invincible* were at the bottom of the North Sea. Later we were to learn that the British crews, of 60,000 men, had sustained a loss of 6,097, as against a loss of 2,551 in the German crews of 36,000. One hundred and fifty ships of the British Fleet had been in the battleforce as against ninety-nine German. We had lost three battlecruisers, three armoured cruisers, and eight destroyers as against one German battleship, one battle-cruiser, four armoured cruisers and five destroyers; a total of fourteen British ships as against eleven German.

The bright image of the British Fleet was misted over. Endless recriminations broke out in political and naval circles and were to continue for years. The British Fleet was sunk in gloom and split with controversy. Jellicoe was compared unfavourably with Beatty, but the latter, rash or bold, or both, had had his battlecruisers badly mauled. Within three-quarters of an hour his impulsiveness, together with bad signalling, had cost him the loss of the *Indefatigable*, with over a thousand men, and the *Queen Mary*, with twelve hundred, both at the bottom of the sea; one-third of his battlecruiser strength. On seeing his second battlecruiser disappear, Beatty turned to his captain and said—"There seems to be something wrong with our bloody ships to-day!" In the afternoon following the battle, tired, depressed, having seen eighty of his crew buried in their sea hammocks, he sat down in the charthouse and said, wearily, repeating his conclusion—"There's something wrong with our ships—and something wrong with our system." But at least he had gone all out, said his supporters, while Jellicoe had played for safety. The pro-Beatty and the pro-Jellicoe factions fought each other—on insufficient data, as it transpired.

VII

Slowly the story of the battle emerged. At two a.m. on the morning of May 30th the German High Seas Fleet under Admiral Scheer was told to prepare to sail. At seven p.m. it assembled outside Wilhemshaven. The intention of the German Fleet was known to Jellicoe as early as noon on May 30th, by reason of the fact that a team of cryptographers, created by the genius of Admiral Reginald Hall, was, in Room 40 at the Admiralty, in possession of the German naval code book. On August 20th, 1915, the German light cruiser *Magdeburg* had been sunk in action by the Russian navy in the Gulf of Finland. A few days later the body of a German signalman was washed ashore. He was found to be holding in his arms, faithful unto death, a copy of the German Naval Signal Book. The Russians, aware of its value, sent the book to England. A cryptographer, Fleet Paymaster Rotter, in Room 40, by a piece of brilliant deduction, succeeded in finding the key to the German code.

Thus the Admiralty knew early on May 30th that the German admiral had issued a signal for his Fleet to make ready to sail. Jellicoe, alerted, ordered his Fleet, assembled at Scapa Flow, Cromarty Firth and Rosyth, to put to sea. Thus Jellicoe sailed with the Grand Fleet four and a half hours before the German High Seas Fleet gained the

North Sea. The Grand Fleet was greater in ships, men and experience and filled with supreme confidence. It consisted of twenty-eight battleships and nine battlecruisers, against Scheer's sixteen and five. The destroyer strength was about equal. The total British shell-power was 396,700 pounds against the German 189,958 pounds. Clearly the odds seemed heavily against Admiral Scheer and it was an act of courage, or as some might think, of suicide for the German Fleet to emerge. It could only hope to win a battle by superior tactics and gunnery.

Almost before the smoke had cleared from the battle in the North Sea, and before Jellicoe had got back to Scapa Flow, the Germans had issued a communiqué claiming that they had won the battle. The Kaiser boasted of a great victory. The British Admiralty's communiqué, issued on the evening of June 2nd, by its admission and omissions seemed to endorse the German claim. Only slowly was it revealed that they had not won the battle, they had not become masters of the seas; their great object, England at their mercy, had not been achieved. The Germans claimed they had inflicted heavier losses than they had suffered, which was true. Moreover, they had eluded Jellicoe's Fleet and slipped away in the darkness preceding the dawn of June 1st. They had gained a tactical success.

Our own belated communiqué, brief and perturbing, made a vague statement on enemy losses. The German communiqué was specific in its claims. It blazed round the world the news of a great victory, supported by a long list of ships they had destroyed and damaged.

Were the stupendous German claims true, we asked through the following black days. It was not until June 18th that Jellicoe's full report was released, accurate in detail. The losses of the opposing fleets were now seen in true perspective. It revealed the meretricious nature of the German communiqué, but the Germans had already established the legend of a naval victory. It took years to demolish it. Who was responsible for the incredible incompetence that enabled the Germans to jump the gun and keep the British nation sunk in gloom for sixteen black days? The fault rested with the Admiralty, dilatory and devoid of any sense of publicity and news value. The man chiefly responsible was A. J. Balfour, the First Lord of the Admiralty. His behaviour shocked his naval assistants. He only slightly modified a proposed communiqué after a brief consultation with them. He sent it to the Press without submitting it to the Secretary of the Admiralty, and gave the public the blunt truth in a fashion that seemed to endorse the German claims. Only very slowly did the actual truth emerge, namely, that the German Fleet had suffered a reverse from which it never recovered. Except for an abortive sortie nine weeks later, the only time the German Fleet emerged in force again was when it went on November 21st, 1918, to the Firth of Forth to surrender itself to Admiral Beatty, now in command of the intact Grand Fleet. Only the imperturbable Balfour could have survived such inept conduct.*

VIII

When the true facts of the battle were assembled it became clear that neither side could claim an annihilating victory. In the first hour the Germans had badly hammered the British. They had shaken even Beatty's confidence, but they had not gained supremacy or come near to it. The Grand Fleet, baffled, still controlled the North Sea though the great opportunity for which the Fleet had been waiting had not been seized. Was Jellicoe at fault? Churchill, weighing the evidence available from both sides eight years later, comes down heavily against the Admiral. Jellicoe had been over-cautious, he said. He had not revealed 'The Nelson Touch'. A fleet greatly superior to its opponent in numbers, tonnage, guns, speed, had been offered, three times in twenty-four hours, a chance of victory which it had not seized. "Three times is a lot," commented Churchill, acidly, in his account of the battle in *The World Crisis, 1914–1918*.

This verdict is unjust, surely, and should not be allowed to stand. Churchill is inconsistent in his argument. He had accurately assessed, earlier, the great responsibility that rested on Jellicoe's shoulders. "The standpoint of the Commander-in-Chief of the British Grand Fleet was unique. It might fall to him as to no other man, Sovereign, Statesman, Admiral or General, to issue orders which in the space of two or three hours might nakedly decide the war. The destruction

* The last sortie of the German Fleet into the North Sea, on August 18th, 1916, was marked by a singular incident. Jellicoe was on shore near Dundee. When the news of the German sortie came the Grand Fleet put out from Scapa Flow without Jellicoe. Captain Meade, of H.M.S. *Royalist*, off Dundee, picked up the Commander-in-Chief and took him, on a pitch-dark night, to a rendezvous with his Fleet in the middle of the North Sea, and by means of a whaler transferred him to the *Iron Duke*, without lights and with a heavy sea running. The German Fleet hurried back to port.

of the British Battle Fleet was final. Jellicoe was the only man on earth who could lose the battle in an afternoon."

Churchill of his very nature was aggressive and ever prepared to take risks. His three counts in the indictment of Jellicoe were that he failed to annihilate the German Fleet at a moment of deployment; that an hour later, when Scheer made a bad error in his manœuvres, he had not engaged it; that he ignored an Admiralty message that could have led him out of the mists and brought him into full contact with the German Fleet. All this ignores one overwhelming fact already emphasised by Churchill—"We could lose the battle in an afternoon." It was no occasion for 'The Nelson Touch'. If Nelson had lost the battle of Trafalgar defeat would not have sealed England's fate, or gravely affected it; his fleet was only part of the Navy. He had no deadly submarines to contend with. Had Jellicoe suffered defeat with a wild throw, the results would have been appalling. England's coasts from Scapa Flow to Dover would have been wide open to bombardment. The German Navy in control of the High Seas could have cut off all supplies of raw materials and foodstuffs. The army in France, deprived of munitions, would have been paralysed. Defeat would have been total. All this Churchill knew. He contradicted himself in reproaching Jellicoe for not taking a grave risk. The basic prejudice he nursed against the Admiral was revealed in a letter he wrote on November 11th, 1924, answering Beatty's congratulations on his being made Chancellor of the Exchequer by Baldwin. He alluded to his time at the Admiralty during the war. "How I wish I could have guided events a little better and a little longer. Jutland would have had quite a different ring if the plans already formed in my mind after Dogger Bank for securing you the chief command had grown to their mature fruition. I am one of your greatest admirers and I can never cease to proclaim you as an inheritor of the great tradition of Nelson."

That is hardly the state of mind for an impartial historian.

Jellicoe had ignored an Admiralty signal, charged Churchill, but the Admiral had already received in the mists of the North Sea one message that was wholly inaccurate. It was not unreasonable for him to suspect the accuracy of the second. In the result he remained master of the seas. The enemy never again dared to challenge the Fleet. Its ships rotted in harbour, with deteriorating crews. It was forced to resort to unrestricted submarine warfare which in turn failed and brought in the U.S.A.

In the course of time some disconcerting facts emerged concerning the quality of our ships. It transpired that they had revealed grave errors of construction. The armour of the battlecruisers, *Queen Mary*, *Indefatigable* and *Invincible* was only six inches thick. It succumbed to the German shells. Also our shells proved to be inferior to theirs in armour-piercing power. There were serious defects of design in the turrets of the battlecruisers. It is surmised that the *Queen Mary* and the *Indefatigable* blew up from shells penetrating their inadequately armoured turrets, and that the flash of shell-bursts roared down the hoists into the magazines, creating fatal explosions. The turret roofs were only three inches thick, the German five. Again, the Germans kept their cordite charges in brass cases, the British in silk covers vulnerable to fire. Such were the defects of construction revealed in action.

Besides faults of construction, we now know there were other defects; an antiquated and too rigorous traditional centralised control by the Commander-in-Chief that choked initiative in subordinate commanders. To inferior projectiles, and anti-flash protection in the battlecruiser turrets, must be added the failure of the Admiralty staff in London, whose handling of the 'intelligence', which would have enabled Jellicoe to intercept the German Fleet on its retreat home, contributed to the enemy's escape. It left Jellicoe blind in the mists. "The whole situation was difficult to grasp," wrote Jellicoe in a letter to the First Lord. "I had no idea what was going on and could hardly see anything except flashes of the guns, shells falling, ships blowing up and an occasional glimpse of an enemy vessel."

IX

When on that memorable evening in my office I held in my hand the galley proofs with its list of our losses, the name of one ship more than any other stood out: H.M.S. *Invincible*. It was incredible that this magnificent battlecruiser and all her crew no longer existed. In a sense she had been my own particular ship. I could still see her, powerful, beautiful, shining on the calm waters of Scapa Flow. The faces of three vivacious boys haunted me, young Portal, Johnstone and Hodgson. I must have been the last person from land to have seen them. I recalled handsome Rear-Admiral Hood who flew his flag on her, and that young rating, name unknown, who had invited me to put my head in the breach of the twelve-inch gun when it opened, hissing, and seeing me a little reluctant, cried, "Why, I'd make my bed in it, sir!" Whereupon I put my head in and looked down the great smooth barrel. Poor lad.

It transpired that the *Invincible* had gone in a few seconds. Her turret was hit by the *Derfflinger*. A great flame had enveloped the ship, the masts collapsed, the ship broke in two. When a black mass of smoke cleared she was gone. Not wholly. When she was struck she was in thirty fathoms of water (180 feet) and since she was 576 feet long, the ends of the two halves stuck up out of the water for about one hundred feet. At 6.31 p.m. she was seen swinging into line with two other battlecruisers, opening fire abreast of the *Lion*. At 6.40 she and her crew did not exist. Of 1,026 officers and men only six survived.

Sitting in my office with the casualty list in my hand I reflected on the waywardness of Fate. The Grand Fleet had sailed urgently out of Scapa Flow for battle. Had I been in the *Invincible* on that day, instead of a few days earlier, it might have been that I should have sailed in her, excited by the thought of gaining a wonderful story. It took three-quarters of an hour for the tender to make the journey from the ship to shore. No ship under urgent orders to sail would have wasted time getting rid of me. Had I sailed in the *Iron Duke* I should have survived. Had I been in the *Invincible* I should have been lost. So much are we the playthings of Fate. There was a twenty-year-old Sub-Lieutenant in the *Collingwood* who, if he had been with those three other boys in the *Invincible*, would not have lived to become King George VI.

Since, possibly, I had been the last to see them, I wrote to the parents of the three lost boys, recalling all the minute details I could of those pleasant two hours I had spent with them in the *Invincible*. They invited me to visit them. Young Johnstone's mother, a widow, lived in one of those delightful houses, balconied, in the leafiness of London's Brompton Square. In the long upstairs drawing-room she showed me photographs of her son. She had last seen him, home on leave, after the Battle of the Falkland Islands, when his ship had chased the doomed *Scharnhorst* and *Gneisenau*. She showed me some of his letters concerning that engagement. After the two German ships had been despatched with an almost total loss of their crews, the *Invincible* had only twenty-two rounds left for their twelve-inch guns. Those German ships had met their doom only one month after they had wiped out, with no survivors, the outpowered British

Squadron at the Battle of Coronel. And, turn by turn, in a day not far distant, the *Derfflinger*, which had fired the fatal shot at the *Invincible*, would herself go under the waves. All young, all gallant, all doomed by Fate.

Later I was the guest of the Hodgsons in their country house in Hampshire. My host was a country doctor whose practice was spread over adjacent villages. The local vicar was Admiral Jellicoe's brother, and in the same village 'Ian Hay' had been sent to train with 'The First Hundred Thousand' that he had made famous in a book of the same name. My host and his wife had lost both of their sons and were now childless. There was a hush over the old Georgian house and the garden where the boys' voices had sounded so often. The elder, Jack, was seventeen, at Rugby School, and Teddy, fifteen, was at Dartmouth as a cadet when war was declared. Jack was killed fighting in Palestine. Dr. Hodgson produced a bundle of letters from Teddy, a very young midshipman's account of the Heligoland and Falklands actions in which he had taken part.

Walking in the garden, my host told me that he had it in mind to place a memorial plaque on one of the garden walls. Could I compose some suitable lines for it? I wrote them. They might stand in many English gardens once known to boys who will never return.

Stranger, pause here and think of us awhile
Who loved this garden in our boyhood's days,
Brothers in death as life, whom many a mile
Has sundered; for amid the pathless waves
Where northern waters roll, one rests, and one
Sleeps in the desert 'neath a tropic sun.

Laugh softly, children, in your mirth for we
Were once as you; remember us who knew
The golden summer noons, who loved to see
The moonlight on the roses, and the dew:
Remember us, and leave a votive sigh;
It was for England we went forth to die.

The passionate controversy, Jellicoe versus Beatty, that followed the Jutland Battle, evoked some discreditable incidents. Beatty succeeded Jellicoe as Commander-in-Chief, Jellicoe being recalled to the Admiralty to deal with the submarine menace. In turn Beatty became First Sea Lord and used his position to suppress and manipulate in the Harper *Record*, commissioned by the Admiralty, passages that criticised his strategy in the battle. Beatty added a Foreword, praising the part played by his battlecruisers to the detriment of the Battle Fleet. Jellicoe, hearing of this *Record*, insisted on seeing the proofs and strongly objected to the biased passages. Finally, the *Record* was pigeon-holed.

The German Official History brought fresh light to the controversy and criticised Beatty's tactics. Churchill's comments on Jellicoe in *The World Crisis* added fuel to the flames. Time has lessened the acrimony of this unsavoury controversy. Geoffrey Bennett, in his book *The Jutland Battle*, wrote, soothingly:

> Beatty may have made use of his position as First Sea Lord to distort the truth about Jutland in his own favour, but lesser men have suffered *folie de grandeur* with smaller excuse. He had to carry more than the heavy burden of his Admiralty office after the incessant strain of four and a half years of war at sea; he bore without complaint the nagging worry of a neurotically sick wife to whom he remained patiently devoted. There are aspects of Nelson's life which are open to harsher criticism, but no one questions his right to look down on the heart of London from the summit of a column in Trafalgar Square.

A generously expressed opinion, though we may question whether *folie de grandeur* is the right excuse, or a neurotic wife should extenuate a biased judgement on strategy. Naturally, Jellicoe objected to the tampering with the Harper *Record*. It was compiled after he had left the Admiralty where as First Sea Lord, in December, 1916, he was primarily responsible for introducing the convoy system which by October, 1917, was so effective that our merchant shipping losses were enormously reduced. In December, 1917, he found a note on his desk at the Admiralty, signed by the First Lord, Sir Eric Geddes, Lloyd George's hammer-fisted nominee, summarily dismissing him without a word of explanation, an act of the grossest injustice. The Press that glamourised Beatty had always treated Jellicoe coolly.

Despite the regrettable argument that raged over the years regarding the merits of the two Admirals, *au fond* they had a great respect for each other. Jellicoe always found Beatty 'splendid'. Once, when he took a short leave to consult his doctor, Beatty wrote to him:

"Take good care of yourself. What we should do without you the Lord only knows." Perhaps it lay on his conscience that he had not invited Jellicoe to be present at a historic scene in the forecabin of H.M.S. *Queen Elizabeth* on November 16th, 1918. H.M.S. *Oak*, still the destroyer on duty with the flagship, had brought Admiral Meurer from the *Konigsberg*, in a thick fog in the North Sea, to the Firth of Forth, to sign the terms drawn up for the surrender of the German High Seas Fleet. In the cabin of Beatty's flagship sat Sir John Lavery, the official artist, making sketches for a painting by which to record that tremendous scene. (Illustration, p. 192.)

"As I was in mufti a uniform had to be found for me," he recorded. "The Commodore dressed me up in a post-captain's discarded uniform that happened to fit. My paintings were hidden behind flowers on a side table where I was unobserved by the delegates."

One looks in vain for Jellicoe among the group of high officers seated at the table. It would have been a fitting gesture by Beatty, his successor in the command of the Grand Fleet, to have invited Jellicoe to be present at that great moment in British naval history, or, failing this, to witness the actual surrender of the German High Seas Fleet on the morning of November 21st, when Beatty, with all his ships at the appointed rendezvous in the North Sea, led the German Battle Fleet to an anchorage in Aberlady Bay, on the Firth of Forth, prior to its internment at Scapa Flow.

Death began to take its toll of the chief protagonists in the Battle of Jutland. Admiral Scheer died in 1928 just when he was looking forward to being Jellicoe's guest in England. Jellicoe died in November, 1935. A naval escort carried his body to St. Paul's, to be placed beside his peers, Nelson and Collingwood. In that procession I saw Beatty, on foot, very feeble, in full dress uniform, wrapped in a boat cloak. It seems that, suffering from influenza, he had defied his doctors to pay respect to his old colleague. He walked, beside the gun carriage, through two miles of the streets of London. As the procession moved along Fleet Street a journalist from *The Star*, seeing how ill the Admiral was, stepped out from the crowd to give him some brandy. Beatty drank it and walked on. Four months later he was dead, and was taken to lie beside Jellicoe in St. Paul's.

Fifty years after the Battle of Jutland, on May 31st, 1966, some of the survivors went to St. Martin-in-the-Fields, for a memorial service. Afterwards they proceeded to lay wreaths in front of the busts of Jellicoe and Beatty, disgracefully hidden away in Trafalgar Square.

Among this company walked the sons of the two admirals, Earl Jellicoe and Earl Beatty, and a delegation of German veterans. At the same time in the North Sea, H.M.S. *Defender* and H.M.S. *Dainty*, and the West German frigates, *Karlsruhe* and *Braunschweig*, approached the site of the battle off the Danish coast. Arriving there, they threw wreaths into the sea, remembering their dead, and the ships' bands played their national anthems.

One thought arises from this anniversary and the conjunction of former foes. Should we regret that the British Fleet did not achieve an annihilating victory? In that battle 6,097 British and 2,551 Germans lost their lives. Had there been a complete engagement some thirty thousand might have been lost fulfilling their duty to their respective countries. So costly a victory would not have brought the British any better result. At Jutland the German Fleet had ceased to be a menace.

X

Soon after my return from the Grand Fleet the Managing Editor of the *Post*, who was actually the owner-director, sent for me. It was my first meeting with Sir Alexander Jeans, withdrawn in his Holy of Holies. He was very genial, asked me a few questions, and told me that my articles had been most favourably commented upon. He would increase my salary to £4 a week and make me literary editor. I went out of the office walking on air. I could now fulfil a hope I had been nursing. I could bring my mother to Liverpool and escape from my lonely lodgings and cheap restaurant meals. I had not once been able to see her in the course of six months. It clearly was impossible for me to run two homes. I now suggested that she should sell up at Nottingham and join me in furnished lodgings. As it turned out this was an error but I had no idea what Fate had in store for me. It was characteristic that she showed no hesitation in accepting my suggestion.

I found good furnished lodgings—a sitting-room and two bedrooms for twenty shillings a week. The house was within walking distance of my office, in a pleasant street. It was owned by the widow of a merchant marine officer. We were allowed to have our Skye terrier. So one day my mother arrived, in a strange city where she knew no one. I fear I did not realise what a sacrifice she had made. She had left all her friends. Happily our landlady was a cheerful old soul. When she was unwell my mother insisted that she should remain in bed during the morning and took breakfast to her. "Who'd believe it! I've never had breakfast brought to me in my life." My mother said slyly to me, "Well, it gives me the kitchen to myself."

One thing worried us. The framed photographs on the walls were frightful. Dead aunts, uncles and lost sea captains had a mortuary stare. Little by little we unhooked them and stacked them in a cupboard. As no comments were made we thought our landlady had not noticed but one day, standing in our sitting-room and surveying the walls, she said—"I see you don't like my relations—to be candid I never liked them myself but once they were up they somehow stayed up." She had a married daughter. "We're not on visiting terms," she said, without any explanation. She also had a son. "I've not seen him for ten years and he seldom writes. He lives on one of those cannibal islands. He never could leave the girls alone. There's something keeps him out there and it's not work, which he never liked." One day she showed my mother an old letter of his. The 'cannibal island' was Ceylon. He worked on a tea plantation. Her husband had been drowned at sea in the loss of his ship. She had a small pension, and owned her house. She cherished and talked at length to a parrot he had brought her on his last trip home. "Polly's not got her language from me or my late husband, who was a God-fearing man," she said.

Our lodging had one drawback. It was a long climb to a windswept height. One caught the full force of the wintry winds that swept the city, blowing up from the River Mersey. My route from the office after midnight led me past the gaunt edifice, scaffolded, of the new Anglican cathedral, designed by Sir Giles Gilbert Scott, a Catholic. How well I came to know every tower and pinnacle of this new cathedral growing very slowly in war time, to be unfinished even fifty years later. It reared up dun-brown and macabre, unroofed against the wintry night.

All my life strange things have happened to me. A lonely, obscure young man, a stranger in the somewhat forbidding city where an old commercial aristocracy, typified by the Gladstones, Rodneys, Roscoes, Huskissons, by the oligarchs and shipping tycoons, held sway, I could not foresee that twenty years hence I should be reading the Lesson from the pulpit in the great high transept of the still-uncompleted cathedral. The manner of it was this. I had been invited to be the Guest Speaker at the dinner of the Dickens Fellowship, holding its annual convention in Liverpool. The Dean of the Cathedral was among the speakers. After the dinner he was very complimentary about my address. I was surprised by what followed. An afternoon service was being held on the morrow, Sunday, for the delegates. Would I give him the pleasure on that occasion of reading the Lesson? I consented, hesitatingly. The Dean wrote down for me the Lesson. Back at the Adelphi Hotel I asked for a Bible. In the remotest down-at-heel hotels in the United States one always finds on the bedside table a Bible placed there by the Gideon Society. In later years it extended its distribution to hotels in Great Britain. But now, the luxurious Adelphi Hotel had some trouble in finding a Bible for me. When, towards midnight, I read the prescribed Lesson I was dismayed by the names I found in the text; their pronunciation was a problem. Immediately after breakfast the next morning I enquired if there was a clergyman staying in the hotel. No. I went into the great lounge and looked around. A second glance raised my hopes. My eyes fell on a rather grim-looking elderly man, neatly dressed, sitting alone. He had his long hair plaited and curled on his head. Obviously he was one of the sect of Jehovah's Witnesses. I approached him and explained my need. He was polite and obliging. His accent proclaimed him to be an American. The Bible had no mysteries for him. He read the passage through. I listened to his pronunciation carefully and read the passage back to him. I thanked him and went to my room where I rehearsed aloud until I was word perfect.

In the cathedral, after they had gowned me in the Vestry, I was escorted to a seat near the Bishop's throne. When the moment came for the reading of the Lesson, I was ceremoniously conducted by a verger with a gold-tipped staff to the pulpit up on a pillar at the corner of the great transept. When I mounted the steps I was astonished by its height above the ground. The congregation below looked like small birds. The great fluted columns swept up to the immense groined roof. As soon as I began to read, two sentences told me that the acoustics were perfect. I gave my voice full volume and the rotund phrases of the Old Testament prophet went rolling out under that resounding roof. What a platform! What a pity I was confined to the printed text! At the conclusion of the service, back in the Vestry, unrobed, the Dean shook me warmly by the hand. "Splendid! Beautifully read!" he exclaimed. "I feel you are a loss to the Church."

Ah, if that dear Dean only knew what a heretic I was. The ghost of my agnostic father smiled faintly at me. That experience made me wonder still more about Anglican clerics and their diction. What superb opportunities they have. For some years, through early manhood, in pursuit of the art of public speaking, I had listened not only to politicians and famous advocates but also to divines in the pulpit. What incomparable settings they inherit in the architectural beauty of our cathedrals and with the preamble of those English choirs, angel-voiced, finely trained, unmatched anywhere in Europe, even considering the much vaunted *Sängerknaben* in the Vienna Hofburg Kapelle. How often, alas, after this noble preamble, came the disillusionment of the Lesson when the priest at the lectern proceeded to travesty our English tongue with a bumbling, inarticulate performance. Once, guest of a Fellow of King's College, Cambridge, I sat in a choir stall beneath the glory of stained glass and Tudor vaulting, lifted to high expectation when the preacher announced his text. His enunciation was deplorable. He had not the faintest sense of the majesty of the Authorised Version in that golden age of English prose. I have also heard renowned clerics amble through the service, giving me the impression that they were rather bored with the Apostles. 'The hungry mouths look up and are not fed.' Rarely am I rewarded. There are some unforgettable occasions. I was the house guest of the Dean of Windsor, Dean of the Order of the Garter, of which the robes are stored in a corridor of The Deanery at Windsor Castle. Going to service through the private door that leads into the noble royal chapel, I was placed in one of the knights' stalls, where the name and achievement of the knight were engraved on a brass plate under his resplendent banner. The choir touched divine heights and then, to my surprise, not the Dean but a young clergyman preached the sermon. I could not credit my ears. He had a bell-like voice, a fluent delivery and an evangelical fervour that made me accept, as he asserted, that we were miserable sinners and there was no health in us. After the service I commented on the preacher, praising his address and the excellence of the delivery. "Yes, yes," agreed the dear old Dean, "but a little too ardent!"

The Liverpool pulpit with its superb acoustics made me wonder about clerical speech. Is there a tradition of deflation of emotion in the ecclesiastic schools? Are they afraid of the herd-hypnotism exploited by the Billy Grahams in vast arenas? Does the Greek admonition—*ΜΗΔΕΝ ΑΓΑΝ*, 'Nothing in excess', prevail? And has the microphone, that adjunct of the mumblers, wrought ruin in public declamation?

Even today the Anglican cathedral at Liverpool is unfinished, though not as skeletal as when I passed by it, eerie in moonlight, in 1916. It now has a Roman Catholic companion some eight hundred yards away, grandiosely planned originally by Sir Edwin Lutyens. It was to have had a dome larger than St. Peter's at Rome. When Lutyens died the estimated cost had risen to £7 million. In 1952 the estimate had risen to £27 million. The brother of Sir Giles Gilbert Scott, architect of the Anglican neighbour, was called in. He cut back the cost to £4 million in 1955. Later it reached £10 million. In 1960, the planners, desperate, awarded the job to a new architect, the designer of London Airport, who built a circular cathedral, completed in 1967, for £1 million. Its singular shape has caused it to be called 'The Mersey Funnel'. When I saw it I was glad it was the Anglican and not the Roman Catholic cathedral in which I was asked to read the Lesson. I should have felt like a robot.

XI

Every week my friend George Burrows came to Liverpool to give his singing lessons. One day he said, "I'm taking you to lunch with a very nice woman. She reads your reviews." We arrived at a large house in an exclusive residential district. My hostess proved charming. There were three delightful children, a girl and two boys, about nine, eight and five. Her husband was absent in London on some Government mission. When I met him we were in immediate accord. His name was Burton Chadwick. He was a partner in his father's shipping firm. He had begun his career by sailing before the mast and gaining his Master's Certificate. Handsome, tall, twenty-three years my senior, he had already distinguished himself. He had fought in a Yeomanry regiment in the South African War and been awarded the Royal Humane Society's certificate for saving life. He was absent from Liverpool, giving his services as Director of the Overseas Transport Division in the Ministry of Munitions. He lived at the Thames Yacht Club in London where he came to know Arnold Bennett, who had retreated there from domestic difficulties with his wife. To know Arnold Bennett seemed more remarkable to me than gaining the R.H.S.'s certificate for gallantry.

Mrs. Chadwick had a warm heart. She entertained splendidly and

I became a frequent guest. The moment my mother arrived in Liverpool Mrs. Chadwick called on her and took her out. "You must feel very proud of your son but that doesn't make up for loneliness," she said.

I was now extremely happy in my work. I had something of a home, and my mother with me. Clearly I had progressed on the paper. I staked out my claim on more and more space, and all Liverpool came to know my initials appended to articles and book and theatre reviews. More and more I was in demand as a speaker on literary subjects and now particularly for my account of naval affairs. The Repertory theatre gave me continuous delight with its excellent productions. Particularly enchanting were the visits of the Irish Players. For the first time I saw the plays of Yeats, Lennox Robinson and Synge. In Liverpool the Irish influence was everywhere. The Repertory Company spread its wings, producing Barrie's *Quality Street*, Zola's *Thérèse Raquin*, Chekhov's *The Cherry Orchard* and Laurence Housman's magical *Prunella*. In many of these my new friend William Armstrong acted.

Then one day I had a thrill. Sarah Bernhardt came to give a matinée performance in Liverpool's largest theatre. It seemed incredible that she could be so dynamic. She was seventy-three and had had a leg amputated two years previously. That spring she had visited the Théâtre aux Armées, acting for the *poilus* on the Western Front. For years she had been near bankruptcy, supporting a weak, spendthrift son she adored, and somehow maintaining a house in Paris and a château in the country. She was now living on the sale of her jewellery. Since the amputation she had had to be carried everywhere. She was en route for a tour in U.S.A., to raise money. She was within four years of her death in Paris. But Death seemed a stranger to the Divine Sarah; the vital flame still fiercely burning. Very little was left of the famous *voix d'or* but she was living history. Every seat in the vast theatre was sold out even though ninety per cent of the audience could not understand a word of French. William Armstrong had a delightful account of her visit to Manchester. She had driven out one day in an open landeau, wrapped in furs, in order to see the country. She halted the car to watch some youths playing football. Fascinated, she looked for a time and then said to her companion as they went on—"*J'adore ce cricket, c'est tellement anglais!*"

I went to see the manager of the theatre. I was writing a notice of the performance. Could he arrange an interview for me? He thought that was difficult. She had to conserve her strength and refused all interviews, but she would receive a few dignitaries in her dressing-room after the performance. He would try to get me in, if only to salute her.

The great day arrived, the atmosphere was electric. English and French soldiers were falling in thousands on the Western Front. This performance became a great demonstration of the *Entente Cordiale*. Everyone of eminence in the city was there. She appeared in a one-act play, *Mort au Champ d'Honneur*, playing the part of a young officer, dying, who was carried wounded from the battlefield and deposited beneath a tree. At his request they brought the French flag to him and holding it in his hands he apostrophised the survival and glory of France. At the fall of the curtain there was not a dry eye in the house. Her voice, the movement of her hands, the dedicated passion were soul-stirring. The curtain rose and fell to tumultuous applause and before the curtain fell finally the stage was a flower garden, with Sarah, on the arm of a supporting actor, bowing and bowing.

I hurried round to the dressing-room. All the big-wigs of Liverpool seemed to be there. To my dismay I found myself at the end of a queue. The door of the dressing-room kept opening and closing. I was almost at the head of the line when the manager emerged. "I am very sorry but Madame Bernhardt is very fatigued and regrets that she cannot receive any more visitors," he announced. I went up to him, desperate, "But you promised me—you promised me! I want to write something about her, I'm not here just to mob her!" I protested.

He looked at me and saw how tense I was. "A moment," he said, and disappeared into the room. A woman in front of me, befurred, with diamond earrings, turned on me indignantly, "Who do you think you are?" she demanded. I made no reply. The door opened. The manager appeared, letting two visitors out. She went forward, pushing me aside. "Sorry, madam," he said, blocking her way, then turned to me and let me slip in. I found myself near a screen in the dressing-room in a bower of flowers. As I came in Sarah's back was towards me. She lay on a chaise-longue, a sable fur thrown over her. There were half a dozen persons in the room. Sarah was reflected in a large illuminated mirror over a dressing-table. There was a strong scent of roses. As she reclined there she was still in the French officer's

The old *Nottingham Journal* office in Victoria Street. From 1883–5 James Barrie was editor-leader-writer. This was his first and last post as a journalist. He went to London to free-lance. On the ground floor was the Northern Insurance Office in which John Drinkwater was an office boy, aged 15, in 1897–1900

Richard Le Gallienne. Caricature by Max Beerbohm

uniform. There were some hurried words between the manager and a Frenchman, presumably her manager. He spoke to her and I gathered that she refused to see another visitor. I heard him say something about the *pauvre jeune journaliste.* "*Jeune—est-il jeune?*", she cried, and made a gesture of assent. The manager beckoned me forward to the chaise-longue. I had carefully rehearsed a little complimentary tribute in French, but owing to the commotion at the door it had quite gone from me. I heard my introducer say something about *le premier critique.* Sarah looked at me with coal-black eyes, her eyelashes loaded with mascara, her face heavily enamelled under grease paint, her small mouth almost violet in hue. She held out a frail bloodless hand. I bowed and kissed it. She smiled on me then, and turning her head towards her manager said huskily—"*Comme il est jeune! Un bébé!*" Smiling through her mask she dismissed me with a gracious wave of her hand. I left the room.

As the door was opened for me the befurred, bediamonded woman rushed in, jolting me. The door closed behind me. What they did with her I don't know. Well, I had seen the Divine Sarah. I had kissed her hand, I had heard her comment on my youthful appearance. It was nothing much to write about, but I had a memory for my old age.

With all my new activities I had not deserted my muse. In September, 1915, I had published my third book of verse, *The Youth of Beauty and Other Poems*, I had begun to contribute regularly to *The Poetry Review*, the monthly journal of The Poetry Society which had been formed in 1909 and had organised that memorable dinner at the Cheshire Cheese in Fleet Street, where Stephen Phillips had taken the chair. But one thing was obvious, there was no money in all this. Poets who rely on their poetry for a livelihood are doomed. It did happen that about this time there was a young man who had captured quite a large public with his work, by name Alfred Noyes, but he was the rare exception to the rule. So I kept my unprofitable muse subservient to my general work.

What industry the young and enthusiastic are capable of! I was writing ten or twelve columns a week. I addressed all kinds of meetings, twenty-two in one year. Alas, these occasions seldom carried a fee, but it was all great fun. One day I received an invitation from the Captain of H.M.S. *Conway*. She was an old masted wooden man-o'-war, contemporaneous with Nelson's *Victory*. Stationed at

Rock Ferry on the River Mersey she served as a nautical training ship for some two hundred cadets destined to become officers of the merchant marine. Accepting the invitation, I lunched with the Captain and addressed the cadets. Before I left he said—"I like the verses you've written at the head of your naval articles. We want a school song. I wonder if you could write one for us? For years we've been trying to find a suitable one but the better the poet the worse the song." Ignoring the uncomplimentary logic of this, I wrote the verses the next day and they were set to music by a gifted girl of seventeen, Muriel Herbert, a friend of mine. A few days later we set off together to the *Conway*. The Captain assembled the cadets and we 'tried it on the dog'. They swallowed the song avidly. Over and over again they sang it, and as the cutter rowed us ashore the old man-o'-war echoed with the refrain of *Carry On*. The *Conway* had found its school song. It brought me a good bonus in later years for whenever I sailed in a liner which had an old Conway boy among its officers I found myself treated with special favours.

One day, three years later, when I visited John Masefield, he asked, "Are you the Cecil Roberts who wrote the *Conway* school song?" Surprised by his question, I said I was, wondering how he could know. He looked at me and in his humble, quiet way said, with a sad little smile, "You know, I'm an old *Conway* boy. They asked me to write them a school song. I did—and they didn't use it!"

XII

I had put aside the poetic drama I had written those first lonely days in my lodgings at Seacombe. Then one day I heard that Sir George Alexander was coming to Liverpool in a one-act play at the music-hall. I wrote to him outlining the nature of my own play and asked him if he would be interested in it. He replied that when he arrived in Liverpool he would ask me to read it to him.

His career had been remarkable. I did not know then that he had made his first appearance on the stage at Nottingham, where he joined Sir Henry Irving's Lyceum Company then on tour in 1881. He had a reputation for having encouraged English dramatists as against foreign ones who were having a vogue in England in the Nineties. In his long reign at the fashionable St. James's Theatre he had enjoyed considerable artistic and financial success. He married a French actress, Florence Theleur, who long after his death, turned eighty, astonished London by her appearance. She was seen everywhere, wearing the most astonishing creations. Being tiny and delicate, she looked like a little French doll that had danced out of *La Boutique Fantasque*. Sir George Alexander was the idol of the West End stage, handsome, courtly in manner, a finished actor. As an actor-manager he had scored a notable success in *The Second Mrs. Tanqueray*, in which he appeared with Mrs. Patrick Campbell. He produced and acted in *The Prisoner of Zenda* and also in Oscar Wilde's *Lady Windermere's Fan*. He played John Worthing in the first production of *The Importance of Being Earnest* in 1895. He was acting in this play when Wilde's conviction caused it to be withdrawn. There is no truth in the story that he behaved badly to Oscar Wilde. He gave him a cheque for £1,000 for his defence, Wilde having sworn he was innocent. Another of Alexander's successes had been his production of the poetic drama he had commissioned from Stephen Phillips, then at the height of his fame, *Paolo and Francesca*. It was because of the renown of this production that I had approached him.

The appointed day, October 16th, 1916, came. Very nervous, my play in hand, I was ushered by a page boy into his sitting-room at the Midland Adelphi Hotel. It was a chill, grey day and there was a fire burning in the grate. He greeted me, easy in manner, retaining off stage the air of courtesy he presented on it. He was beautifully dressed in golfing tweeds, put me at my ease at once, and drew up a chair for me in front of the fire.

"You don't wish me to read all this play to you, sir?" I asked, fearful that he would be wearied before the end.

"That depends—how many acts?"

"Four."

"How many characters?"

"Nine."

"How many changes of scene?"

"Two."

He looked at me thoughtfully for a moment and then said, smiling, as he crossed his neat legs. "That's a good start. Who taught you that?"

"What you you mean, sir?" I asked.

"Young dramatists who write verse plays invariably write them with seven acts, thirty characters, and twenty changes of scene—Shakespeare sets them a bad example. How many dead bodies on the stage at the end?"

I laughed. "One," I said. "But how do you know there's a dead body?"

"There's always a dead body in a poetic drama—and a speech over the corpse—from *Hamlet* on. When the stage becomes a morgue, like in *Romeo and Juliet*, I get fidgety."

"I'm afraid there's a speech over the corpse in my play," I confessed.

"Very well. Now let's hear it. I shall stop you if I don't like it," he said with a charming smile as he poked the fire.

So I began, somewhat nervous at first. I read and read. After I had been reading for almost an hour he interrupted me and stood up. "We'll have some tea," he said, ringing. "Go on!"

I went on, stopped when the tea came, and after we had had it, began again. It was a quarter to five when I came to the end.

"You read well—been on the stage?" he asked. I shook my head.

"Your diction's very good. Tell me, why have you come to me with your play?"

"I thought you might like it—you produced Stephen Phillips' *Paolo and Francesca*."

"I like it and it might suit me but do you realise what a luxury it would be? Phillips' play was a great artistic success but two more successes like that would have ruined me. Beerbohm Tree was the only man who could make poetic drama pay. You know why he did Phillips' *Nero* and *Herod*? He saw in them spectacles. Even Shakespeare can be made to pay if he's well-dressed."

This was a blow. I had thought *Paolo and Francesca* had been a gold mine. I remained silent. Sir George looked at me. "The only reason why we actors put on poetic drama is sheer vanity. We like to do something for art's sake to show we can do it, and that we have a soul above the social drama. I'm rich enough to be vain. I'd like to consider your play. Can you wait? At present I've let the St. James's and I have two plays in hand."

I would have waited until he built a theatre. In parting he walked down the corridor with me to the lift. I felt the happiest lad on earth.

At his request I sent him the typewritten play. He acknowledged it and said he would be writing to me. I waited and waited. At last there was a letter that raised me to heaven. He would like to produce my play, but he could not consider this for a year as he was committed to two plays in hand. I answered expressing my willingness to wait.

Alas, it was not to be. One morning, a year later, I picked up a newspaper and read of his death, aged sixty-five. It was a blow to all my hopes. I put the play in a drawer. Six years later it was produced by the Compton Comedy Company, then run by Compton Mackenzie's mother. One of his sisters appeared in the cast, and the play was published by Heinemann. It was called *A Tale of Young Lovers*. It was set in Genoa in the sixteenth century.

CHAPTER FOUR

A Wonderful New World

I

A MONTH AFTER reading my play to Sir George Alexander I was sent off on another naval mission. I found myself on a jetty at Dover, boarding a torpedo-boat-destroyer, one of the T.B.D.s keeping the perilous vigil of the Dover Straits. Their task was to block the passage of the German U boats into the Atlantic. The route via the north of Britain was a long detour which took eight days of the fourteen-day cruising range of the smaller U boats, and six days of the larger boats with a twenty-five day cruising capacity. The Germans therefore took the risk of passing the Dover Straits. To prevent this we had a patrol operating from Dover. Towards the end of the war, when Admiral Keyes succeeded Admiral Bacon, a mined barrage, brilliantly lit, was thrown across from the English to the French coast. It was so brilliantly lit that it was nicknamed Piccadilly, but when I arrived to visit the Dover Patrol, early in December, 1916, there was no illuminated barrage. The Dover Patrol was not only given the task of blocking the passage of the U boats; on it depended the safety of our transports constantly crossing to and from France. It was a task that wore down the strongest nerves. Although our Navy had thrown a mined barrage, submerged, across the Straits, it was not wholly successful and the U boats penetrated it at the rate of some twenty a month. The patrol had to be increased although the destroyers could ill be spared. The greatest menace was the floating mine. They were sown by the enemy and borne down by strong currents upon our ships. The destroyer to which I was assigned carried three four-inch guns and two twenty-one-inch torpedo tubes. She did thirty-three knots with a tonnage displacement of 1,000 tons.

Admiral Sir Reginald Bacon was in command of the Patrol, with his office at Dover. We received a briefing from him. I am not by nature a brave man, burdened with too vivid an imagination. I never had, like 'Tiny' Freyberg, the inborn *dono di coraggio* which makes the first-class soldier, sometimes the 'dumber' the better. I belonged to that despised cohort denounced by Shakespeare—"Cowards die many times before their deaths, the valiant never taste of death but once." The finest speech ever made on courage came from the mouth of Sir James Barrie, possibly the most timid of men. Nevertheless, I had great willpower and could mask my own timorous nature. I went to the Dover Patrol in its darkest hours, and could find no words adequate in commendation of the steady cool courage of the men of this Patrol.

Our gallant little vessels were tossed about in the vile wintry weather of the Channel. Grimly they kept on their twenty-four hour elliptical patrol, up to the barrage and back. In the last light of evening and in the first glimmer of dawn a destroyer on the upward patrol passed its colleague on the downward. Sometimes the twenty-four hour patrol was prolonged, violent gales preventing the relief of the vessels. Life on board a destroyer stripped for action did not offer the amenities of a battlecruiser. A crew of sixty or eighty in confined space had little diversion. If you cannot put up with your fellowmen in a stuffy little wardroom then life is Hell. There are moments when a destroyer's crew is ripe for murder. It was the risks undertaken in common that held these men together—the brotherhood of the brave.

Leaving the Dover jetty that cold grey December afternoon I descended the hatchway to find myself in a small low wardroom with an atmosphere of tobacco, anthracite and cooking, a veritable fug. Wicker chairs faced the stove, a leather divan ran along two sides of the low wardroom which served as temporary bunks for officers going on watch. As almost everywhere in the Service the walls were hung with alluring houris by Kirchner, a Viennese artist, and nude studies from *La Vie Parisienne*. A gramophone blared above the beat of the engines.

My skipper was Lieutenant-Commander E. K. Boddam-Whetham. Tall, thin, I don't think he was a day older than thirty. He was responsible for a ship costing a quarter of a million pounds and for some eighty lives. Long watches on the bridge, cat-naps in the charthouse below, for at sea he never went to bed, had robbed his face of all signs of youth. The other officers consisted of an engineer, a lieutenant, a gunner, a surgeon-probationer and a sub-lieutenant. The Doc, as he was called, was an ingenuous young Scot who upon the slightest excuse exhibited his case of gleaming knives. He was pining for action that might entail operating on someone.

I was prepared for going on deck. I put on a prodigious amount of clothing lent to me, two pairs of thick woollen stockings, halfway up the thigh, a pair of heavy rubber sea-boots, a thick waistcoat, a fur-lined bridge-coat, a pair of wool gloves, over them a pair of leather gauntlets, and a balaclava wool headpiece. If we got into the sea I was a lead plummet. An icy wind caught me as I emerged from the fuggy wardroom. I walked warily along the steel deck, with its torpedo tubes swung athwart, clutching the lifeline as I clambered towards the bridge. Sometimes I waded in water, the deck swept by the washing sea. I gained the charthouse, the 'brains' of the ship, for here voices sounded from pipes that ran like nerves through the vessel. It had an iron door that automatically switched off the lights on opening. Above was the wireless room. The charthouse was the skipper's living-room, dining-room and bedroom when at sea, with the bridge immediately above it.

When I went up on to the bridge we were well out to sea on our way to relieve a fellow patrol boat. The wash from the propellers marbled our wake. Dusk fell over the grey waters, a gull cried, flying westward against an angry red-streaked sky. A desolation of peril spread around us. My muffled skipper stood by the compass. Silent, he peered through the half-open windscreen on which the sleet rattled. Beyond was nothing but the blackness of a restless sea that flowered into a white line as the wind whipped its wave-spume. The engines throbbed, driving our grey ship through the darkness. In a manner it was like a grim dream but when later I crawled along the deck the stern reality of our mission was revealed; by each gun and tube crouched a tarpaulin-covered figure. At any moment a bell might break the silence and the men by the guns would be galvanised into activity. Without warning the sea might carry down on us a deadly mine, with a sinister possibility—a hit, a flash, escaped oil covering the sea, men struggling in it, then a sheet of flame as it caught fire.

We reached our patrol beat, the relieved destroyer slipped away. She reported a patch of mines to the east. Through the next twelve hours we would plough from darkness to dawn on our elliptical orbit, up to the barrage and back, alternately spaced with our companion destroyer. We carried a device to protect us from the mines that was fitted like a wishbone on our bows. It fended off a submerged mine, ran it along a steel wire to a groove with a cutting neck. The mine, severed from its sinker, then bobbed up and could be shot at and destroyed. Nearly half a century later my weekend host, Everard Gates, motored me across Surrey to dine with a friend. In the large hall of a beautiful country house there was a highly polished piece of steel mechanism of a curious shape, akin to the freakish work of a 'modern' sculptor. Our host led us past it. "Will you please tell me why you have a paravane in your hall?" I asked him. He looked very surprised. "Now, how would you know it's a paravane?" he asked. "I invented it and this is my exhibition model." I then learned that my host was Sir Dennis Burney, the son of Admiral Sir Cecil Burney of First World War fame, an ex-naval officer and M.P. A man of considerable genius, he not only invented, when quite young, the paravane, but he also designed and was the constructor, in 1924–1928, of the airship R. 100. It created a sensation by making in August, 1930, an acceptance flight from England to Canada and back. The return journey from Montreal was made in fifty-seven hours, a record in those days. Burney travelled with the airship, representing the contractors.

Motoring home from Sir Dennis's my host said to me—"He got a whacking award from the Inventions Board after the war for his paravane." He richly deserved it. It saved thousands of tons of shipping and hundreds of lives. What a strange meeting, after all those years, with the paravane I had first seen on the Dover Patrol!

II

On the bridge I was horribly sick. I hung on in wet misery. At last it was the middle watch. The Sub came up with hot ship's chocolate for us. Then I went below for four hours, lying in the bunk allotted to me, listening to the swish of the water on the other side of the quarter-inch steel hull. Each time we reached the end of our beat the ship slowed down, rolled when she turned on her course and then, as the engines speeded up into their familiar hum, we set off along our track again. I dozed, then woke. 'Four bells' sounded. I got up and clambered on deck. It was still pitch dark. The air was bitterly cold. A heavy sea broke over us and swilled round the gun mountings. I saw a rating clutch the line under a heavy sea. I watched him. He emerged from the passing wave. This reminded me of a story I had heard at Dover that morning. A midshipman went overboard in one of those seas. The officer of the watch saw the poor lad go. When another great wave buried the ship he was amazed to see the returned midshipman clinging to a gun mounting. The miraculous event was wirelessed around. The next morning, back in harbour, word came that Admiral Bacon wished to see the lucky Mid. It was his hour of glory. He made a careful toilet and emerged shining. Ushered into the Admiral's office, he came to attention and awaited congratulations. The Admiral looked at him sternly and said, "I wish to receive from you, sir, an explanation as to why you vacated your post of duty *without leave*!" Even the great of the earth indulge in leg-pulling. A few minutes later the midshipman went forth in glory to lunch with the Admiral.

I arrived safely on the bridge. Messages were popping out of the wireless-room hatch. Was something astir? There was yet another flimsy which the skipper looked at and showed to the Sub as they glanced at me. Obviously they were keeping something from me. As tactfully as possible I asked if anything was happening. The skipper was evasive. "Do please tell me if it's anything . . ." I began. He pulled the flimsy out of his pocket. I read: "H.M.S. *Locust* to H.M.S. *Lennox*—"Is your damn journalist still sick? Ours is."

There was a glimmer of dawn at last. The destroyer kept her course throwing water from her as from the shoulder of a strong swimmer. It was snowing now. The darkness gradually lifted its veil, the horizon changed from iron grey to purple and then cold white. The skipper went down into the charthouse, inviting me to follow. They could now take the shutter off the door, on which there came a knock. It opened, bringing a whiff of cooked kippers. His man appeared with our breakfast. The skipper went out for a few moments. When he returned he asked, "I puke every morning before breakfast—what about you?" I had nothing left in me to puke but my breakfast went untouched.

The weather cleared, the relieving destroyer came out to us, we turned and began a homeward course. The Sub appeared with a bright morning face despite the fact that he had kept the middle-watch. The blessed white cliffs of Dover loomed up, the gulls wheeled over our stern. Half a dozen planes roared and swooped above us like swallows. We passed the home buoys, the engines reduced speed, the grey destroyer slid into her berth, the engines shook a little then fell still. The officers left the bridge. It was time to say goodbye. One of them asked me if I would write something in his autograph book.

I returned it the next day with some verses, *The Dover Patrol*, that were destined to enjoy something of a vogue.*

I had taken a great liking to my skipper, Boddam-Whetham. It seemed mutual. We promised to meet again. I sent him my articles when they were published. "I must say we think you're a top-sawyer at your job. You seem to pick up facts like a magnet in a packet of needles," he wrote, "but our Sub is looking for you with a hatchet. You called him 'A rosy-faced Ganymede'. He's looked up 'Ganymede' and finds he was Jove's peculiar boy-friend!"

Our promise of reunion was never fulfilled, but it almost came about. Fate played us a trick. Thirty years passed; we were in the Second World War. I was on a mission in the U.S.A. One day in New York I called on an American lady who had a terraced apartment high up on Fifth Avenue with a wonderful view of Central Park and the circumambient skyscrapers.

"Oh, I wish you had been here a few minutes ago," she said. "I've just had a visit from such a nice British naval officer. He's taking some food parcels for me to friends in England. I wonder you didn't meet him in the hall, you came up just after he'd gone down." I asked about him and how he came to be here in New York. "His ship's in Brooklyn Navy Yard. He told me he'd retired but came back into the Service with the convoys. Here's his card. It's a funny name," she said. I looked at the card. The name was Boddam-Whetham! "My God! I know him!" I cried. "He was my skipper on the Dover Patrol!"

I rushed to the elevator and was soon on Fifth Avenue. I raced along but he had disappeared. All that evening I tried to trace him. You could not then call ships in the Brooklyn Navy Yard, and also I did not know its name. I appealed to our Naval Liaison Officer. The next morning at nine he called me. "Sorry, we traced Boddam-Whetham but too late. His ship sailed at six this morning."

The next year I read of his death in *The Times*. In 1939 he had been placed on the retired list. Five weeks later he was back on duty. In 1942 he gained a C.B.E. 'for bravery and resolution' as a commodore of the Second North Russian Convoy, which was attacked by air at intervals for eight days. "The Germans claim we cannot use the northern route but the answer is we do!" he said.†

* Appendix II, *The Dover Patrol*.

† It was a murderous convoy service to Murmansk and Archangel conducted through Arctic seas in winter, and in summer through Polar days of

I learned from a friend something of his career subsequent to the Dover Patrol. When the Second World War broke out my old skipper, although then fifty-two, had returned to the Service and became a Commodore of Convoys. He had been awarded his D.S.O. in 1917 for action with German destroyers off the Belgian coast. Later he was torpedoed off the Dutch Coast. He then commanded the *Swallow* in the Mediterranean and the Black Sea, and was promoted Commander. He was the first officer of that rank to qualify as an observer in the Fleet Air Arm. From 1929–1931 he was the senior officer of the gunboat flotilla in the West River, China, and in 1934–1936 was Captain in charge of the Dockyard at Bermuda, and, until being retired in 1939, Captain and King's Harbour Master of the Chatham dockyard. He died while on duty at Gibraltar in 1944. What astonished me most in his obituary notice was that he was born at Kirklington, Notts. So he, too, was a Nottinghamshire lad. If only I had known. What a gossip we would have had!

III

Soon after my return from the Dover Patrol I had an attack of neuritis in the right shoulder that confined me to bed for two weeks. I was still able to do my literary page, having books for review sent to me. My mother read some of these to me while I lay in bed. One book particularly pleased me. It was a travel story by a man who had made a journey across Asia Minor on foot from Samsun on the Black Sea to Amasia, a fortified stronghold known to Timūr the Terrible (Tamerlane). I little knew then that it would fire an imaginative train when, three years later, I began to write my novel, *Scissors*, but I brooded over the theme it had suggested while in Liverpool. Exciting events now imminent were to make any concentration on the task impossible. I had talks with Burton Chadwick when he made flying visits home from his Ministry post in London. We liked each

light which exposed the vessels. They were attacked by German aircraft, destroyers and submarines. The PQ 13 convoy lost 5 out of 19 vessels and the cruiser H.M.S. *Trident*. PQ 14, 15 out of 33, PQ 15 and 16, 20 out of 60, and loss of the cruiser H.M.S. *Edinburgh*. Churchill horrified, called off the convoys but was compelled by violent Russian criticism to resume them. PQ 17 met a terrible fate: 23 out of 34 ships perished. PQ 18 lost 13 out of 40. Fogs, storms, darkness, Arctic seas, ice, German shells, bombs and torpedoes, took a ghastly toll, but the convoys persisted and arms reached Russia.

other from the first but it was his wife who conceived the idea that I should join her husband as his assistant in London, an idea he endorsed but which I opposed, alluring as it was. I had my own career to follow and my feet were now well planted on the ladder. Unknown to me, Chadwick approached my employer. Between them they agreed to share my services. I would work during the day at the Ministry of Munitions as Chadwick's assistant in the Department of Overseas Transport, of which he was Director. In the evenings I would be roving correspondent in the London office of my paper, doing theatres, concerts, art exhibitions, book reviews, and contributing to the London letter. I should also be available for special correspondent work as it arose. The *Post* would undertake to pay me £156 a year, and Chadwick another £156 for acting as his assistant. We should thus both be honorary workers at the Ministry.

My first reaction was to reject the proposal. I feared the prospect of riding two horses. It seemed too complicated and arduous. I had to consider another fact. If I tore up my roots in Liverpool what was to become of my mother who had sacrified her home to join me? On £312 a year it would not be possible for us both to live in London. On the other hand there was the immense allure of London, a bigger and more thrilling field of opportunity and of unpredictable contacts. But I resisted the allure. It might prove a mirage.

Mrs. Chadwick now made a personal appeal to me. She was convinced that I could be of considerable service to her husband for whom she was highly ambitious. It was most likely they would move to London. A warm-hearted, charming woman who had shown me much kindness, she made my situation difficult. I turned to my mother, gifted with infallible common sense allied with courage. She thought I should seize the opportunity. She would return to Nottingham. With no house, no home? Yes, she would find a cheap lodging. So once again she unhesitatingly sacrificed herself. She estimated that she could manage on £1 a week. I believed that I could live on £3 a week and save £1. There was also what I might earn with my pen, although my independent time was likely to be very little. I had already some capital behind me. I had saved £180.

When we left Liverpool our landlady burst into tears. She had never been so happy in all her life, she said. In Nottingham my mother found a bed-sitting-room at six shillings a week. How nomadic her life had been, uncertainty ever at her shoulder. Never once had she quailed before the ordeal. "I shall be able to be near your brother," she said brightly. My elder brother—'Speak, speak, speak to me, Thora', as I had dubbed him from his constant singing of that deplorable love song—was now a semi-invalid. In the second year of marriage he had been operated upon for a duodenal ulcer. Two years later he had a second, more drastic operation. He looked a wreck at thirty-five but he had my mother's courageous tranquillity. A long life of operations and invalidism faced him.

IV

I went to London in March, 1917, with some apprehension. I knew no one there and a few brief visits had revealed its hard countenance, but the flame of ambition sustained me. I was twenty-four. I arrived there in an unusual period when London, tense with a war for survival, had an air of almost hysterical gaiety. Soldiers home on leave from across the Channel, including men from the remotest corners of the earth, madly spent there a few days' respite from the trenches. *Goodbye Piccadilly, Farewell Leicester Square.* They chanted the nostalgic song in the face of death and sourly enjoyed the ironic agnosticism of:

> The bells of heaven go ting-a-ling-a-ling
> For you but not for me,
> O Death, where is thy sting-a-ling-a-ling,
> O grave, thy victory!

So they spent like mad, for a corpse has no use for money in the bank. A strange London, yet with a wonderful exhilaration, touched with the light of the Day of Judgement.

Emerging from the railway station I bought a newspaper and studied the 'Rooms to Let'. There were very few, for London was crowded. I found my first lodging in Claverton Street, Pimlico, that depressed, low-lying area between Victoria Station and the Thames Embankment. I found a back bedroom in a boarding-house run by a cheerful Irishwoman. It recalled a music-hall song once in vogue, the lament of a bachelor who had married. "Oh, why did I leave my little back room in Pimlico!" I paid £1 10*s.* 0*d.* a week for room, breakfast and evening dinner. It proved a rich experience from which I drew later many of the characters in *Scissors.* There was a broken-down colonel, addicted to the bottle, with a room full of canaries. There was a pair of young 'queers', the first of the species I had encountered. One was a hairdresser's assistant, the other worked in an interior decorator's shop. They were a chirpy pair who addressed everyone as 'My dear', which infuriated the colonel. But they were witty and very kind. When I fell ill with influenza they carried all my meals up to my bedroom and brought me flowers. I heard later that one of them was 'called up' and died of pneumonia in a training camp, and that his friend drowned himself in despair. There was an overwhelmingly pretty girl, a typist in one of the Ministries. She was an Irish beauty with a shock of black curls, a little robust for twenty-four. She rippled with laughter, twitted the 'Tomtits' as she called 'The pair', and mercilessly flirted with the old colonel who adored her but was dismayed by two things. She walked out with a young guardsman, a Devon farm lad—"Your social inferior," he complained. And she was on good terms with 'The Pansies' as he always called them. "They stink!" he said. "Not at all, and you might have been born one," she retorted.

The Colonel met his Waterloo. He broke an ankle and was in a plaster cast. 'The Pair' helped him up and down stairs, brought birdseed and groundsel for his canaries, and changed his library books—"I hope you'll like this one, dear." They had rather aristocratic names which I am sure were assumed. In *Scissors* I called them Wellington and de Courtrai—the interior decorator had a Roman nose and the hairdresser liked to scatter odd words of French. He had worked in Paris for a time until the war broke out.

In later years I felt ashamed of the manner in which, in my novel *Scissors,* I had derided those two youths handicapped with an abnormality. One does not kick a blind man or mock a cripple, and nothing angers me more than our witch-hunting of those on whom Nature has imposed a deviation from normality. When I read the trial of Oscar Wilde I felt revolted by the monstrous sentence given to that vain and foolish man of genius whom our legal system murdered. We have marched a long way from that barbarism.

We had a real aristocrat in our boarding house, an old spinster who was an Honourable. "Bogus," said one of the boarders, a Customs clerk who was very 'Left', and always referred to the Royal Family as 'that German crew'. Our Honourable was shy and retreated after dinner to her bedroom. Obviously she was pinched in means, and was shabbily dressed. She was not bogus. When I came to talk with her she informed me that her father had been a First Secretary at our embassy in Washington. How came she to be dragging out an existence in a Pimlico boarding-house? I never discovered. She never spoke of money or complained. There was a monthly cheque, I assumed, in a long envelope that bore the name Coutts and Co., which lay with our letters on the hall table, and bore the prefix 'The Hon.' I was fascinated by this as I had been told by my father that this bank had, locked up in its safe, the marriage certificate of George IV the royal bigamist and Mrs. Fitzherbert.

There was also in the house a flashy middle-aged man, a 'know-all', very exacting about his food, who talked of his 'Place' near Malvern. Observing that he was missing from the dining-room for several evenings, I asked if he had left. My landlady drew me aside. "The police have taken him," she said. "Such a disgrace for us. The Colonel says he stole some gold cuff-links of his—took them from his drawer while he was in the bathroom. He owes me sixteen pounds. He's an escaped convict. Just think, sitting at table contradicting everybody, and always complaining the bath water wasn't hot! It's cast a shadow over the house and I don't feel the same."

I liked my back bedroom. It looked out on to the tall chimney of the Army Clothing Factory. This had been built in the form of a campanile. When there was a blue sky it gave me an illusion of Italy. The bed was very comfortable and the landlady put into my room a Victorian writing desk with a sloping top that could be raised and had a drawer underneath. I had a gas ring on which I could make my own tea, and a good wardrobe with a long mirror. On Sunday mornings the hairdresser's assistant had what he called a 'Pressing Session' and he volunteered to press my trousers, a service I gratefully accepted. Once, coming from the bathroom, he saw I had a tear in my dressing-gown. "Let me have it, I'll mend it, dear," he said. He mended it beautifully. "And if you've any socks, I'm a dab at darning!" I thanked him but I did my own, being a 'dab' myself.

I used to walk to my office in Whitehall, sometimes along the Embankment, but if I was pressed for time or tired I took a bus. I loved the London buses. They had open tops, and a leather apron you could draw over the twin seats if it rained. Flirting couples loved this arrangement. You had a splendid view from the top of the bus. It cost twopence to go from the end of Claverton Street, via Victoria Street, Westminster Abbey, and up Whitehall to Trafalgar Square. What a magnificent twopence-worth of English history!

I was sad when my nice landlady told me she was giving up the

My dear Cecil Roberts
Affectionately Yours
Joseph Conrad

Joseph Conrad. Portrait by Walter Tittle

Brigadier-General Critchley addressing Royal Air Force cadets at Hastings

The Handley Page Bomber at Lympne, 1918—the author faces the camera. "We were all of us gargantuan in our padded flying suits and life jackets"

boarding-house—it had become difficult to run. She had developed 'water on the knee' and the stairs were too much. After some searching I found a room, with only breakfast served, in Upper George Street, off Marble Arch. This rooming house was kept by an Indian woman with a diamond in her nose. Sometimes she wore a sari. I was rather doubtful at first but she proved to be very kind and did my laundry. Shy and reticent, she lived in the basement.

As soon as I had arrived in London Burton Chadwick made me a member of the Royal Automobile Club in Pall Mall, next door to his, the Carlton. It was a magnificent new building, splendidly furnished and equipped with a large Egyptian-style pillared swimming pool. On the second floor there was a delightful library with deep easy chairs and a coal fire. French windows opened on to a long wide terrace that overlooked the trees of Carlton House Gardens and the Mall. I could see Big Ben with a light above when the House of Commons was sitting. To the left rose the Nelson column in Trafalgar Square, to the right were the stables of Marlborough House in which the Dowager Queen Alexandra was living. The club servants were dressed in blue liveries, with tails and silver buttons, but these were all elderly, the younger ones having been called up.

At six o'clock every day I went down to the swimming pool in the basement. It was a centre of gaiety. The club had been thrown open to overseas officers on leave. The youth of London congregated there. We swam and then, swathed in bath towels, sat around drinking and gossiping. Adjacent to the pool there was a Turkish bath, a rifle range, a bowling alley and squash courts, with showers, locker-rooms and a bar. It was there that I met a young American who was a vice-consul at the American Consulate, with rooms in St. James. When I went to America in 1920 he was my host at Harvard University where he was taking a law course. But my most memorable encounter had a note of comedy. Swimming in the pool, I was amazed to see emerging above the water the bearded face of one of the most famous men in Europe, George Bernard Shaw. I gasped and exclaimed involuntarily—"You're Shaw!" He pierced me with his eyes and in a flash retorted—"Young man, I'm certain of nothing!" The next moment he had vanished under the water. It was a flippant contradiction for there never was a man more certain of himself.

It is an exciting experience for any young man reared in the provinces to find himself living in London. The sensation was heightened by the drama of the World War, London being crowded with Missions and famous personalities. Despite the great battles being fought on the Continent and on the high seas the amenities of life in the capital were not seriously disturbed. The theatres and restaurants were booming, packed with young officers on leave with accumulated pay to spend. Everyone knew what awaited them after two weeks of Blighty, with its good food, soft beds, gay entertainment, reunion with relatives and friends—the water-logged, rat-infested, freezing trenches, the desperate sorties and murderous shell-fire, the blasted landscape studded with riven trees, the grim rain-soddened plains, the shattered villages, the bumping ambulances, the corpse-collecting, the squalid burials; hell and heaven separated by only twenty miles of mined water. It was to be the last war with a 'front line', civilians immune from destruction, the skies scarcely troubled, a homeland unscarred.

V

The Ministry of Munitions was housed in a number of palatial hotels in Whitehall. It had been founded by the dynamic Lloyd George who was succeeded in turn by Montague and Addison. The latter was Minister when I joined a staff of some twelve thousand assistants. Lloyd George had left a legacy of ambitious plans for the creation of munitions. Warfare ensued between various directors whose share of operations encroached upon each other's. One was aware of the contest, over which Addison had poor control. The demand for munitions became hourly more desperate as the Western Front called for more and more ammunition, a demand inadequately met. The powerful Northcliffe raised a clamour in his Press. Lloyd George, now Prime Minister, succeeding the ousted, lethargic Asquith, decided upon a bold change. He challenged public opinion in July, 1917, by appointing Winston Churchill as Minister of Munitions.

Churchill was still regarded as the culprit responsible for the Dardanelles disaster. He was now a hunted dog with a tin tied to his tail. After his fall he had proceeded to the Western Front where with the rank of Lieutenant-Colonel he commanded the Royal Scots Fusiliers for a few months. He was an embarrassment to the Army authorities. They could not ignore the fact that this officer was an ex-Cabinet minister with a formidable history, or that, while in the trenches, he was in touch with the Prime Minister and members of the Government. The situation was preposterous. Meanwhile something had happened. The Dardanelles Commission published its report. It reprimanded Asquith, it exonerated Churchill. His bold project might have succeeded had there not been disastrous delays which gave the Turks warning, and, finally, had not de Robeck, the Admiral in charge of naval strategy at the Dardanelles, lacked the will to risk his ships in forcing a passage, a feasible enterprise in more resolute hands. But even when the Report appeared the slur remained; Churchill was a dangerous, impetuous fellow. Lloyd George's appointment of Churchill to the Ministry raised a storm. Naturally, all of us in the Ministry were agog. "There'll be fireworks," said my chief.

I had seen departments of the Ministry proliferate in the manner of all bureaucracies. A controller to increase his importance appointed a deputy who in turn appointed an assistant, who in turn appointed more clerks and typists. In any Government office twenty per cent of the staff is usually superfluous. Our Ministry was no exception. A hasty temporisation resulted in bewildering categories and departmental congestion. Through the Registry passed the swollen dossiers. The D.N.F.M./M.M. wrote a minute to A.S.D./B.T. complaining that A.D.I.T./M.S. had authorised a shipment of spelter per the B.M. in S.A. without consulting M.S./A.T. The result was that the spelter arrived at Cardiff from South America at the bottom of the hold, with a shipment of tungsten, for Liverpool, on top of it. The ship, therefore, had to be diverted to Liverpool to unload its tungsten and then proceed from Liverpool to Cardiff, to unload its spelter. En route the ship was torpedoed and lost.

Officials confronted with a swollen dossier, with a minute-sheet attached looking like a medieval palimpsest, finding the problem too much, passed the dossier to another department, marked "Action please." There was the case of a ship that had loaded a cargo of iron ore in Spain. Enquiries about her whereabouts, she being long overdue, were made for four months. Finally the dossier came back to the registry with a laconic note written by the Ministry of Shipping. "Informed torpedoed. Complete loss, off Lisbon, six months ago. No further action."

Nevertheless there were first-class brains at work in the Ministry. There were heads of great companies who gave their services. There were also some high-grade civil servants. One of these, a young man of thirty, was an organising genius. He carried a load of 'somebodies' on his shoulders until he broke down. There was a brilliant young man named Layton who became later Lord Layton, a statistical wizard. The *Daily Mail* conducted a witch hunt against what they called "Cuthberts in funk holes". There were not a hundred young men in the whole Ministry, all 'combed' and rejected for military service, except some two dozen 'key' civil servants with very special qualifications; but it had become an offence for any young man to be alive in civilian clothes.

Churchill dealt vigorously with the departmental confusion he found on his arrival in July, 1917. There were fifty departments. He reduced them to ten and formed a General Council which met daily under his presidency. He was alert to the verge of rudeness, and ruthless. I was present at one of these Councils and heard him dress down a tremendous bigwig in shipping circles because he had not some figures at his finger tips. Churchill was denied a seat in the Cabinet, but his influence was felt immediately. A number of heads fell. He had arrived at a very critical period. We had sold a thousand million pounds worth of securities in America; our transatlantic credits were exhausted. The vast Prudential Insurance Company and others had pledged all their foreign assets. Unrestricted submarine warfare had begun in July, 1916, and our losses had risen in April, 1917, to 847,000 tons of allied shipping a month. The outlook was grim.

The Minister's room was on the first floor of the Metropole Hotel, along a carpeted corridor that was called 'The Holy of Holies'. I saw Churchill arrive and depart, a stocky, hunched figure in black vicuna coat and striped trousers, wearing a flat-topped bowler hat. Oddly enough I never saw him smoking a cigar; it had not yet become a part of his public image. He went to his office quickly, never looking at anyone. At the entrance of 'The Holy of Holies' stood a uniformed porter who knew the elect and allowed them to pass. This was the only carpeted corridor in the vast building. There has always been a magic about the Order of the Carpet, as a symbol of power. Whether a Cabinet Minister, a managing director, a town clerk, an editor or a headmaster, he rates a carpet on the office floor. It has given birth to the term 'on the carpet' which generally means an unpleasant interview of a subordinate with his chief. Let me confess that I can recall vividly my vanity when I walked upon an office carpet of my own.

Down the corridor, having passed the lynx-eyed guardian, you were intercepted, if called by the Minister, in an outer office occupied by two secretaries. One of them, by constancy to Winston and to Art and Literature, had become almost a national figure. This was slim 'Eddie' Marsh, soft-voiced, quick-eyed, monocled, famous as the founder-editor of *Georgian Poetry*, and as the friend of Rupert Brooke, newly among the immortals. I had already encountered Marsh when he had come to my poetry recital at the Bechstein Hall in June, 1914, but I was shy about making myself known to him as a colleague in the Ministry. Presently an occasion arose. Marsh published a Collected Edition of Brooke's *Poems*, then having a tremendous vogue following his tragic death at the Dardanelles in the flower of his genius. Marsh had written a biographical preface. I had reviewed this book at length in my weekly book column in *The Liverpool Post*. I sent him the review together with my copy of the book, asking him to be kind enough to autograph it. He returned it, autographed, with a friendly note: "Did we not meet many years ago when you gave a reading of your poems? Perhaps as we are colleagues and neighbours you will look me up some time in my room, 275."

I accepted the invitation. He was most affable and enquired about my history since Lord Henry Bentinck had brought him to that recital. Our conversation was interrupted by a telephone call. Suddenly a door behind him opened and Churchill walked in, holding some papers in his hand. I stood up. He gave me a keen look, and paused while Marsh ended the phone conversation. Churchill said something to him about the papers. I half turned, avoiding intrusion. He looked at me again and was leaving when Marsh said—"This is Cecil Roberts, one of our young poets." Churchill stopped and addressed me.

"What have you written?" he asked.

"Four books of poetry, sir."

"What are you doing here?"

"I'm in the Overseas Transport Department, sir, assistant to Burton Chadwick."

He nodded, turned and walked out of the room.

"Do come and see me again," said Marsh, picking up the papers.

I thanked him and left. Well, I had seen the great man at last, close up. I had been introduced and he had spoken to me, though briefly. Back in my office I told my chief. "Was he pleasant to you?" he asked. "Oh, yes," I replied. "Good," he said, "You can never tell what mood he'll be in. Sometimes he's *grand seigneur*, sometimes irascible, sometimes puckish."

I memorised every moment of that encounter for this was a man for whom I had conceived an intense admiration since that day in 1909 when I had heard him speak at Nottingham, then a very young Cabinet Minister. I believed, despite all the adverse criticism and political ostracism he had suffered over the Dardanelles failure, that he had been absolutely right and that it had been the Cabinet's procrastination, the instability of the violent and vacillating Lord Fisher, the hesitant direction of Admiral de Robeck, that had ruined his imaginative strategy for the conquest of the Straits. After the Dardanelles he had cried, "I'm finished!" Finished indeed! He had now been a year at the Ministry and I had witnessed the great transformation he had effected, giving it a dynamic drive and a smoothly planned direction.

When I met him in those brief minutes he seemed smaller physically than I had expected. More noticeable than his eyes, with their quick penetration, were his hands, very delicate and beautiful, an aristocrat's hands. He was well dressed, wearing a low white collar against which was pressed a flat black bow tie. His white cuffs protruded the correct length from the sleeves, and his trousers, faultlessly cut, broke over the small shoes. He had the appearance of a man well-valeted without being in any sense a dandy. I smiled to think that my father would not have approved of his deportment, for he stooped badly. He would have brought his stick down over my shoulders for a similar posture.

Did the great man, now at last encountered, seem a great man? I decided that he did, and in those few moments of his conversation with Marsh I noticed an incisiveness of voice and manner that told me he could be formidable, as reports from the Council Room had endorsed. Later, I was to experience this, as also his irresistible charm and emotional character. I put a note in my diary that day: "Met Winston Churchill—a momentous experience."

VI

My first months in London proved exciting. There was all the adventure of a great capital tense with the war though the general life of the city went on with deceptive calm. The public seemed unaware of any real menace. There were some Zeppelin attacks, mostly futile. There were no very calamitous air raids. When raids occurred they were looked upon as exciting diversions. One morning my chief gave a breakfast party at the Carlton Grill, then existing at the bottom of the Haymarket, to which Arnold Bennett came. While we breakfasted an excited waiter came in and told us that an air raid was on. We all rushed out into the street to look at the raiders. The planes were very high up. There was the faint sound of anti-aircraft fire. Later we learned that one enemy plane had been shot down. Their bombs had done little damage. The raid made the breakfast party quite a success. Bennett stammered, "W-what fools to th-think they can w-w-worry us."

But nearby at Charing Cross the reality of war was grimly visible. Every evening lines of ambulances collected the wounded from across the Channel. As they went out into the night people threw them cigarettes and flowers in silent sympathy.

And here is the end of it all, and we count the loss,
Recording the glory, forgetting the human waste
Left by extravagant war, borne away in the night
Swiftly and silently. God, here again at a Cross
Crucified man in a dark world dies; here the sight
Burns in the mind, and I cry, as once One cried—
'My God! My God! why hast Thou forsaken me?'—then
I watch with dumb anguish the endless procession of men,
The remnants picked up from the waste in the field; they who died
Flow no more in the stream, they can rest; and only it matters
That Science should skilfully mend what it skilfully shatters.

Thus I wrote in *Charing Cross & Other Poems*, born of that nightly scene in front of the railway station.

The casualty lists grew longer and longer. The war on the Western Front had bogged down into trench warfare interrupted by costly assaults. By April, 1917, our casualties were more than a million men. It was difficult to believe that only a very narrow stretch of water gave us immunity from the bloody massacre on the other side of the Channel. There was murder also on the high seas. Our seamen, torpedoed, were left to perish in icy waters.

VII

The loneliness that I might have known in London was mitigated by a family into which I had been welcomed. One Sunday afternoon my friend George Burrows, back from a tour in France with an Army concert party, took me to a house in Auriol Road, South Kensington. We ascended steps to the front door of a villa with a semi-basement and garden, and entered a drawing-room that ran through from front to back. It was crammed with people, mostly young. Some of the men were in uniform. There was a loud buzz of conversation. George piloted me through the room towards a woman sitting in a chair by the fireplace. She rose to greet us. "Who's this?" she asked him, smiling. He presented me. She was a large handsome woman with greying hair, a fine brow and kind eyes. She wore a pair of large drop-pearl earrings. This was Mrs. Snowden, the mother and spirit of the house, as I was to find. I was next introduced to her husband, a little thickset man. He looked like Socrates and indeed proved a philosopher. He would ruminate and then very slowly produce his views on the world which he thought a somewhat crazy creation. The family treated him with great respect though it was clear his wife was the dynamo that sent a hum through the vibrant house. Keighley (pronounced Keethley) Snowden was a Yorkshire novelist who had never quite touched success. He produced only after a long labour. It took three or four years for something to come out of him, only to meet a quiet death. Poor man, his novels were rather like those swaddled infants one finds on medieval tombs denoting death in infancy. A loyal family kept up the myth that one day the world would listen to his voice. As I began to succeed, producing one book after another, to be sent off on Press expeditions, to appear on platforms, I often felt a reluctance to announce my little triumphs, fearing that the elation of a youngster out to conquer a world that had ignored him, might hurt him. But he was a man of an enduring sweetness of character. Nothing of envy ever entered his soul. "Yes—how very good, how smoothly written. I wish I had your gift," he would ruminate kindly, puffing slowly at his pipe as I presented some of my work. His earning power must have been very low, though he had a small following in Yorkshire, where a paper occasionally serialised one of his stories. The economy of the house could never have been very easy. They possessed no servant in that four-story house. I discovered that during the week they lived in the large basement kitchen sunk below the front garden. On Sunday afternoon they surfaced in glory. For that gala occasion Mrs. Snowden during the week baked her endless variety of excellent scones and plum cakes.

Through the next five years I returned again and again to that warm-hearted home, always crammed with Sunday guests who gobbled up the cakes that were brought round on trays by members of the family. The guests ate heartily, finding it saved them buying supper. Many of them were students at music or dramatic academies, living on a shoestring. This was my first experience of what might be termed 'a salon'. When in later years I attended those of a duchess in the Faubourg St. Germain, a millionaire on Park Avenue, or world-famous 'stars' in Hollywood, they never offered the cosy warmth and friendly excitement of that suburban villa in South Kensington. If not celebrities of high achievement, they were cadets of promise in a youthful world. There was a sprinkling of journalists, authors, actors, actresses and artists but the prevailing guests were musicians. For this was above all a musical household. These Sunday At Homes given by Mrs. Snowden, presiding like Juno, were dedicated to the presentation of her talented children. The father faded into the background, dear little man, sitting in a corner puffing his pipe. Marion, the only daughter of the house, lean-faced, slender, tall, black-haired, with an angelic smile that lit her dark eyes, was a professional pianist searching for engagements. Her elder brother was a violoncellist, a member of Sir Thomas Beecham's orchestra. The eldest brother was a journalist on a London newspaper, the lively 'kid' brother was a student at a dramatic academy.

Before and after the refreshments Marion and her brother would perform, she at the grand piano, playing solos or accompanying her brother or a singer. They were fine thorough musicians. In the company there were other executants, young, ambitious, reporting little successes. They were given their turn but it was tacitly understood that their contributions were accessory to the family programme. Occasionally an established star made an appearance. I recall the playing of a merry, rotund little Jew, Harold Samuel, a pianist who won some renown and died in early middle-age. There was Albert Salmons, first violin in Beecham's orchestra. There were singers who were appearing in operas in subordinate roles and making concert tours. And of course there was my friend George with his superb talent, the golden voice as yet untarnished, the artistry flawless. He had an actor friend, a New Zealander, an officer just out of uniform, having been wounded. He towered above the company, six foot four, heavy browed. He played in *Chu Chin Chow*, then enjoying a long run at His Majesty's Theatre. At some moment in the evening he recited, filling the room with his great resonant voice. Unhappily, he was doomed to failure despite his talent. He was an ungovernable egotist with a habit of telling the producer what he should do. He had a collision with Matheson Lang, then he fell foul of Oscar Asche and Basil Dean. As a result he got less and less work. He proudly withdrew, bloody but unbowed, into obscure poverty and shocked his friends by dying before forty. Mrs. Snowden grieved for him and wondered if he had died of malnutrition. But in these early days he was full of vigour and arrogant confidence.

In between changing lodgings I lived in the Snowden home for a short time. The closer contact increased my affection for them. One thing I never let them know—that I could play the piano. In all the time that I frequented their house, amid all the guests who showed off their various talents, I never performed. I would not risk pitting myself against the gentle Marion, incomparably my superior. Had I been Rachmaninoff I would not have played. Theirs was a Snowden afternoon.

There was another house to which I was taken by George, where I did perform. It was a house of a very different kind from that friendly abode in Auriol Road. We went to a princely mansion in Holland Park, a sylvan district dotted with the large establishment of famous artists. The great Lord Leighton, G. F. Watts and Alma Tadema had lived there in grandiose studio houses. Their friend and neighbour had been Valentine Prinsep, R.A., a friend of D. G. Rossetti and Robert Browning. He was a dilettante, and an artist of some merit and wrote two novels and two plays. He was commissioned by the Viceroy of India, Lord Lytton, to paint the Durbar in 1877 at which Queen Victoria was proclaimed Empress of India. He married the wealthy daughter of F. R. Leyland, a Liverpool shipping magnate. He was a patron of Whistler and it was he who suggested to the artist the term 'Nocturne' for one of his night pictures.*

Val Prinsep's widow was now living in the Holland Park house where they had lavishly entertained, a veritable museum sumptuously furnished with many works of art. When I rang the bell I often wondered how many times Robert Browning, Rossetti and Whistler

* Whistler wrote to Prinsep—"I can't thank you too much for the name 'Nocturne' as a title for my moonlights. You have no idea what an irritation it proves to the critics and consequent pleasure to me—besides it is really charming and does so poetically say all I want to say, and *no more* than I wish."

had rung it. Mrs. Prinsep kept open house, too open. There were now no servants and she was attended by 'dailies', this is an era when servants were available, and by the oddest collection of youths who occupied this luxurious nest. How they got there, with free lodging, I never learned. They flattered and amused her, chattering like a lot of magpies. Some of them were chorus boys, or ballet underlings. The old lady made odd appearances, often an hour late for dinner. She had a heart of gold, loved music, and was full of interesting reminiscences about the great artists who had frequented her house in former times. One of her sons became a theatrical producer and married the beautiful Marie Löhr, an actress who had a resounding success in the theatre. I was there one day when she called to see her mother-in-law, with a vivacious, pretty, dark young woman. The attraction of the house for me was that there was a Steinway grand piano. I was playing when they arrived and as I got up the unknown friend said, "Oh no! Do please go on!" I detected a foreign accent. I continued and she sat down by the keyboard. Presently I stopped and asked her if she played. "Mm! Mm!" she answered, turning her pretty head coquettishly. I insisted that she should play, and got up. In a few minutes I realised I was listening to a superlative artist. I was nowhere in her class. "But aren't you a professional?" I asked. She replied quietly, "Well, not really—and I'm now on the stage." "But where did you learn to play like this?" I asked. "I studied at the Paris Conservatoire of Music," she answered. I learned later that at thirteen she had won the first prize at the Conservatoire, a young prodigy, and later was a Gold Medallist. But now she had chosen the stage and had made her first appearance in *The Quaker Girl* at the Adelphi in 1911. Her name was Yvonne Arnaud. When she died in 1958 after much success in the theatre Guildford built a theatre and named it in her honour.

In those First World War years I had other musical contacts. Since I was the London music and dramatic critic for my paper I received tickets for most concerts and plays. Sir Henry Wood was then London's most popular conductor and presided over the Queen's Hall Promenade concerts. He had an assistant, young Adrian Boult, helping also with the Russian Ballet. "You were kind to me then," he told me, fifty years later.

The war had driven a number of eminent persons across the Channel. There was Emile Cammaerts, a gentle blue-eyed Belgian poet whom I met at a hospitable house in Prince's Gate, and there was another Belgian, little Arthur de Greef, a pianist. I shall never forget his playing of *The Grieg Concerto* with an orchestra conducted by Landon Ronald at the Albert Hall. Seen from a box in that vast auditorium de Greef looked like a little mouse nibbling at the ivory keys of the immense concert grand. But what passion and sonority that tiny figure evoked, filling the great hall with his poetry. Another of my friends was Sir Thomas Beecham, the magician, already a legend, and incorrigible. One day Albert Salmons, his first violin, entertained us at the Snowdens with the story of an altercation between Beecham and Pavlova and her partner at a morning rehearsal. That same evening they danced *The Bacchanale*, a pseudo-orgiastic *pas-de-deux*. It brought the house down. Beecham played the score at such a pace that the dancers finished on the verge of collapse. As the curtain fell Beecham turned to his first violin and said, "Well, Albert, we made the bastards dance!" I did not then know that I was destined to play a singular role in Beecham's life during the Second World War; a tragi-comic story for another book.

There were four pianists whom I came to know about this time. They were all pupils of the great Leschetitsky of Vienna—Gabrilowitsch, Hambourg, Moiseiwitsch and Schnabel. One day in the U.S.A., a relative of Mark Twain took me to call on the daughter of the author. She was the wife of the pianist Gabrilowitsch. He was very different from a fellow pupil, Mark Hambourg, who was florid, inaccurate, but so overwhelming at the keyboard that after his debut at Vienna, aged sixteen, Brahms toasted him at a dinner as "The youth who played so astonishingly this evening." Gabrilowitsch was the poet at the piano, delicate, with exquisite tone. The third of Leschetitsky's prodigies out of Russia was Benno Moiseiwitsch who settled in England in 1908. He became the favourite pianist at Sir Henry Wood's Queen's Hall concerts. Rachmaninoff looked upon him as his artistic successor. One evening at George Burrows' little Hampstead pied-à-terre he came and played. He had an impeccable lyric phrasing in his playing. He never lost his hold on the London public until he died some forty-five years later.

With concerts, theatres, book reviewing, art exhibitions, odd articles and my duties at the Ministry of Munitions, I was terribly overworked. I rose at 6 a.m., did some reading for my reviewing, making notes, and was at the Ministry by 9 a.m. I left there around 6 p.m. and if there was an evening engagement rushed down to the Fleet Street offices of the *Post*, took a snack, went on to a concert or a theatre, returned to Fleet Street to hand in my copy, which was telegraphed to Liverpool, and reached my lodging after midnight. Somewhere in between all this, on free evenings, I found an hour or two for my own creative writing. I could not have sustained all this had I not been happy, and possessed of tremendous nervous resilience. My work at the Ministry was not exacting but absorbing. I had my own desk in Burton Chadwick's room. As a director he rated a carpet, which I shared. There was a smaller room for the typist-secretary, a pretty young woman, rather nun-like in her manner. She was married and somewhere there was Edward, her husband. We never saw Edward. I began to think he was mythical but I was wrong. They separated and, as fate decreed, she became Burton's second wife after the death of his first.

My chief was very easy to work with. He exuded charm, was popular, always lunching somewhere, and brimful of ideas. One day he decided to write a letter to *The Times*, suggesting that the nation should give up drinking tea. He worked out how much precious tonnage could be saved. In vain I pointed out that all the Ministries would collapse if deprived of their tea. The rattle of tea-cups around four o'clock was as regular as the striking of Big Ben. *The Times* gave the letter prominence. A hot debate followed. Burton had his hour of fame, or notoriety, but the tea addicts won.

The loss of our tonnage grew grimmer and grimmer, how very grim the British public never learned. The Admiralty secret reports were available to us. Our jugular vein was being cut. The shipping losses by submarine warfare brought us to the verge of defeat. From April to October, 1916, we were losing 300,000 tons a month. By March, 1917, the figure rose alarmingly to 500,000 tons. In April, 1917, our losses soared to 849,000 tons of allied shipping. From January to March, 1917, the loss of ships had mounted from 181 to 423 a month. In April, 1917, one in four British merchant ships sailing from the United Kingdom never returned.

The Germans calculated that if they could maintain a steady monthly sinking of 600,000 tons we should be brought to surrender within six months. England would be foodless and the munitions for our armies abroad would dry up. We had now only 1,300 merchant ships to feed the country and import its essential raw material. By 1917 the German submarines were being built faster than they could be destroyed.

In December, 1916, Jellicoe had been brought back from the

Grand Fleet to the Admiralty as First Sea Lord. He armed the merchantmen and established an Anti-Submarine Division of the Naval Staff. The following April he made plans for Atlantic, South American and Gibraltar convoys. By September, 1917, the convoy system had proved so effective that the losses of British merchant ships had steeply receded from their peak. Germany's supreme effort had failed. The Convoy Service was a tremendous achievement. By September, 1918, there were ninety-nine outward and homeward convoys operating, with a loss of only some ten ships in the convoys though fourteen stragglers were picked off.

But in these months of early 1917 when I was at the Ministry the losses were paralysing. Sometimes, leaving my office in the evening and going to a restaurant, I had a vision of a waitress returning to my table, saying, "There's no more food in the kitchens. We're closing down." One night at a music hall, having seen a few hours earlier the blackest of black figures, I watched the audience roaring with laughter at the antics of a comedian. If they only knew what was threatening! But they never knew.

By proclaiming an unrestricted U boat campaign the Germans had committed an incalculable blunder. They sank four American ships in March, 1917. Twelve Americans were lost in them. On April 1st another ship was lost with twenty-eight lives. Then the Germans committed the folly of urging Mexico to make war on U.S.A. The reluctant President, with a divided country behind him, now rode on a tide of indignation. He obtained from Congress the right to declare war on Germany. It was a late decision but it was momentous. The Germans had written their doom.

I was destined to see the convoy system in action. One morning I caught a train out of Paddington being told that I might be at sea four or five days. I was not informed to what port I was being sent, merely that a Naval officer would be at the station to see me off. There I was briefed. I learned that the train was going to Milford Haven. Presently I found myself occupying a carriage with only one other person in it. He was a thickset man in civilian clothes. I made two attempts to talk to him but he snubbed me. His accent told me that he was an American. About noon I opened a lunch basket. Just then we stopped at a station. He called a porter and asked if he could buy any food. He could not. Dismay was on his face as he sat down, closing the window when the train moved on. We had five hours to go. I offered him half of my basket. He gruffly declined and became rude. "You've been trying all the morning to get into conversation with me. I neither want your food nor your conversation," he said. "You'll be very hungry by the time we get to Haverfordwest," I remarked genially. He started, and then betrayed himself. "I never said I was going to Haverfordwest!" he retorted.

"But you are. You're going further—you're going to Milford Haven. You don't want to talk to me because you've been strictly warned not to allow strangers to force you into conversation. My guess is that you're an American naval officer with a convoy sailing out of Milford Haven. Am I right?" I asked. He was speechless. "You see," I continued, "I also happen to be going to Milford Haven to sail with that convoy. Others who've got on this train are skippers or seamen by their looks, making the same connection. There's an American cruiser in the Sound. You are an American, ostensibly an officer, since you're travelling first-class, returning from leave in London. Here are my credentials." I passed him my 'brief' signed by Admiral Brownrigg, Chief Censor, Admiralty. "Now I hope you'll give me the pleasure of sharing my lunch."

He looked at my document. A smile came to his face as he held out his hand. "I'm sorry I've been so rude to you. Thanks. Sure, I'll be glad to accept. My name's Pierce, I'm in command of the U.S.S. *Sacramento*."

After that as he ate he talked. His home was in Baltimore. He had a wife and three children. I was shown their photographs. He had been a cadet at Annapolis. He said his ship was a good one, "But no beauty." Before we arrived at Milford Haven we were warm friends. He invited me to dine on board that evening. I accepted.

When I saw his ship I agreed with his opinion of her. She was an odd-looking craft. Her most prominent feature was her stack which towered up to a prodigious height. She remined me of a Mississippi River paddleboat. But there was nothing wrong with her hospitality. The dinner was excellent as also the company. I reflected that this was the first time that I had been on American territory. In her wardroom hung a portrait of President Wilson. I astonished my host by telling him that when a boy of sixteen I had given the President a lecture on Wordsworth, at Grasmere.

The next morning I went to a school for skippers of the convoy. They were collected from their ships all over the Sound. There were about forty of them of some ten nationalities, British, French, Italian, Greek, Dutch, Swedish, Brazilian and others. Their ships were as diversified as their skippers. They steamed variously seven to twelve knots. The slowest menaced all the rest. The skippers of these kept reminding the Senior Naval Officer briefing them that they could only do seven knots at the best and if they were left behind they would be picked off by U boats. All told, they looked a company of cut-throats. Actually they were all tough men of high courage. Some of them had been in the sea two or three times. The whole violence of submarine warfare fell upon them, but they sailed again and again.

The briefing finished, they were given sealed orders. They had to have steam up and weigh anchor at noon on the morrow. They would have U.S.S. *Sacramento* leading them, a destroyer on each flank and another as whipper in. Overhead there would be four dirigible airships, like silver sausages, that would see them off, acting as submarine spotters. Somewhere off Cape Finisterre the ships would be left to their own devices, Atlantic- or South Atlantic-bound on a patrolled route. The destroyers would pick up an incoming convoy.

I went aboard one of these destroyers that evening for a trip round the Sound. It was to prove my undoing. When I went up on to her bridge I was struck by an icy blast that froze my face. The next morning when I got up, to join the outgoing convoy, I had great pain in my eyes. Half-blinded, I went, against advice, aboard a ship that was to accompany the convoy out of harbour. The convoy moved out, spaced and constricted at the harbour mouth in order to emerge. It was a manœuvre fraught with the peril of collision as the ships moved like a pack of hounds seeking a fence opening. In the open sea we fanned out again. Moving over the water we looked like pieces on a draughtboard. Our ship raced round the expanded convoy, a kind of sheepdog. The moment came for us to leave them. The S.N.O. gave over his command to the Commodore of the Convoy, my friend of the tall smoke stack, wishing them God Speed. We returned to harbour.

By four o'clock I was in such pain with my eyes that a doctor was called. I had conjunctivitis. It would be five or six days before I was cured. The little hotel was impossible. My eyes bandaged, I called a car and motored to Tenby where there was a good hotel on the cliff. There I found two angels. They were the two Misses Graves, daughters of a very popular comedian. They thought at first that I was a blinded hero, but when they learned I was nothing so heroic they were just as attentive. They fed me, they talked to me, they led me about. They did even more, they wrote down the despatches I dictated to them. When at last my bandages were removed I discovered what a pretty place Tenby was, with its cliffs and sandy bays. I also discovered what a pair of pretty nurses kind Fate had sent me.

VIII

Soon after my return from the convoy experience I went to Nottingham to visit my mother. She was somewhat alarmed by my experience. She thought I looked thin and worn. In truth, I was overworking and eating badly in poor restaurants to effect economy. I was unhappy about her own condition. She was living in a small bed-sitting-room, poorly furnished, on a north side of the street. She professed to be quite comfortable but I saw that she was keeping up a brave façade in order not to worry me. She missed her home. I suggested that she should try to find a little house. I would increase her allowance to thirty shillings a week, also I would give her something for furnishing. "Oh no, that isn't necessary. I've thirty pounds left from when we sold up to move to Liverpool and I've thirty pounds left of the Fund," she said. The Fund! She spoke of it as if it were a fortune. Somehow she still had this in hand from the fifty-six pounds that had been our total wealth on my father's death nine years earlier. I had now three hundred pounds capital. No, she would not accept a penny of it. "I'm quite enough of a burden to you," she said. She promised to look for a small house, not an easy quest in those war years. I went back to my larger world with its great variety, its people of fortune all around me, in a somewhat troubled spirit. But one day, I vowed, she should have everything.

My chief had taken a summer house at Machynlleth. Mrs. Chadwick was Welsh. She spent the summer months there with her three children, Noel the eldest, in his first year at Eton. Poor lad. He was expensively reared for killing in the Second World War. The younger children were Gwynfa and lively little Peter who would one day succeed to the baronetcy conferred on his father later. Burton Chadwick went there for weekends. I was their guest for a fortnight. They were a delightful family, full of mirth and high spirits. The house stood in its own grounds, the mountains behind us and the estuary at Barmouth not far distant. At a nearby farm I found a horse to ride, and made excursions over the foothills and through the woods. I worked each morning in my room, preparing a new book of poems and writing articles.

One day in a deep glen by a waterfall, I came upon a small white house. It was open and empty. I went all over it, three bedrooms, two living-rooms, into all of which came the murmur of a nearby stream. There was a built-out terrace under a green canopy of trees. The isolation was complete. The house had never been lived in. What a place to retreat to, eating, writing and sleeping! I nourished an impossible dream. I learned later that the house was for sale for five hundred pounds including two acres of woodland and fishing rights. It had a beautiful Welsh name that meant Dream-in-the-Woods. Perhaps—perhaps—but impossible, of course it would remain only a dream.

I had a friend with a lovely house where I was often a weekend guest. Grant Richards, the publisher, had accepted my *Twenty-Six Poems*. He was the handsomest and most spectacular of all London publishers. He had a genius for spotting authors. Shaw, Galsworthy, A. E. Housman, Mrs. Belloc Lowndes, Warwick Deeping—the list was illustrious. Alas, he had a habit of losing them. His younger authors with first books were Alfred Noyes, Osbert Sitwell, Ronald Firbank, Thomas Burke and Alec Waugh. He was very much amused by me, surveying me through his monocle as a sort of *rara avis* that had perched in his corner office off Leicester Square. He was very hospitable, inviting me to stay at his large house overlooking the common at Cookham Dean, in the very heart of the cherry trees covering the slopes above the Thames. One Easter, touched by the glory of these trees in snowy blossom, I wrote *Springtime in Cookham Dean** which appeared in *The Poetry Review*, and was dedicated to him and his wife when reprinted in *Twenty-Six Poems*. It enjoyed a tremendous run in the United States, where it was repeatedly printed, but it never brought me in a cent of royalties, being just 'lifted' by the American magazines.

Grant Richards had married a second time, a young Hungarian widow with a pretty sprite-daughter. By a former marriage he had a son, a cadet at Dartmouth Naval College. It was a merry household. Richards, middle-aged, was a superlative host. His table lacked nothing, his wine cellar was that of a connoisseur. He loved to have guests and in summer we dined out on the lawn overlooking the Common. The guests were exciting also, well-established authors and visiting publishers from America. One weekend I encountered a small famished-looking youth, Thomas Burke, who had just jumped

* Appendix III.

into fame with *Limehouse Nights,* a story of London's China Town. Charlie Chaplin had bought *Broken Blossoms* from it for a film, and when he came to England he said that Burke was one of those he most wished to meet. Burke conducted him over Limehouse having a great knowledge of the riverside alleys and inns. But the China Town of his book was an imaginary creation and there was less of the real thing than in New York or San Francisco. Burke and I became friends. He told me something of his grim early life. He had fought his way out from the slums and this sudden success rather dazed him. When talking to me he would keep saying—"Of course, you aristocrats . . ." In vain I denied the impeachment; and as for hardship in childhood, I had known something of that too. Poor fellow, he was to die just as life had begun to offer him something.

Grant Richards was a witty, well-informed talker with the art of drawing the best out of his guests. He had written an excellent novel, and been the most enterprising young publisher in London. His weekly advertisement-causerie in *The Times Literary Supplement* was unique and attracted young authors as well as the reading public with its very individual note. Unhappily, he lived extravagantly, a kind of Lorenzo de' Medici, who liked to keep a court of gifted persons about him, without the Medici resources. He had an expensive habit of spending weekends at Monte Carlo, leaving Friday afternoon and returning Tuesday morning after gambling in the Casino. From time to time there were financial crises but, always debonnaire, he weathered the storms. His kindness to me was unfailing. He published my *Twenty-Six Poems, Charing Cross and Other Poems* and my apprentice novel, all within three years. His book production was always notable for its artistry. In July, 1917, two young authors were excitedly awaiting publication of their first novels. "My book is due next week," wrote Alec Waugh, "You know, we have struck a damned fine publisher in Richards." Alec had a resounding success with *The Loom of Youth* and, just twenty, 'woke to find himself famous', while learning to fire a machine-gun in Clipstone Camp, Nottinghamshire. His success deservedly surpassed mine with *The Chelsea Cherub,* which I suppressed. Fifty years later Alec told me that it was his father, Arthur Waugh, Richards' 'reader', who had recommended my novel.

In time I came to feel that the raft I was on would sink and I moved off to a more stable publisher, Heinemann, some four years later. Grant Richards took offence at this. He declared I was an ingrate.

We had words and I said things I was to regret all my life, spiked with that egotism which often afflicts the ambitious young. Conscious of his early faith in me and his hospitality, I made repeated overtures for a renewal of our friendship. When he retired and celebrated his seventieth birthday I sent him a friendly message through his wife, with whom I retained cordial relations. But there was silence, and I thought he was unforgiving to the end, which troubled me. Then long after his death my attention was called to something he had written in his book of reminiscences, *Author Hunting*, which told me that I had been forgiven. Many years later, dining at Lord Warwick's villa on the French Riviera, taken there by Somerset Maugham, I met Mrs. Grant Richards with her sprite-daughter, now a beautiful young married woman. She told me that he had said one day, "I always liked the lad and I'm glad he's had such a success." *Vale.*

That first novel! For years I tried to ignore it. It was so crude that I cannot think why Grant Richards published it. Possibly he did it out of affection for me. Happily he did not lose on it since it sold three thousand copies, which in those days would cover the cost of production. For over half a century I have tried to repudiate that novel but it clings to me like a child of one's youthful indiscretion. For many years I bought up every available copy. In 1919, on a mission to Denmark, I was startled to find half a dozen copies displayed in a Copenhagen bookseller's window. I bought them and borrowed his office fireplace in which to burn them, much to his astonishment. The novel somehow got across the Atlantic, and was presented to me by autograph hunters in Carolina, and Texas. It reposes in the New York Central Library, and is now a 'collector's item'. The last copy cost me £10 to call in. I did not know for a long time that Grant Richards had probably prolonged its life. He wrote in his *Author Hunting*:

"I published, too, the first novel by Cecil Roberts, *The Chelsea Cherub*, a story greatly different in mood and technique from many that have followed it. Some of his admirers should insist on its being made available again. It would have value as indicating his rapid development."

Among the many interesting guests I met at Grant Richards's house was Alvin Langdon Coburn, an American who had won fame with his portraits of famous people, Bernard Shaw in particular. He blazed a trail that Karsh was to follow. "Steichen and Coburn are the two greatest photographers in the world," wrote Shaw in

1912. He photographed Rodin, Matisse, Epstein, Stravinsky, Wells, Henry James, Sibelius, etc. He lived in one of those old balconied houses on Hammersmith Mall, and there I encountered many of the celebrities of the day, including Wells, Bennett, Galsworthy, and Chesterton. One day Coburn opened an album and displayed some of his most cherished photographs, remarkable as works of both art and criticism. One was of a wholly naked Bernard Shaw posing as Rodin's *Le Penseur*. But the most impressive head of that collection was Joseph Conrad's. I exclaimed on my deep admiration for his books, whereupon an American lady asked me if I had met him. I regretted I had not. With singular kindness she promised that I should meet him at the first opportunity. He sometimes came to see her. I thanked her but remained doubtful of fulfilment. Some weeks later I was pleasantly surprised to find that she had remembered her promise. She was giving a house-warming party at a flat she had just moved into and Conrad had promised to come. Her new home was on the top floor of a house in Bedford Square, with an attic window.

Late one afternoon in February, 1918, I found myself crushed in with other guests. The daughter of my hostess was on the stage. There were other actresses and some American university students. We shouted at one another over teacups and sherry glasses. Above the din my hostess repeated the hope that Conrad would come. I began to have my doubts. Was it possible that I should see a legend become flesh? Conrad had emerged in 1907 as one of the foremost novelists of the age. His novel *Chance*, published in 1913, had resounding acclaim on both sides of the Atlantic. I had been entranced by *Nostromo* and became one of his unknown disciples.

Half an hour passed and an hour, then the miracle happened. I can see him now, every detail indelibly etched on my memory. I saw at once that he was even more impressive than Coburn's photograph. And yet how little he resembled the Conrad of popular legend. He bowed ceremoniously as in turn we were presented. Here was no master mariner, no Lord Jim or Lingard. His face was almost triangular, coming to a point where grew a trim beard. His eyelids were slanted, making his dark eyes imperious in their glance. He was handsome not in the virile manner of a sailor but with the air of a diplomat, more familiar with the Faubourg St. Germain than the bridge of a ship. Here was, in short, the Polish aristocrat who belonged equally to a dinner table at an Embassy, or the Bois de Boulogne, the Pincio, or the Prater. He was dressed in a well-fitting double-breasted dark blue suit and had a monocle swinging on a cord.

Life had written much in that singular face but the diversity of the story could not be guessed. As a child he had gone with his Polish father into exile. When a boy he had been ceremoniously presented to the Emperor Franz Josef at the Hofburg in Vienna. He had spent some of his boyhood in Cracow, but he craved to be a sailor, and went to Marseilles and sought service on a French merchant ship. He arrived at Marseilles from Poland, being just under seventeen. As a pupil cadet he made four voyages on French ships to the Far East. He had lost his father early but was fortunate in having a remarkably generous uncle who responded to repeated appeals for money, which seemed to run through the youth's fingers. Poor Uncle Bobrowski, how long-suffering and kind he was, and what a dance young Conrad led him! Handsome, impetuous, thriftless, there was always surprising news from Marseilles. When Uncle Bobrowski imagined his nephew was sailing in the Antipodes he received one morning in Kiev, in 1878, a telegram from Marseilles—"*Conrad blessé. Envoyez argent. Arrivez.*" Uncle Bobrowski rushed across Europe. A brawl, a duel, a love affair? On arrival he found that Conrad, out of hospital, could now walk. What was the truth of the whole affair? It was given out, and Conrad supported the story, that there had been a duel. But the facts appear to have been different. He had been engaged in some smuggling affair on the coast of Spain, at first profitable, then disastrous. Penniless, in debt, he borrowed 800 francs and set off for Villefranche, to enlist in the American Navy, of which some ships were in harbour there. He did not succeed in enlisting. In despair, seeking to improve his finances, he went to Monte Carlo, where he lost everything on the tables. He struggled back to Marseilles and attempted suicide with a revolver. It was a near thing. The bullet just missed his heart. All this was revealed to Uncle Bobrowski, who, nevertheless, did not regard his nephew as a bad boy. He despairingly put his hand in his pocket again, paid all his debts and set him on his feet.

Conrad was now twenty-one. Having trouble with the French immigration authorities, he arrived at Lowestoft in a ship called *The Mavis* and walked on English soil for the first time, in June, 1878. He at once fell in love with the land and the people, with the result that he eventually became a third mate in 1880, and took his Master's certificate, and was naturalised at the age of twenty-eight. He was renowned as a dandy among his fellow officers roaming the East Indies. Out of these voyages, in 1894, came his first novel, *Almayer's Folly*. During a cruise on the three-masted *Torrens*, Conrad, a young officer, showed his manuscript to a passenger, John Galsworthy. Impressed, Galsworthy told him to send it to Fisher Unwin, whose percipient reader, Edward Garnett, strongly recommended publication. He was a late starter at thirty-seven and had a hard struggle ahead, but he was now on the road to immortality.

Nothing of this desperate and romantic background showed in the face of the man, urbane, aristocratic, who now talked with his hostess. Presently by chance I found that he was near me, pinned in the window recess by the guests. He spoke to me—perhaps he saw the adoration in my eyes. We talked of the war at first. He had been with the mine-sweepers, writing articles for the Admiralty. We were able to exchange naval experiences. Had I published anything? Yes, some articles and poetry. Poetry? I named my four books. Ah, how interesting! He had never been able to write poetry. It was a craft beyond him. We had a long talk and then he said—"My dear young man, we shall be very unpopular if we don't mix with the company." He asked for my name and address. We parted, to the relief, I am sure, of our hostess who felt I was monopolising her lion. Before Conrad left the room he came over to me and with the formal courtesy that was so marked in his manner asked, if I was not too busy, whether I could come to dine with him one evening. If I was not too busy! He left me with my heart thumping.

Within a few days I received a letter from Conrad asking me for dinner the next Sunday evening. He had taken an apartment for a few weeks in the Marylebone Road, coming up from his home in Kent. On the appointed evening I found he had other guests. Conrad had the simplicity of all great natures and assured me on introducing me to his wife, Jessie, that she was a wonderful cook. The evening was enjoyable but I had no opportunity for private conversation with my host. We talked of everything except literature and his work. Then there was a terrific noise. The Germans had bombed St. Pancras Station not far distant. It rather ruined our pleasant evening.* He must have been aware of my disappointment. A few days later a note arrived at my lodging.

* Replying to a letter of condolence I wrote Mrs. Conrad on her husband's death, she replied: "Your name recalls so vividly that night of the raid, and that one night is equal to months."

"Next Friday is our last in town, and it is Edward Garnett's evening. E.G. has done a lot for literature in the 90's and anyway is an interesting and worthy personality. If you would like to meet him, come in about seven and we'll have a three-cornered talk."

When I arrived I met 'Edward' as he was affectionately called. He was a delicate elderly man with grizzled hair and a diffident manner. He had not been very successful in the way in which the world ranks success. His own work had not met with deserved acclaim, yet he was an *éminence grise* and had sponsored the birth of many literary reputations. Conrad owed a great deal to him. Most of his subsequent work had the aid of Garnett's constructive criticism. On the very evening that I arrived they had been in conference over a manuscript and as Conrad put it aside he said—"Then I shall leave it in," referring to some passage in the new work. Garnett left immediately after dinner. "Poor Edward!" commented Conrad, returning from the door. I was not quite sure what aroused this compassion. But many years later I found a clue. Spending a weekend at Norman Birkett's, I took down from his crowded shelves a privately issued volume, *Letters from Conrad*, edited by Edward Garnett. It seems that for some reason Garnett had been worrying over the possibility that he might be called up for military service! He was elderly and there could have been no such possibility but he pressed Conrad to write to me and ask if I would use my influence to obtain for him a post in one of the War Ministries. By ill chance I never got that letter which Conrad had sent to my club. "I hear nothing from young Roberts. He is either sick or gone away," wrote Conrad to Garnett.

I saw this gentle and gifted man of letters leave that evening with much regret. The talk of one who had sponsored Conrad and Galsworthy would have been worth hearing. His gifted son had not yet come up over the horizon as the author of *Lady Into Fox*. When dinner was over Jessie left us together in the room. Conrad asked how many words I could write a day. I said, "Two thousand." He repeated my answer, astonished, and then said, "Do you know that I am utterly exhausted if I manage three hundred words a day—that is good going for me."

"But what a difference in the product!" I exclaimed. He smiled gently and said, "Well, there are others with your facility. Bennett says he writes four thousand words a day with ease. Wells also. Writing is always agony for me, sometimes I wonder why I write!"

I observed that surely of all living authors he could rest assured of his position. He shook his head despondently. He would feel rewarded if one book of his was destined to survive. He was standing with his hand resting on the mantelpiece as he spoke. I insisted upon his enduring position, if anything out of this age was likely to survive. He was silent for a while and then he turned to me exclaiming earnestly—"My dear young man—if I could think that!", and after a pause added, "In what book do you feel that I've done this?"

"*Nostromo*," I answered. The deep steady eyes that had scanned the horizons of the Malayan archipelago rested on me. I saw that I had moved him. He put a hand on my shoulder. "Ah, my dear fellow —my poor *Nostromo*; it cost me so much labour, and the public don't like it—it's a failure. They talk about *Lord Jim* and say so little of *Nostromo*, immeasurably a greater creation."

A strange picture of success. Here was a world-famous novelist, to whom recognition, if tardy, had come in full measure, saddened by the perversity of the public. When towards midnight I came to leave, a small incident showed the degree to which he had been moved by my preference. "Can we strike a little bargain?" he asked. "Will you give me one of your books and I will give you one of mine to remember this evening by?"

I gladly assented. He asked me to wait in the hall for a moment. He returned, holding a wrapped up book. We parted. When I got out into the street I could not wait to see what he had given me. Under the first lamp-post I unwrapped the parcel. It was a copy of *Nostromo* with an inscription.

Future events prevented our meeting but he never lost an opportunity to celebrate any little achievement of mine. His letters bore signs of the physical pain of writing. He was crippled with gout in the hands and they were written in a large scrawling script. Sometimes they were typed but always opened and closed with a few handwritten words. "A gouty wrist prevents me writing more than a line or two at a time. Hence this typescript for which I apologise." Often a little of his philosophy, slightly despondent, slightly agnostic, as is that of most men who look on the whole of life and do not seek refuge in some *credo* or *mystique*, would be expressed in response to an observation of mine. He wrote to me:

> . . . The sentiments, the opinions, the phrases, the emotions, and the very catchwords of our time are as old as the hills. The voices

of today are but the echoes of dead voices that were moved by the same thoughts, the same doubts, the same anguish and the same passions from which we suffer to-day.

The doubt that dwelt in him concerning his work is the doubt that lies deep in the heart of every sincere writer. Conrad was never sure of himself for all his mastery. Towards the end of his life, saddened by domestic events and the illness of his wife, he laboured over *The Rescue*, making a supreme effort to express his sensuous conception. The story was published serially. I followed the instalments and commented on them, wondering whether he could sustain the degree of suspense. He answered:

> Yes, I am not, myself, without some anxiety as to keeping up the same pitch. I have thrown into that tale, as into a desperate fight, all that I am, all that I have, in the way of romantic vision, experience and feeling. That is the artistic aim of the story. I am telling you this, but you need not communicate it to the world at large. Treat it as what it is—a confidence. Years hence when I am no longer among you young men who think of me so kindly, and the subject happens to turn up in a reminiscent conversation (everything is possible) you will be able to speak with authority. "Yes, Conrad wrote to me about it before the story was actually finished." For it is not quite finished yet. And this is also a confidence. Only a few friends know, and by this confidence you are enlisted in their ranks . . . Your generously appreciative letter compels me to confess that those pages of which you speak have been written a long time ago. This book was begun really before I knew my business. But I knew enough to feel this and to lay it aside. It was taken up from time to time till I felt that the time had come to finish it. What had been written has been severely revised and pruned; but I think that storm description is still too long and it appears, unfortunately, still longer because, as it happens, it fills the whole instalment. However, you like it and it is not for me to argue against an opinion that gives me so much pleasure.

When he wrote this letter he was nearing the end of two romantic stories, the one fictional and the other real. And when my play *A Tale of Young Lovers* was produced I was just in time to dedicate to him the published version. He died, aged sixty-seven, with no sign of any diminution of his remarkable gift. To have known him, to have had his confidence when I was young and unknown will always be for me a thing of good fortune.

IX

The consequences of life are unpredictable. In the year in which I came to know Conrad I began a friendship with another famous man of letters for whom I had a deep admiration. When I was nearing twenty I had made a return visit to Ambleside in the Lake District, still engrossed in Wordsworth. I spent two very inexpensive weeks in a mansion with a mountain-side garden, a little out of the town, run by the Co-operative Holidays Association. We were about fifty, all young, and we tramped the dales together, taking our lunches with us. The cost of this was twenty-five shillings a week. Such is the miracle of youth, I recall it with great pleasure. One could walk twenty miles a day in that mountain air, with good company, for all the world was young. I was certainly the most intense Wordsworthian of the group and I remember how outraged I was when a little Yorkshire youth, with a surprising knowledge of Wordsworth, told me that Coleridge had been in love with Dorothy Wordsworth and had neglected his wife for her, that Wordsworth had had an affair in France during the French revolution, and had had an illegitimate daughter by his French mistress, and also that Dorothy, at the end of her life, had become mental. I indignantly denied all this and, erroneously as it turned out, I vowed it was all sheer scandal. I could not bear to have my god besmirched.

There was a very tall young man in the party, Claude, with whom I formed a quick friendship. He invited me to his home in Kidderminster. His father was a prosperous carpet manufacturer whose family consisted of his wife, two sons and a daughter. They were all vegetarians and addicted to a health cult. They lived in a long bungalow which they had built on a hillside commanding a fine view of the valley. All the bedrooms had sleeping-out porches. There was a long verandah and in the evening we sat there, watching the moon rise up over the woods, while Dorothy, the daughter who had a good voice, inside the sitting-room sang *Who is Sylvia?* and other songs, to her own accompaniment. They were lovely evenings with a touch of romance. The mother of my tall friend was very tiny and very frail. She floated about like a bit of thistledown. She was all spirit and confided to me that she longed to escape out of her body. She had a deep love of poetry and I, the budding young poet, found in her an encouraging spirit. They were a warm-hearted family and it was like a second home to me.

In this era, before the First World War had come to shatter an easy and unharassed life for the middle-classes, the motor-car began to appear on the dusty roads. The young bloods dashed about on something simpler and less expensive. To their motor-cycles they attached a thing called a sidecar. It was a sort of gondola on one wheel, fastened to the side of the motor-cycle. You sat in it, covered with a waterproof apron. It had no windscreen and you were exposed to the wind, dust and rain. At a speed of forty miles an hour, maximum, you bounced up and down beside your goggled driver. It was perilous and exciting.

Claude and his elder brother, Lancelot, each possessed one of these roaring outfits, and they took us out, my hostess or Dorothy in one sidecar, me in another. In this manner I saw those beautiful counties, Worcestershire, Herefordshire and Shropshire, up to the Welsh border, and the upper reach of the Severn, where it glided under the arches of lovely Bewdley Bridge. We were in the Housman country, 'In summer time on Bredon'. We ate our lunches looking down on the 'coloured counties' of *The Shropshire Lad*. We walked in lovely Ledbury where John Masefield was born. In its street of gabled houses I looked for 'The Widow in the Bye Street'. Most enchanting of all were our visits to the Severn Valley, below Arley Castle. In May, in apple-blossom time, I was deeply stirred and wrote *Dedication, lines written on attaining the age of twenty-one*. It had an echo, of course, of *Lines written above Tintern Abbey*, and I was elated when Arthur Waugh, reviewing the poem said, "Wordsworth might have claimed it, with pride."

Along the valley May has blossomed forth
Giving with prodigal beauty to these hills
A splendid coat of many-coloured green;
While 'mid the wealth of Spring the Severn rolls
Gently among the pasture lands that lie
Laughing beneath the sunny heaven of May.
Here deep in boughs of scented, white and red
Cherry and apple-blossom, peering through—
As though a world so fair should not be made

A place for common habitation—gleams
A white-walled cottage from whose ancient tiles
A wreath of purple smoke through the still air
Like incense upward winds amid the trees;
While all along the valley, softly heard,
The murmur of the swollen river joins,
With undertones of minor melody,
The glittering flights of song that, from the birds,
Fall through the air like pearls from Heaven's gate.

In the manner of things this cherished friendship led to another. Returning from Kidderminster to London in the summer of 1918, a small, neat man got into my carriage at Oxford. He was about forty, quietly dressed. I started when I saw him sit down opposite me. There could be no doubt that this was John Masefield, whose portrait as England's foremost living poet was to be seen everywhere. He opened a book and began to read. I palpitated with repressed excitement. At Reading he put down his book and peered out of the window. I could restrain myself no longer. "Excuse me, aren't you John Masefield, sir?" I asked. He looked at me, smiled and replied, "Yes, I am." I told him how much I admired his work. We talked for the rest of the journey to London. When we arrived at Paddington he asked me if I could lunch with him one day. He was working in the Ministry of Information and dealt with the entertainment of the American soldiers billeted in England. I was so excited by this encounter that later, on the Underground, I was carried two stations beyond my destination. So to the friendship of Joseph Conrad I now added that of John Masefield, a lovely friendship that was to last until he died, forty-nine years later.

One of the chief literary figures around London at this time was Arnold Bennett. When I encountered him at Alvin Langdon Coburn's house it was not our first meeting. He was friendly with my chief, Burton Chadwick. They both lived for a period at the Royal Thames Yacht Club. When my novel was accepted by Grant Richards and I received my first publisher's Agreement, Chadwick suggested I should show it to Bennett, to have it examined by his experienced eye. So one June morning in 1917 we all breakfasted at the club whose pleasant rooms overlooked the leafy glory of the Park. Bennett put the Agreement in his pocket and said he would go through it carefully. A few days later I was astonished to receive a two-page letter along with the Agreement. The penmanship was so beautiful that the letter was a work of art. I learned that all his manuscripts were written in this beautiful, unhurried hand. A prolific writer, it is almost incredible that his calligraphy never deteriorated. His comments on the Agreement were so scathing that I never dared to show the letter to my debonnaire publisher; moreover, at this point in my career, I was not prepared to jeopardise publication.

"This agreement is in my opinion very vicious," he wrote. "The first clause is the worst as it gives the publisher absolute control of the book anywhere . . . On the other hand Richards is very clever in his advertising and he has a reputation for publishing clever things."

I still remember with gratitude the great trouble Bennett took with a tyro's Agreement. I was fortunate in having Bennett's advice. Grant Richards published the first novel of Philip Gibbs, when he was a young unknown author. He paid him £25 down for all rights. Thirty years later, when Gibbs was famous, Richards demanded £500 to buy back all rights, otherwise he would republish the novel. "This was sheer blackmail," said Gibbs, telling me the story. "I refused, so Richards republished the old novel as a new one by me, which seriously jeopardised the sales of my new novel."

About this time Arnold Bennett's marriage to his French wife was developing strains. In 1967, on the centenary of Bennett's birth, I presented his letter to the Society of Authors, in whose offices it now hangs, a model of kindness and calligraphy. It recommended membership of the Society to me. He often stayed at the Royal Thames Yacht Club. I found him, that June morning, reserved and, I thought erroneously, a little pompous in his manner and posture. He was self-conscious over his stutter but deliberate in not letting himself be frustrated by it. His pompous manner of walking was caused by the boots he had to wear because of weak ankles. He appeared to proceed balancing backwards, and a cockatoo quiff of hair emphasised his deportment. But he was obviously a kind man, unassertive, generous and trustworthy, qualities I was to have proof of on future occasions.

"What makes you want to be an author?" he asked.

"Because I feel it is the one thing in the world I want to be."

He looked at me steadily for a moment and then said, "That's quite enough reason. It is my own."

Burton Chadwick had given him a copy of *Twenty-Six Poems.*

"I've enjoyed your poems. I'd like to write poetry but I just haven't the gift. How do you write—does it just come or do you create it?" asked Bennett.

"Sometimes all at once, but more often I polish and polish."

We somehow got on to the subject of Henry James. I was reading *The Turn of the Screw*. "I can't read him," said Bennett, "I get bogged down in his books—those awful involved sentences. They've as many folds as a box-pleat kilt. He just can't write a plain sentence and his novels never seem to be about anything. But he was a great and delightful man to know."

I asked him, diffidently, what he thought was the most important thing to be observed in writing—grammar?

"No. Wells and I have poor grammar, we're always finding flaws in one another's sentences. Interest and paragraphing are the two things to watch. Have you a stomach?" (He pronounced it 'stomick'.)

"No," I replied.

"You're lucky, I have. Watch your stomach and every morning, immediately after breakfast, evacuate the bowels."

Many years later I was to learn how right he was about a writer's stomach. After Bennett's separation from his wife she wrote a book about him. There were embarrassing details concerning Arnold's stomach and her service of hot water bottles when he was writing.

As we left the club Burton Chadwick said, "Well, what do you make of the great man of letters?"

I replied, "I like him. He's very downright."

"Yes, he's bumptious and self-assured," said my chief. "But if I was in trouble I'm certain he would prove a sound friend."

It was the verdict of everybody.

CHAPTER FIVE

The Royal Air Force is Born

I

EVENTS HAD SEVERED me from my old friend and patron William Kiddier. Soon after my arrival in London two other men came into my life, whose generosity and experience proved invaluable at an impressionable age. A lively, highly ambitious young man, inclined to rush my fences, I had little *savoir faire*. Deprived of a father at the age of fifteen, when one is most deeply in need of guidance, coming up from the provinces, I was callow. At that time social life was very much controlled by 'Thou shalt' and 'Thou shalt not'. One was encompassed by subtle shibboleths. Today, two wars have demolished most of the conventions but at the time of my youth there were powerful unwritten laws. You must leave the last button of your waistcoat undone. Your coat-sleeve must have four button-holes that were real. You could not wear brown shoes with a blue suit. You might only wear a black bowler with a black jacket and pin-stripe trousers or with a very dark plain suit; and wearing such in the West End you must carry a rolled umbrella. The umbrella had to be very thin. Cartoonists gave their victims thick umbrellas. If you wished to go forth without any nervousness and not raise the eyebrows of butlers at houses where you called there were certain shops you must patronise that were caste-proof; you bought your bowler hat at Locke's in St. James's Street, next door to where Byron had had his first lodgings and woke up one morning to find himself famous. You bought your umbrella at Brigg's, in the same street and, nearby, in Jermyn Street, you ordered your shirts, made to measure. If you could afford it you had your shoes hand-made at Lobb's. I never did. Being easy to fit I got very well-made shoes in Coventry Street for thirty shillings. They would have been passed by my connoisseur father whose ghost was always near me in a shoeshop. There were many good tailors, but valets who took your clothes away in the morning in order to brush them while you were in the bath, sniffed if they did not have Savile Row labels. There was at this time one superlative tailor who made suits for the handsome young Prince of Wales—Scholte. You had to be introduced to this autocrat, and the price was high. Ambitious to be faultless, I achieved this introduction and the price. The result was superb. Almost thirty years later, in Madrid, with pesetas in hand from blocked Spanish book royalties, I asked a Spanish Grandee if he could recommend a good tailor for it was a post-war restriction age when you could only get suits in England if you had coupons. He gave me the name of one. I ordered two suits and an overcoat. They were excellent. I congratulated the tailor. "They are as good as anything made by Scholte," I said. Very quietly he replied—"We have a cutter from Scholte, señor."

In the beginning of the century Scholte was an autocrat. The tale is told of how a certain duke went for a fitting accompanied by his wife, a rather domineering lady. She suggested alterations to the vest and jacket, which Scholte patiently listened to. Weeks passed and, the finished suit not arriving, the duke's secretary requested delivery. The suit arrived, in its unfinished state, with a covering note from Scholte. "As Her Grace has no confidence in my tailoring she may like to finish the suit herself."

Clothes, shirts, shoes, hats and umbrellas were not the only caste-marks. You must not wear a ring with a diamond; foreigners could, but foreigners were 'different'. You might have a dark stone in a gold ring but only if it was carved with your crest. The ring must be worn on the little finger of the left hand. Such, I learned, were some of the hurdles one must take properly if one did not want to come a cropper. There were stiffer ones, almost unsurmountable. It was a grave obstacle not to have been to a public school, however minor, and a university, which meant either Oxford or Cambridge; the others did not rank. Without these, no matter how impeccable your speech and manners, you lacked a school tie and could not get into a good club. This imperative went beyond clubs. Etonians held almost a monopoly of book-reviewing on the best London papers. It was surprising where the Bourbons turned up. There were, of course, side-doors and some 'doubtfuls' got into White's, the Carlton, or Boodles. How very strange it all seems in these latter days when exclusive clubs are touting for members, trying to avoid bankruptcy, and when most of the best tailors and bespoke shoemakers have gone out of business! A young clerk to-day can buy a ready-made suit whose cut does not make him look like a lout, and, conversely, there are well-bred, well-to-do young men who patronise Carnaby Street shops that specialise in supplying lout-clothes. "What do you think of my Burton suit, off the peg?" asked Lord Brocket at his cocktail party in the House of Lords, in 1965. "A very good fit," I replied. It was.

I am amused, fifty years later, at my Beau Brummell period. I recall the thrill of buying my first fancy waistcoat in Burlington Arcade, but surely it was a superior folly to the Beatle-era of long-haired, unwashed youths with pin-pointed unpolished footwear, grubby shirts and atrocious manners? One day in 1966 I found myself emerging from a Piccadilly shop beside a shining, well-groomed young man. I could not forbear asking him how he came to be so smart. "Sandhurst, sir!" he replied, raising his bowler hat to me.

When I first went to live in London I was just twenty-five, a young man who knew nothing of *le beau monde* that, after Edwardian extravagance, was under a cloud with barriers toppling. My friend Duncan Macpherson gave me a letter of introduction to a Major Cunningham Brodie whom he had met during war service. I presented my letter and was asked to call one evening at the Reform Club in Pall Mall for a drink. It was to the Liberals what the Carlton Club next door was to the Conservatives. It prided itself on housing political intellectuals as against classicists and clerics in the Athenaeum on the corner. Not bishops but Cabinet Ministers haunted it. The Liberal sun still shone in the political heaven, with Lloyd George at the centre of its solar system. The wealthy Sir Alfred Mond, later Lord Melchett, H. H. Asquith, W. H. Massingham, editor of *The Nation* and A. J. Spender, editor of *The Westminster Gazette* were notable progressives. H. G. Wells and Arnold Bennett were the chief literary luminaries.

I was shown into a large, dark, pillared hall with an upper gallery. It had an Egyptian air like a scene in *Aïda*. While I nervously waited by a ticker-tape that clattered away, breaking the silence, and looked at life-sized oil paintings of Liberal statesmen, I heard a page going round calling "Major Brodie!" After a long wait I saw a dapper figure come down the red carpeted stairs. He crossed the marble floor, held out his hand and said—"How d'you do?" As I answered he looked at me critically, asked after our mutual friend, and said—

"You are very young. I expected someone about twenty-five!" "I am twenty-five," I replied. That was my trouble these days. Six feet tall, slender, with a pink and white complexion and chestnut hair, I was always taken for about twenty, a handicap in my man-of-affairs role.

"Now where shall we have a drink—ah, in the gallery," he said. We mounted the crimson stairs. There were dark leather chairs and small tables round this upper gallery which was very dark, with shaded lamps throwing pools of light. I had taken a quick measure of my host. He looked forty-five, of medium height, balding, with a cropped military moustache. He had laughing eyes. His manners were perfect. His suit, shirt, tie, shoes, were obviously fashionable, and expensive, without ostentation. He was *grand seigneur* without arrogance. I knew only a little about him. He had been in a cavalry regiment in Egypt in the early part of the war. He was now in one of the Ministries. He had been for ten years a Liberal member of Parliament for Reigate. He was married, with two small sons. His wife was the daughter of the famous Sir Robert Hart who had made a name in China where he had resided most of his life as Inspector General of Customs. It was Hart who had introduced General Gordon to the Empress's famous minister, Li Hung Chang, when the former went there during the Taiping Rebellion. Hart spoke fluent Chinese and lived for many years in great state in Pekin. Later, I met Mrs. Brodie, his daughter, a lethargic, amiable woman with a beautiful voice, destined to end her life as an invalid, attended with the greatest devotion by her husband.

Having finished our drinks in the gallery of the Reform Club, Brodie said, "I hope you can stay and dine with me?" I accepted with repressed eagerness. We descended to the long stately dining-room with windows overlooking the lawn and trees of Carlton House Gardens. Lord Curzon lived in a house across that green oasis, with A. J. Balfour almost a neighbour. These gardens and mansions overlooking the Mall had not yet been shattered by the "developers" with their concrete monstrosities. The shade of Gladstone, who had once lived there, haunted the leafy gardens.

As soon as we were seated a steward brought the menu card. My host screwed a monocle in his eye and surveyed it carefully. Obviously I was the guest of a connoisseur. We started with oysters and a Soave wine. A half-bottle of champagne went into an ice pail. We had just begun to eat when a very tall, slender man came up to our table. He greeted Brodie with a dominant voice and accepted an invitation to join us. He had a sharp eye and formal manners. His name was Charles Prescott.

"And what does your young friend do?" he asked, ignoring me.

"Master Roberts is in one of our Ministries and has published several books of verse," replied my host. For a considerable time he always referred to me as 'Master Roberts', as if I were on holiday from school.

I came to know the formidable Charles quite well in the course of years, until he died, a paralysed querulous old man who had succeeded to his brother's baronetcy. He somewhat tyrannised over Harry Brodie who was always gentle and acquiescent. Still in vigorous middle age, a wealthy bachelor, a connoisseur of wine, art, literature, Prescott lived in luxury off Eaton Square, his large drawing-room carefully spaced with paintings by Canaletto, Guardi, Cézanne, Renoir, Utrillo, etc. His taste in literature was precise and restricted. "Dear boy, there is very little worth reading after the eighteenth century. Goldsmith, Fielding, Boswell, above all Gibbon—and then, perhaps in the nineteenth century, Jane Austen—and shall we admit a work or two of Thackeray's, say, *Esmond*, *Vanity Fair*?" His knowledge of eighteenth-century French literature was extensive. 'The Moderns'—Gide, Claudel, Cocteau—interesting but not really first-class. Proust was an objectionable *arriviste*, an interminable bore and snob, who wrote exquisite French. "But how inferior to Voltaire!"

When I knew him better I dared to challenge him. He misquoted a line from a sonnet by de Hérédia. It was *lèse-majesté*. "Your young friend is rather pert," he observed to Harry Brodie. When, fifteen years later, he came to lunch at my cottage at Henley-on-Thames and saw apples standing in a sideboard dish, he admonished me. "Dear boy, you should never allow fruit to remain in a dining-room. It's odour pervades the room!" "But, Charles, I like the odour of fruit!" I retorted. He gave me a look that suggested I had a low origin and simply did not know. He saw on my wall a Van Dyck portrait of Henriette, wife of Charles I, and immediately delivered himself of a long monologue on the stupidity of the Queen and her disastrous effect on the King, largely bringing on the Civil War, as if I had not read all about the lady. I let him enjoy his omniscience. Educated at Wellington and Magdalen College, Oxford, he was a brilliant, witty talker, though rather domineering. He had great knowledge in spheres that interested him. He had started life with much promise and had been Chairman of the National League of Young Liberals. He had stood for Parliament unsuccessfully. He had been the young private secretary of the Marquis of Lincolnshire, President of the Board of Agriculture, and in the same role to Earl Beauchamp, First Commissioner of Works. He was in the Life Guards, 1914–1916. Wounded in France, he then became private secretary to Lord Emmott, Director of the War Trade Department. He held this position when I met him. He had been on the editorial staff of *The Saturday Review*. His posts in official life were memorialised by the red leather despatch box, embossed in gilt with the royal arms, that had a permanent place between the fine Renaissance bronzes on his Louis Seize writing-table. And after this achievement, nothing, just talk. Highly cultivated, he lived in blinkers. He would not admit that any Americans were civilised. "They seem steeped in vulgarity. A few educated ones come over here and become good Europeans, like Henry James." Demurring, I quoted Abraham Lincoln, Jefferson and Emerson. "They had moments of lucidity, dear boy. But Jefferson, an aristocrat who posed as a democrat, perpetrated that crowning absurdity, written into their Declaration, 'that all men are created equal'. What nonsense, which they never believed themselves! No man was more conscious of his superior rank than Jefferson, and exercised it. And what of the pretensions of the Brahmins of Boston?"

One day I took a Rhodes scholar, a F.F.V. (First Families of Virginia), to call on him. The visit was a great success. A few days later Charles said—"What a charming young man your friend is! So intelligent, such good manners! Very surprised to find he's an American. I might change my opinion if I met more like him. I hope you'll bring him again."

When I put Prescott in my novel *Scissors*, which I dedicated to Brodie, I was a little fearful of my gentle caricature—"His attire was as precise as his flat in Mayfair. He hoped he was the last to preserve the traditions of the Augustan Age." When he had read my novel he wrote me a letter of congratulation. "How proud Harry must be of the dedication. No one ever dedicates a book to me!" I showed the letter to Harry, saying, "Evidently he didn't recognise himself in it." "Oh, yes, he did!" replied Harry. "He's rather proud about it. I heard him telling someone 'Young Roberts has had a little fun with me in his novel. Really amusing and rather clever'." With all his absurdities and severities, he was held in much affection by his friends and after his death half a dozen of them wrote tributory memoirs and had them privately printed.

On leaving the Reform Club, following an excellent dinner, I wondered if I had been approved of and would see my host again. I very much hoped so. Here was the English gentleman, a Wykehamist who endorsed his school's motto. Two weeks elapsed and then I was invited to lunch one Sunday at his house. It proved to be an establishment such as I had expected. There was a company of ten. Mrs. Brodie was affable and easy to talk to. The lunch was deftly served by servants perfectly trained. When coffee followed in the drawing-room, a bower of flowers, two adorable small boys, dressed in white silk blouses and black shorts, their hair pomaded and well brushed, were brought down from the nursery by their nannie. Their names were Alexander and Patrick. I was to see them grow up, one a Colonel in the Black Watch, the other a director of his father's business.

I became aware in the ensuing months that I had again found an incomparable friend, a man of the world who took me in hand and tactfully instructed and polished me. Our friendship lasted until he died, aged eighty-one, in 1955. What fun we had together down the years! He was ever a boy at heart. I recall his good advice and a thousand kindnesses. We had our upsets, of course. I was too temperamental to be always 'set fair' but he never took offence. There were certain shibboleths, certain sacred cows belonging to his age and background that I could not understand. Every birthday and Christmastide there was a well-chosen present from him—a walking stick from Brigg's, an ivory brush from Asprey's, a leather stud-box from Finnigan's, and ties and scarves from Sulka in Bond Street. He was embarrassingly generous to all. One of these scarves caused a storm. It was a long black silk muffler with large white dots. Harry was a member of a number of clubs, the Union, the Reform, The Cavalry, the R.A.C., the St. James's and Hurlingham. One evening he invited me to dine at the St. James's Club. It was a mecca of diplomats and I recall seeing Axel Munthe there, later to win fame with his fantasia, *The Story of San Michele*. Out of compliment to my host, I wore the black and white Sulka scarf with my dinner jacket and a snappy Borsalino black felt hat. I imagined I looked very smart and debonnaire. On asking for my host, the hall porter left me standing in the hall while he went to search for him. When Harry came he gave me a sharp look and hustled me along to the cloakroom.

The dinner was excellent, the setting beautiful in the long upper dining-room overlooking the Green Park, its walls adorned with the eighteenth-century paintings collected by members of the Dilettante Society. There was a party of eight and I enjoyed myself immensely. When we left Harry said, "I'll give you a lift." No sooner were we in the taxi than he turned on me. "How dare you come dressed like that! That preposterous scarf! You wear a white scarf in the evenings. No wonder the steward left you standing in the hall. He must have thought you were a Piccadilly street boy!"

"But Harry, I'm wearing the scarf out of compliment to you! It was your Christmas present!" I protested, dumbfounded. But he would not be appeased. I was just a callow young man to appear in such a fashion. Always a white silk muffler with evening dress, etc. Then, exasperated, I turned on him. "How can you be so silly about such trifles, a spotted scarf instead of a white one! Here we've just emerged from a war with over a million dead, and you are fussing about a spotted scarf! There are many things I find absurd in you—your scrub military moustache faked with a curling iron, your unbuttoning and turning back your coat sleeves to display silk cuffs and gold studs, the enormous handkerchief you flourish when you blow your nose! You've got a bohemian streak!" I cried, growing hot in my tirade. "It doesn't go with a cavalry officer!"

He looked at me, surprised by my indignation, and said quickly, "Dear me, dear me! Yes, perhaps you are right. I should not do these things." His sudden humility was so touching that I felt contrite at my ill-mannered outburst. "Harry, I wouldn't have you alter one jot," I said, pressing his arm. We both broke into laughter. The storm passed.

One day he saw on my desk a letter addressed "Hon. Mary Melton". He picked up the letter. "You must write 'The Hon. Mary' and you address her mother as 'The Rt. Hon. the Lady Balmain', 'Lady Balmain' would mean she is a baronet or a knight's wife." "Does it really matter The or not The?" I asked, a little annoyed at being caught out. "Anyhow I don't know the Lady Balmain." "It matters a great deal. A form of address, if used, should be correct," he replied.

Harry had a great sense of humour and a warm natural interest in all kinds of people. In this he reminded me of my father. At the time when his younger son Patrick was a student at Christ Church, we journeyed to Oxford to see him. At Slough a fat red-faced woman carrying a large heavy basket struggled to enter our compartment. Harry helped her in. The basket would not go on the rack. Presently he got into conversation with her. She had a farm and was taking some poultry to Reading. "Look," she said, raising one lid of the basket. There were half a dozen limp, plucked fowls in it. She raised the other lid disclosing packets of butter and a mass of sausages. As we neared Reading the farmer's wife asked, "Do you like sausages, sir?" "I love them!" said Harry, with gusto. "You're a very kind gentleman and I'll give you some." She held up a string of sausages and wrapped it in a sheet of waxed paper. "I hope you'll enjoy them, sir. They're fresh, I made them myself." Harry accepted the limp package with a bow, as though he had received an accolade. At Reading he helped her out of the compartment. When we arrived at Oxford I asked, "What will you do with the sausages. Will you take them to Patrick?" "Not at all," replied Harry, holding the damp packet in his gloved hand. "I don't think Patrick would appreciate them. We'll deposit them at the luggage office and collect them on our return." So they arrived in Eaton Square, and were reported to be excellent.

Little by little, ever tactful, he taught me the hundred little things a father passes on to his son. He was an excellent man of affairs, holding several directorships, and was tremendously industrious. I discovered that he was a sensitive critic and I profited by this, reading my manuscripts to him. Once, reading a chapter of my forthcoming novel, *Victoria Four-Thirty*, I looked up and saw tears running down his face. Nothing was too much trouble in service to others. As a point of honour he stayed in London throughout the Second World War. His house was on the corner of Eaton Square and when a bomb fell, damaging the façade of St. Peter's Church just across the road, his windows were blown in. Although seventy years of age he was a member of a fire-watching corps and took all-night duties despite the pressure of a business that became understaffed and faced with problems arising from its colonial nature.

I had lost my father at fifteen but a kind Fate brought me two wonderful friends, William Kiddier and Harry Brodie, in my crucial, formative years.

II

I experienced nothing of the bombing of London in the Second World War but I was bombed once, in London, in the First. I had become friendly with a young Canadian Army doctor who, invalided, was given the care of the Chelsea Hospital Pensioners. He had delightful quarters in one of the buildings in the grounds of Charles II's Foundation. I was often his guest. One Saturday evening in February, 1918, after I had dined with him, there was a tremendous blast. To my utter surprise I found myself on my back, quite unhurt. My host called to me out of the total darkness. He and his other guests were also unhurt. We picked ourselves up and went out into the dark avenue littered with broken glass. A glow in the sky told us there was a fire nearby. We discovered that the German bomb had utterly demolished a small house in the grounds. The occupants, an invalided officer and his wife, two children and a servant were killed. A German plane had succeeded in breaking through the London defences, had followed the visible rivercourse, and dropped a bomb. The bodies of the victims were not retrieved from the debris until Monday.

Bombing from the air was then a novelty so that there was always a rush of spectators to the site to look at the damage. When a Zeppelin was brought down by a young airman at Potter's Bar in October, 1916, there was such a movement of cars to the spot that the police had trouble in controlling the traffic. Mathy, the German commander of the airship, had made seven trips over England. This was his last. The first raid in January, 1915, over Yarmouth and Cromer by two of the German dirigibles killed only five persons and injured fourteen. But the raids mounted and the death toll grew. These Zeppelins, erratic in behaviour, and vulnerable, were withdrawn after the Potter's Bar fatality. Something more menacing followed when in November, 1916, the first enemy aeroplane attack was made on London. At the close of the war 1,413 persons had been killed and 3,407 injured. The most serious fact arising out of these aerial bombardments was that two hundred planes had had to be kept at home for defence though badly needed on the Western Front. One would have thought that the writing on the wall would be plain to all. England had lost her island immunity, but the bigots in the Army and Navy, unwilling to recognise their diminished roles, were derisive of this new arm.

There was a distinguished major who, before the beginning of the war, foresaw that neither the Army nor the Navy would be capable, henceforth, of saving England from destruction. His name was Hugh Trenchard. In July, 1912, when nearing forty, he wished to learn to fly and join the new Flying Corps. His seniors were scornful but he succeeded in getting two weeks' leave in which to qualify for a pilot's certificate that would enable him, though approaching the age limit of forty, to join the Corps. He paid down £50 of his own money, went to a flying school and earned his wings in thirteen days. On August 16th, 1912, just the right side of forty, he was transferred to the Military Royal Flying Corps. His fellow officers thought him crazy. Such was the early history of the Father of the Royal Air Force which saved England at the momentous Battle of Britain in 1940.

On the outbreak of war in 1914, until April, 1918, when the R.A.F. was born and had a separate existence, the Army and the Navy regarded it as an illegitimate child. They had fought an angry duel over who should control the brat. The Royal Flying Corps had come into existence almost unnoticed when Trenchard arrived at the Central Flying School. Its foster parents, the Army and Navy, treated it with suspicion. It was the incomparable Churchill who had a clear vision of its tremendous future. He backed the free status of the air arm. "British policy is to develop the independent conception of the air . . . We think that to keep this new arm, with its immeasurable possibilities, in perpetual thralldom to the Army or Navy, and confine it solely to ancillary and auxiliary duties in relation to these two older services, will be to rob it of its most important development."

This sounds a commonplace to-day but when the R.A.F. achieved its independence, it already had behind it the great achievement of the Royal Flying Corps built up by those valiant young men wearing their wings on the fold-over uniform nicknamed 'maternity jacket'. Until that morning in July, 1917, when the members of Burton Chadwick's breakfast party had rushed out of the Carlton Restaurant to look at German raiders over London, I had not seen an aeroplane in action. My earliest awareness of the aeroplane, as that of many others, was when a daring Frenchman named Louis Blériot, on July 25th, 1909, flew over the English Channel from France to England. It was a nine-days' wonder. Few foresaw in that flight that a colossal shrinkage of the globe had begun, and that a devilish, murderous instrument had been born of man's ingenuity.

Trenchard and Churchill were not alone in their prescience. In the Ministry of Munitions in 1916, Lloyd George had noticed a taciturn Scottish engineer, whose firm had been turning out engine parts in a Glasgow factory since 1914. When a Ministry of Air was created, this engineer, William Weir, was made Secretary of State and President of the Air Council. It was his ambition to build bombers and carry the war over Germany. The new Ministry had its headquarters in the Hotel Cecil in the Strand. Weir felt that to build up the image of the flying arm some publicity would help. Thus it was that I was sent off on a tour of the R.F.C. establishments in England. I followed the training of the airmen from cadet to wing-decorated pilot. The new corps started with one great advantage. It had the pick of young England for its recruits. Its standard of recruitment was high and severe. The course took six months, the distance between the status of a sixth-form schoolboy and that of a fully qualified pilot. It was six months' concentrated pressure and ruthless elimination. The candidate could be nearly eighteen or thirty. He might be slightly lame, for walking was not a strict test, but sight, lungs, sense of balance, quick hearing and, above all, indomitable pluck were essential.

I first went to a large house in Hampstead, formerly the home of a millionaire pillmaker. There the fresh-cheeked cadets, like eager puppies, were processed. Their lungs were tested in a manner that threatened suffocation. They were spun round in an arm chair, and then asked to walk a line that would have given the staggers to an alcoholic. They were jerked, subjected to sudden noises and expected to show no surprise. I saw one eighteen-year-old with the muscles of a panther hold his breath so long that the examining officer thought of writing to the *Lancet*. The recruit did not flinch when a sudden bang made us jump. The tell-tale tuning fork held upright in his hand did not make even 'the little noiseless noise' of which Keats spoke. He marched down a straight line with eyes closed. He did it backwards, then he stood on one leg as though he had been metamorphosed into a stork. A specialist with the eye of an eagle and the mouth of a judge looked up the candidate's nose, down his throat and into his ears. He called the candidate 'laddie' with such fatherly affection that one comprehended the spirit that had made him forsake a remunerative Harley Street practice to become a colonel in a bare room. One could see by the manner in which he asked for a repetition of unsatisfactory tests how it grieved him to disappoint the eager spirit of a boy.

Safely out of the specialist's room, our young candidate had not finished with his examination. He was led into a dark chamber where oculists had cunning devices to prove that he could not see straight. Little holes, lights, letters and revolving columns assailed him. Clear vision seemed as impossible there as in a theological council; only those of great faith could possibly survive betrayal by their senses. Next came the final review of the medical assessors, with a black scarf, a stethoscope, thermometer, etc. Triumphant, the candidate emerged, to be seized by a sergeant. One boy who had passed every test with flying colours fainted from relief. Two months of strict discipline were before him. He was given a little breathing time ere he received his kit. His income would now be one shilling and sixpence a day, with uniform, messing and quarters. So a special telegram with the good news was sent home, coupled with a request for a little extra cash. But one exultant candidate I talked to had his doubts. His father was a naval Commander. "This'll knock the old man. The Air Force gripes him," he said.

III

Having witnessed the selection process I was sent to Hastings. In 1966 Hastings celebrated the great battle of the Norman invasion that changed our social system and established the feudal nobles and a French culture nine hundred years ago. But Hastings has known other invasions, in 1914 and again in 1939. In each of these years the town emptied almost overnight. The landladies shut down for the war, the pier was boarded up, the shelters on the promenade had no one to shield. The streets had a graveyard silence. Then, in 1916, Hastings was invaded in a fashion it had never dreamed of. It became the Cadet Brigade Headquarters of the Royal Flying Corps. Suddenly down the empty streets there was a tramping of feet, not of the Germans but of the youth of England. It had become a Citadel of Youth. Two thousand bright-eyed boys with bare knees and open necks, tanned by the sea air, filled the streets with laughter. These cadets were experiencing the sheer joy of life. For two months they were drilled and disciplined with the traditions of a Brigade of Guards. There was not an aeroplane in sight, no flying instruction. They were here for one purpose only, to be toughened and made radiant with physical fitness before they were marched towards their destiny.

The man who held these two thousand boys in hand was himself a boy. He was only two years older than myself, a Canadian born of a British emigrant father, and educated in England. He returned to Canada and joined the Army. An expert horseman at twenty-one, he captained the Canadian polo team. On the outbreak of war in 1914 he came to Europe with the Canadian Division, was wounded at Ypres and awarded the D.S.O. He next started a battle training school, with live ammunition, which shocked his supervisors. By 1917 he was given charge of the physical training of the Royal Flying Corps cadets. It was at this stage that I met him, with two thousand eager youths under his command. He captured those lads. His smile was intoxicating, his voice confidential but his hand was iron. He was now twenty-eight, a Brigadier-General. His name was Alfred Cecil Critchley.

"When I came here we had fifteen court-martials a week, now we haven't five in three months." Clearly the cadets worshipped him. In due time they would earn 16 V.C.s, 235 D.S.O.s, 266 D.S.C.s and 905 M.C.s. As I lunched with Critchley he had one complaint. He was angry with the Public Schools. "They have the type we want but they don't join up. It's the parents' fault. They send their boys off to the old well-established firms—the Army and Navy—family tradition and all that. My God, when are they going to wake up and see that we are what matters most to-day. The horses have gone, the cavalry have gone, trench warfare is a stalemate—the destiny of the human race will be settled by the bomb, and the lads who are sent out to drop them. And here they are, pushing the boys through Sandhurst, Woolwich and Dartmouth." He stopped suddenly, dropping his knife and fork and looked at me. "Do you think I'm frothing?" he asked, "How old are you?" "Nearly twenty-six," I replied. "Then we're nearly the same age and my name's Cecil, too. Well, I'm really in earnest, and with luck you'll live to see I'm right for the next war."

"Surely not another war!" I protested.

"There will always be another war. Nations like wars. The whole history of mankind shows they like them. Wars break the old moulds and redistribute power and money. All nations are better off after a war, whether they win or lose it. I know this sounds heresy. The best vineyards grow round volcanoes. But don't report me as saying this or a thousand mothers will cry I'm not fit to handle their kids!"

I did not record this but I never forgot. I recalled his words when, after the Second World War, I saw the mobs of German tourists buying gold jewellery, and the Italians converting their shabby hotels into modern marble palaces with money given by former enemies. And as for the bomb, his opinion was singularly corroborative of what the officer in H.M.S. *Oak* at Scapa Flow had said to me. It was the bomb that pulverised Germany and weakened her for defeat, demolished Hiroshima and brought Japan to her knees.

After lunch we proceeded to a parade ground and from a platform I looked down on a march past of the cadets. They came, the ground resounding under their young feet, rank on rank in perfect formation, superbly virile and beautiful. Tears blurred my vision. I recalled something I had heard of another march past. "Why do you cry, General?" asked a visitor at a review of new troops before embarkation. "God bless them, they are so young!" he replied, and I understood and felt his emotion.

I left Hastings, following the next stage in the life of the cadet at Oxford. I did not see Brigadier-General Critchley for another forty years. After the war he had gone into business, had become the Vice-President of the Portland Cement Association and the leading figure in the promotion of greyhound racing. Despite some official opposition, he opened the first greyhound racing track in England. In 1934 he entered Parliament as Member for Twickenham, canvassing the constituency in an autogyro. Forceful, outspoken and not given to suffer criticism, he soon ran into opposition and lost his seat. When the Second World War that he had foretold broke out, he was made an air-commodore in command of 54 Group and was responsible for the training of air crews. Once again his genius for organisation was demonstrated in the youngsters he handled at camps situated at empty seaside resorts, as once at Hastings. In 1943 he was selected by the Government to take over as chief executive of the British Overseas Airways Corporation. Two years later he resigned, having opposed the Government's plans in the creation of international air lines. In that short period he had established the London Airport and turned a heavy loss into a profit. Later in life he took up golf and soon was in the front rank. The wife of his third marriage was Diana Fishwick, the Ladies' National Golf Champion. At the age of sixty-three he became blind, an affliction he met with characteristic courage. He built a hut at the bottom of his garden where he trained himself to be self-sufficient. He made one or two attempts at hitting a golf ball but he found it too difficult and didn't continue. Nevertheless, he wrote, though blind, an autobiography, publishing it two years before his death in his seventy-third year.

In the winter of 1947 I was a house guest of a friend in Palm Beach, Florida. My hostess took us one morning to lunch at the Golf Club. There was a buffet lunch set in brilliant sunshine in a room looking out on the course. The Duke of Windsor, wintering in Palm Beach, came off the course and proceeded to help himself at the buffet. He greeted me in his unfailingly affable manner and said, alluding to another golfer at his side, "Do you know General Critchley?" I looked at the Duke's companion, who looked hard at me and then exclaimed—"My God!—Cecil Roberts—Hastings, 1918!" I also recognised him, and so two now elderly gentlemen recalled their young ghosts across twenty-nine vanished years.

It was a very different Oxford in 1918 from that of 1913. It had sent many of its sons to die in the mud of Flanders, under a desert sky or in the treacherous seas. And now here came another flood of young voices that sounded in college quadrangles and along stone corridors. Here and there an ancient figure emerged with fluttering gown, but khaki not black cloth was the predominant garb. The University had 'joined up', in a sense. Colonels sat at the high table in Hall, sergeants filled the lecture rooms with unacademic speech. Their audiences were Air Force cadets, there for a six weeks' course in aeronautics.

Could ever a don have dreamed that his lecture room would be used for teaching youths to fly at an altitude of 10,000 feet? Even the principles of Euclid seem changed. A straight line was no longer the shortest distance between one point and another. He who would fly in a straight line must fly at an angle; there was the problem of drift to be solved.

From the back of a college where formerly nothing louder than the thud of a ball on a cricket bat or the whirr of an undergraduate's motor-cycle was heard, came the noise of high-powered engines. In long sheds they were assembling and dismantling them. The cadet must know the very heart of the machine to which he would entrust his life. He learned with surprise that while under the plane the wind exerted one-third pressure, on top of it the air contributed two-thirds suction in the total lifting power. I found myself in a classroom whose floor was covered by a large model map, as true in its colouring as in its modelling. Farmhouses, villages, fields, highways, streams and bridges were shown in admirable detail—an exact replica of a Western Front battlefield. In a gallery running round the room, just under the roof, sat twenty cadets, notebook in hand, watching the model battlefield. Level with the model stood an officer. He pressed a button and fired an ammunition dump or blew up a camp. The flashing of red lights denoted a battery in action. The students had to record the latitude and longitude of the sites, thus making an imaginary reconnaissance flight across the battlefield.

When the lunch hour arrived I followed a Colonel and his staff into Christ Church Hall and presently we were seated at the high table. For a brief space I was a don and looked down on the cadets who quietly seated themselves at the long tables after we took our seats. 'Scouts' of immemorial respectability ministered to our needs. The sunlight streamed in through the long glass windows—those windows known to Matthew Arnold's Scholar Gypsy who, from Cumnor Range on a winter's evening, saw 'the line of festal light in Christ Church Hall'—and glinted upon the college plate decorating the high table. And this table, no longer sacred to dons, was now thronged with khaki-clad officers who under solemn portraits by Kneller, Romney, Lawrence, Millais and Watts, talked of rotary engines, Constantinesco synchronised fire, bomb-releases and Immelmann turns. One of the company, a major, had been a Christ Church undergraduate and pointed out, as we left hall, that only one portrait showed a man in armour. This was William Penn, the founder of Pennsylvania.

My next place of call was at the School of Armament. It was in a country house. Here the cadets learned vital gunnery. It was wholly by his gunnery that twenty-year-old Captain Ball, V.C., made his amazing record and joined the immortals of the R.F.C. He was a poor pilot and in training had so many crashes that at one time his career was imperilled. As a gunner he was unsurpassable and the deadliest of fighters.

At the School of Armament the cinema was part of the training. The cadet watched the screen. He had to bring his gun into alignment with the bead in the centre of a ring round the enemy plane. Any error, too late or too wide, was shown on the screen but if he made an accurate shot he had the thrill of seeing the enemy plane toppling down the white screen. Elsewhere in the bombing sheds he learned how to release bombs in mock-bombing over a moving panorama of country reeling below him. He was told to bomb a bridge as it came beneath him, operating a model bomb-release.

At last, the armament course finished, the cadet was out in the open

The second Marquess of Milford Haven (formerly Prince George of Battenberg) with his wife, Nadeja, daughter of the Grand Duke Michael, cousin of Czar Nicholas II, and their children, Lady Elizabeth, and infant son, David, Earl of Medina, later third Marquess and best man at the wedding of his cousin Prince Philip and Princess Elizabeth

The surrender of the German Fleet. Admiral Sir David Beatty reads out the terms to Rear-Admiral Meurer in the forecabin of H.M.S. *Queen Elizabeth*, Rosyth, on November 16th, 1918. Behind Beatty hangs a portrait of Nelson; on the table before him is a bronze lion. This painting was sketched on the scene by Sir John Lavery, R.A.

Leonide Massine and the author, Rome, 1967. In June, 1919, at the Alhambra, London, Leonide Massine, of the Diaghilev Russian Ballet Company, created and danced in the first performance of *La Boutique Fantasque*. In December, 1967, at the Opera House, Rome, Massine again produced his ballet. At the rehearsals of 1919 and 1967 the author was present. They are here seen on the stage of the Rome Opera House, celebrating a friendship of forty-eight years air with a real machine. In six weeks, if he had air sense, nerve, and was able to loop, nose-dive and half-roll, he could get his wings. It was a swift life—and death. His record was registered in hours. "We live in heart beats, not in figures on a dial," the airman could say with *Festus*. I talked to a young instructor, a major with three decorations —"How long were you at the front?" I asked. "Four hundred hours," he replied. That was a long life.

From Oxford I went to the School of Special Flying at Gosport, founded by Robert Smith-Barry.

"How long have you been flying," I asked a pilot whose stunts left one breathless. "Nearly two hundred now." He meant hours. A Captain with an M.C. ribbon, a calm, debonnaire young gentleman, invited me to go up with him. A devilish young man. What he did to me! He turned me over a dozen times, he did an Immelmann, he threw his machine about like a tennis ball, the whole universe went whirling round our heads. He ended with a 'falling leaf', putting his machine out of control as it spun to earth, to retrieve it only a few yards, it seemed to me, short of annihilation. When he gained the tarmac he turned to me in his seat. "All right?" he asked. He well knew I could not possibly be all right; my stomach was still up in the clouds. He eased me out of the fuselage like a baby being lifted out of a pram and guided my tottering legs to a canvas chair. Later we went up to town in the train together, he was on weekend leave. Lean, tall, handsome, assured, I speculated what might be his future, if he survived. I felt he had his hands firmly on the driving wheel of life. His name was Balfour. He had joined the R.F.C. in 1915, being then on the verge of eighteen. He served in the war for the next three years, emerging with a Military Cross and Bar. In the last year he had been an instructor at the Smith-Barry School, an experienced pilot at twenty-one.

Almost fifty years after we had parted at the station in London, a friend reading the typescript of this book in 1967 said—"I wonder whether your Captain Balfour is now Lord Balfour of Inchrye, who became Under Secretary of State at the Air Ministry in 1938. I was told he'd been a flying ace in the First War." So I wrote to Lord Balfour and asked if he was the young pilot who took me up at Gosport. Back came this letter:

> I was delighted, and flattered, to receive your letter. I was delighted because I have always been an admiring fan of all you

write, and flattered because you have rightly linked me with your flight at the School of Special Flying, Gosport. Certainly I was the pilot who gave you your Gosport experience and it was on a 100 h.p. Gnome-engined Avro. I was one of the Flight Commanders at the School where we tried to teach Instructors how to instruct. Bob Smith-Barry, who died in South Africa just a few years ago, was a wonderful man to whom aviation owes much. He was really the pioneer of 'Analysis in the air'. What he did was to work out exactly why an aeroplane did certain things when certain things were done to it. The result was the pilot felt he was the master and not the servant of the machine, and that the controls were there for him to exercise that mastership under every circumstance and condition, knowing, as he did, what was happening and what was required for that particular manœuvre.

Balfour stayed in the R.A.F. until 1923 as one of the original Flying Instructors when Trenchard opened the Royal Air Force Cadet College at Cranwell. He then went into business and journalism. In 1929 he entered politics by winning a seat in the House of Commons. From 1938 to 1944 he was Parliamentary Under-Secretary of State for Air. He then became Minister Resident in West Africa, 1944–45. The next year he was President of the Federation of Chambers of Commerce of the British Empire, having previously been made a peer as Lord Balfour of Inchrye and a Privy Councillor. By 1955 he was a Member of the Board of the British European Airways. So my speculation on that spring day in 1918 at the Gosport Flying School had not been sheer fantasy.

IV

The Royal Flying Corps, like the race in Kipling's *Recessional*, had not only taken dominion over palm and pine; it had spread the shadow of its wings over land and sea. I was picked up one chilly morning at Milford Haven by a Captain of twenty-one and whisked off by car to meet a Commander of twenty-four. He was in command of a convoy station, equipped with dirigibles or 'blimps' and for the protection of convoys sailing out and coming in. Dirigibles, seaplanes and aeroplanes were the eyes of the Fleet. They were swans and swallows. When they spotted a ship they had to know what it was, no easy thing when a ship often looks like an insect on a pond. It would not do to drop a bomb on a British submarine, or go home jubilantly after a victory over a minesweeper. When a convoy put to sea, ten abreast, twelve deep, it was irresistible to a U boat lurking off the port. The dirigible and the seaplane herded the flock like sheepdogs. Height gave deep and wide underwater visibility for any lurking submarine. The seaplane carried a torpedo, swung underneath. To launch it called for supreme skill. High overhead floated the spotting blimp. Wider in range, swifter, roamed the seaplane. It descended to drop its depth charges, seeking to shake the life out of the U boat. There were many deadly duels.

I went up in a seaplane over a convoy. The sea looked like the skin of an old elephant. It was difficult to believe that those waterbeetles below were ships and that the little strips of steel, flashing like the blades of an open knife, were escorting destroyers with white tails. The navy regarded this branch of the air-arm as its own particular show. In this game with death, the weather took part, the gale was everybody's adversary.

I came to know four boys in this gamble. They were out in their 'blimp' or 'gasbag' as they called their S.S. Twin dirigible. They carried a gun. Spotting a submarine, they came down and opened fire. They succeeded with a lucky bomb that knocked the enemy out. But the Admiralty never accepted hearsay reports. So they went down lower, to within photographic range of the wreckage and were so engrossed that they failed to observe a companion U boat that had surfaced some distance off. Their first knowledge of her presence was the whistling of shells. The U boat had trained its gun on them. Their own was no match for this fellow. They rapidly sought altitude. An odd game now ensued between the boys in the air and the commander on the sea. A bomb induced the submarine to submerge. The moment her conning tower closed the boys brought down their gasbag and gave chase. The submarine met the fate of its fellow. A second time they made a photographic record of oil patches. In a high state of elation they got back to the aerodrome just in time for tea.

I was told this story by a lad of nineteen who wore a D.S.C. ribbon, the skipper of the dirigible, with a record of four U boats. We were seated outside a great hangar housing the airships, having just returned from watching a convoy out to sea. He pointed out one of his crew. "Do you know, when we got back at tea-time old Ginger would go off and wait until the film was developed and was real mad when he came in the mess and found all the cake gobbled up!"

I came to know very well one of these bright lads in this arm of the Royal Naval Air Service, as this branch of the air arm was termed. One Sunday afternoon in the summer of 1917 I was one of a crowd of guests gathered in the studio of a house in St. John's Wood. Our hostess was a beautiful and gifted woman, Mrs. Eyre Macklin. She set up as a publisher with the result that her Sunday At Homes were thronged with a host of persons, young and old, critics, writers, artists, musicians, publishers, etc. It was, so far as such a thing can be achieved in London, a 'salon' over which Mrs. Macklin, a linguist, presided. That particular afternoon I found myself wedged down on a lounge beside a youth in the blue and gold uniform of the R.N.A.S. Pink-faced, chubby, bright-eyed, good-looking and vivacious, I noticed that he had a nervous stammer as he eagerly talked. Gradually I extracted from him some of his story. He was very much better now, he said, after a harrowing ordeal, and convalescent. The Service was sending him round lecturing on the work of the R.N.A.S. But he did not want to talk about flying, he was interested in literature. When we left the house together and came to a bridge over a canal he asked me if I knew Compton Mackenzie's *Sinister Street*. Of course I did. Every young writer those days was enthralled by this new masterpiece. Well, here was the canal mentioned in the novel. He knew Sinister Street also, he had identified the very house in which the heroine Sylvia lived. I soon realised that he worshipped at the shrine of Mackenzie. I asked him if he was writing. Yes, he confessed shyly, he was trying his hand at it. He had just published a book of poems, *The Dawn Patrol*. From that moment, having guessed his secret, I had his confidence. Three years his senior, with my fourth book, *Twenty-Six Poems*, just published, he regarded me with a touch of awe. His name, he told me, was Bewsher, Captain Paul Bewsher, D.S.C., aged twenty-two. I learned later that he was the son of the headmaster of Dean Colet School, the preparatory school attached to St. Paul's School, whose boys were known as 'Bewsherites'. One of the earliest at this new school had been young Compton Mackenzie. Doubtless this fact explained some of Bewsher's enthusiasm for Mackenzie. *The Dawn Patrol*, published by our hostess, had won the praise of Laurence Binyon in *The Times Literary Supplement:*

"He describes in vivid detail an air raid at night. He feels that he is desecrating the night's beauty and stillness; he spares a thought for the sleepless below him, who lie listening to his droning engine; he describes how he comes above a city all ablaze with lamps which suddenly dies into utter darkness at the fear of his approach; and then he espies the furnace he has come to wreck, and among the blinding searchlights, outlining every wire of his machine, drops his bombs—'such fearful death with such great ease'. But though so glad to hurry back to the friendly West and home, he is pursued by remorseful thoughts of those he has killed 'like a thief in the night'."

We met again and then, in the manner of those days, the war swallowed us up. Our next meeting was wholly unexpected. I was crossing from Boulogne to Dover in December, 1918, at the close of the march to the Rhine, in my role of war-correspondent. Embarking at Boulogne in the dark afternoon, I heard my name called and turned to find Bewsher, as rosy and bright-eyed as ever. He too was returning to England, and I recall how instantly his eager personality captivated my colleague Philip Gibbs, to whom I introduced him as we sat at tea in the London-bound train. We picked up the threads and found that our tracks had crossed when he told me of his bombing of the Luxembourg Bridge. Only a month previous I had seen the demolished railway bridge as we passed through Namur, now liberated, on the march to Cologne.

Soon after Bewsher had returned from convalescence in 1917 he was sent for by his squadron commander, a pioneer of night bombing. He was to bomb the Luxembourg Bridge at Namur. He and his pilot loaded four bombs, each weighing 250 pounds. After a quiet dinner and a half-jestful making of their wills, they clambered into their plane and roared off through the night 200 miles to Namur. They were soon over Dunkerque. They passed a searchlight at Thourout, dodged Very lights, and knew that Brussels, Aix-la-Chapelle and Cologne had been alerted. Soon they struck the Meuse, and on its banks Namur. They turned, throttled the engines and glided down parallel to the railway lines. Bewsher left his seat by the pilot and lay on the floor of the plane. Through a trapdoor he saw a square of moonlit country, the curve of the river, the black thread of the railway bridge across it. The plane dived. Before Bewsher were three buttons, light direction indicators to the pilot's dashboard. He pressed a handle, the bomb door opened with a clatter. He watched the bombs' fat, dusky shapes hurtling towards the bridge. Then flashes leapt up, but they missed the bridge. The explosions woke up

Namur. They turned for another down run over the target. They were dangerously low now. Two bombs again, their last. They waited what seemed an eternity and then two flashes appeared on the thin black line of the bridge; A direct hit! "Priceless! Priceless!" yelled the pilot.

"What did you do? How did you feel?" I asked Bewsher. "Oh, bucked no end! Wrote letters and verses, read Dickens, drank tea, ate sandwiches all the way back." Five weeks later a repatriate reported the destruction of the bridge. It was the one I saw later, marching into Namur.

Bewsher had one more adventure to relate, the last and most tragic, during a raid on the Bruges canals. Engine trouble brought them down over the sea. The plane was smashed with the impact. They struggled in black icy water, lit by the oil flares they dropped. Bewsher, dragged down by his flying kit, fought his way to a projecting wing but found nothing to cling on to on the slippery surface. Sinking, he discovered a crevice. High above him his pilot, Roy Allan, a fearless red-haired youth from Montreal, sat astride a wing. They hung on, death imminent. Then a boat answered the flare signal. As Bewsher was dragged in he called for them to save the pilot. Down the wing the figure slid. It was not Roy Allan, it was their gunlayer. Roy was missing. The next morning the two survivors were landed at Dunkerque, the gunlayer in his stocking feet, Bewsher all bloody, with hair plastered over his eyes, distraught with the loss of his friend. Two officers sitting at breakfast stood up in amazement at this return of the 'reported missing'.

By ill-luck I saw Bewsher only once more after our Channel crossing, when he came, a year later, to a farewell dinner for me, in December, 1919, on my leaving for my first lecture tour in America. He had published that year an excellent book on his exploits called *The Adventures of a Night Bomber*. It showed a real writing gift. Forty-four years later, again crossing to Dover, I bought an English newspaper on board and in it was the announcement of Bewsher's death. A friend, Trevor Allen, reading the manuscript of this book, filled in a gap. "I knew him in Fleet Street. We used to meet on murder stories, etc., as rival feature writers. Remarkable fellow—he never wanted to be anything but a reporter on late night turns, and stuck it for years."

Bewsher became a leading feature writer for the *Daily Mail* and wrote a very remarkable article on the interment of The Unknown

Warrior in Westminster Abbey. Like so much good journalism it is lost in an old newspaper file. Another friend, a Squadron Leader who led eleven night-bombing raids over Germany in the Second World War, on my mentioning Bewsher, observed, "It was just the same gambit with us. Twenty-seven years later I bombed that very bridge!"

V

I was to have a brief, unpleasant experience of the bombing plane. Trenchard had formed the Independent Air Force after he had been evicted by political intrigue from the position of Chief of the Air Staff. He and Weir created hundreds of planes for reprisal raids and carrying the war over Germany, something new in warfare. The De Havilland and the Handley Page machines were the result of this plan. I was sent to write about the new Handley Pages (H.P. 42s) on the Kent Coast, at Port Lympne, where there was a splendid mansion owned by the spectacular millionaire-politician, young Sir Philip Sassoon, A.D.C. to Field-Marshal Haig during the war. An adjacent aerodrome had been made a R.A.F. acceptance depot. It had suffered an amazing transformation. When you looked in a hangar you saw packing cases with 'Basra', 'Cairo' and other names stencilled on them. From these labels one gathered that we were operating not only in France, but also in Egypt, Palestine and the Near East, etc. An engine has two thousand parts. Somewhere in Palestine it loses a bolt or a rod. There is a message and from a lettered rack the required replacement is on its way.

In various places in England the planes were tested. The tour of some of these places ended at this old mansion. Here was the last halt before the pilot and machine took off for 'foreign parts' and incredible adventures. Lympne was really an inn on the way to the Continent. I was continually surprised in the messroom. A lad in a hurry came in and sat down for tea. He hoped to be in Paris for dinner. "Have you come far?" I asked. "From Edinburgh this morning—pass the jam, please." Such answers mean nothing to-day. Then, not ten years after Blériot had astonished the world by flying over the Channel, they carried an element of magic. There was a staff of ferry pilots on hand. In order to obtain maximum deliveries a Handley Page went across the Channel at intervals to collect a dozen pilots, who were brought back to ferry over new machines.

It was at Lympne that I encountered my first monster Handley

Page bomber. The very look of it was frightening. It was an ungainly elephant. Would it ever get off the ground, and stay up? I felt doubtful and I was due to fly across to St. Malo in it. We started, having got into it through a hole in the floor of the fuselage. We taxied. The noise, the vibration, the dark turret-like interior cabin, a huge dimly lit box, were unnerving. I clambered up and sat by the pilots. We rose unsteadily, I thought, turned and circled over the Kent countryside. It was the first time I had been in Kent and I saw an oasthouse, bird-beaked, diminutive, below on a draughtboard of fields. Then at some three thousand feet we went seaward, over a Channel that looked a boiling cauldron. We had not gone far when something hit us. It was a terrible impact. The lumbering creature shuddered from nose to tail. In a few seconds we were on end, in a few more seconds we were on our tail. Failing to secure myself, I travelled down that long dark fuselage with a packing case that had come loose, and a mascot cat. As we shot over the grid by which I had entered, I had a swift glimpse, at an odd angle, of a farm, haystacks and a pond. I was hauled back to security by a long-nosed lad. We were all of us gargantuan in our padded flying suits and life jackets. Clearly things were not going well. We shook, heaved, and bobbed about as if gravity had been abolished. I had already vomited, in company.

I have no clear recollection of what happened next. There was a terrific roar of the engines, and a mad creaking as if the plane were splitting apart. Next, before I had realised it, the sea was somehow the ceiling. Sweat was running down the face of my near pilot. I saw him exchange a grim wild look with his co-pilot, who whistled loudly. Then we steadied and I learned we were ordered home. A violent gale was blowing up the Channel. Obviously Handley Pages didn't like gales. Somehow we had got very high and were half way over to St. Malo, I learned, for we could see no land anywhere in that black cloud-torn heaven. Going home? It didn't seem to matter which way we went. I was not sure that all of me would arrive anywhere. I prayed for a landing on either side. So back to Lympne we went. I stumbled out of the plane with shaking limbs. One of the pilots, his face wet with sweat, pulled off his helmet and wiped his brow. "Well, that was a bugger!" he exclaimed, and I heard another voice explain to someone, "We had to loop the bloody bus." Trying to seem courageous, I asked if we had been in danger. The co-pilot gave me a wry look. "She might have broken her back—you can't go looping in this mangle, kind sir!" (Illustration, p. 145.)

I sent Joseph Conrad my articles on the convoy service and the airmen, thinking they might interest an old sailor. Back came a letter from his Kent house.

> Your R.A.F. paper is very good—but I don't think the age is so very wondrous unless perhaps in spots like the curate's egg. Otherwise humanity is at its old game, the same old game from the beginning of ages, and I really believe that the invention of the bow-and-arrow was a much more wonderful feat than the invention of sewing machines—when you dispassionately think of it. But the young men are all right.

VI

My visits to the R.A.F. completed, my articles published, Lord Weir, as he now was, Secretary of State for Air, sent for me. I went to the Hotel Cecil and found this grim little Scot very complimentary. It was then that I had an idea. I asked him whether, if I collected my articles and had them published, he would write a preface to my book. He agreed most affably. I called it *Training Our Airmen.* Murray published it. So here I was a Murray author, entertained to lunch by Sir John Murray IV, in his historic house in Albemarle Street. Shades of Byron and Moore!

Lord Weir's preface was short and generous:

> When the full history of this war is written, no part will be found more absorbing in interest or thrilling in episode and none as a whole more creditable to the nation than the record of the Royal Air Force. I welcome Mr. Cecil Roberts's articles as a very admirable contribution to this record . . . Now that the fighting has ended, I think that the Royal Air Force may count itself lucky in having secured so accurate and picturesque an account of what has been so essential a part of its war organisation.

CHAPTER SIX

An Editor, A Poet, A Ballerina

I

I WAS IN love with London, in love with life in these morning years. Every vista enchanted, every day brought a new delight, new friends. I quoted Wordsworth: ''Twas very bliss to be alive', and, on Westminster Bridge—'Dull would he be of soul who could pass by a sight so touching in its majesty'.

It was at about this time that I found another good friend, Holbrook Jackson, a man of some genius. He was one of the most remarkable figures in London's literary life. I never met a man with such a passion for books, or of greater erudition concerning them. He was *homme de lettres* in the truest sense of the term. Born in Liverpool, he drove a tandem in London, harnassing literature and business with singular success. For some years he was the acting-editor of T. P.'s Weekly, a popular literary paper founded and owned by T. P. O'Connor, known in the House of Commons, affectionately—for he was 'a broth of a bhoy'—as Tay Pay. A member of the Irish Party, he was in demand on public platforms with his embroidered stories of the potato famine and the wrongs of Ireland. "Tay Pay's up", the word would go round the lobbies of the House. He could reduce an audience to tears and cry with it. He was for many years a Member for a Liverpool constituency. In 1877 he founded the London evening *Star*, became a Privy Councillor in 1924, and was one of the first film censors. He was an excellent journalist and became famous for the front-page reviews in the Weekly he founded. He was lazy and extravagant in his later years and left the running of the paper to Holbrook Jackson, a tall, dark, curly-headed young man who soon made his own mark on London life.

O'Connor mercilessly milked his paper and there were recurrent crises when the printers refused to go to press unless their bills were settled.

One day the end seemed really to have come. Twenty-four hours before publication the printers struck. The bills must be settled or there would be no issue. Jackson hurried off to see Tay Pay at his chambers near the House of Commons. Pleading great urgency, Jackson aroused him from his bed. Putting on his slippers and dressing-gown he listened to Jackson's dire news. At the end of the recital he said, "You're a verra young man, and there's something you don't know—papers take a hell of a toime dying, so don't be so agitated. They'll go to press." They did, and the paper staggered on for some years.

Meanwhile, Holbrook Jackson looked for a safer ship on which to sail. He had already drawn notice as a Shaw disciple and gave great pleasure to G.B.S. with a monograph on the dramatist. With his third book published in 1913, *The Eighteen Nineties*, Jackson wrote a classic that has stood the test of time, and remains without a rival as an assessment of an era. He had a masterly knowledge of typography which he demonstrated in two fields: literature and business. The man of letters, an excellent essayist, was also the editorial director of The National Trade Press, a company that produced trade publications. He founded and edited from 1917 to 1923 a literary monthly called *To-Day*. Its contributors were as distinguished as its format. It was more vigorous, healthy and comprehensive, and lived longer than *The Yellow Book* of the nineties.

One evening in 1917 a friend took me to a place called Prince Henry's Room in a timbered house, dating from 1610, in Fleet Street. There was a literary meeting over which Holbrook Jackson presided. It was the first time I had seen him although I knew his name and work. A discussion followed a lecture. I made a contribution. He recorded that first encounter in an article just before I left on my first American lecture tour in 1919.

> Half an hour later this intruding youth had taken control of the meeting. When I first heard Cecil Roberts I felt like the man who had seen a giraffe for the first time. I felt inclined to announce that I didn't believe it; even after seeing him it was difficult. Tall, lofty-browed, serious and colossally self-confident, you might write him down at forty. But indications of youth intervene especially in a boyish enthusiasm which disavows over self-confidence. He is

still a boy despite his tradition. He enjoys life and is immensely pleased with himself. Not conceit, though he is by no means lacking in that necessary tonic gift, but sheer delight in being himself, doing things, dashing about, writing poems, making speeches, flying in aeroplanes and dirigibles, sailing in dreadnoughts and destroyers, in fact anything and everything that is alive, and the nearer the vortex of things the better. He walks down the Strand as if its vast energies were due to him, and the fact that he is going to New York next week might indicate that he has exhausted London.

From that first encounter we became warm friends. He was very hospitable to me in *To-Day*, printing my poems and articles. It was a great good fortune to be among the list of his contributors, some already famous, some on the verge of fame. Through him I met many of my contemporaries. He was a generous host and a gourmet of the first rank. His conversation was sheer delight. It was rich with knowledge culled from many sources, and founded on an encyclopaedic memory. Between 1920 and 1931, he produced his *magnum opus*, the finely printed two-volume *Anatomy of Bibliomania*, a *tour de force* of scholarship and literary omniscience. Its reception placed him firmly in the niche he had carved for himself as a man of letters. With all this he was also an exceptional man of business. He derived an impish delight from sly derision of his business colleagues. "Good dull, tough fellows," he would say before introducing me to some of them. "Don't frighten them by being clever, be patient with them. Of course they haven't the faintest conception of my real life, or of my mind." He presided ably over Board meetings, planning campaigns for advertising textiles, etc. His editorship of mammoth trade magazines showed his flair for lay-out, his high technical expertise in illustration and typography.

Jackson lived a secret life in a house at Mill Hill, with his wife and daughter. Here he was the *littérateur* with a valuable, choicely selected library. Its resources seemed inexhaustible; editions de luxe, some Aldine first editions, together with such 'moderns' as James Joyce and that master of scurrility, Baron Corvo, revealed in a packet of unprintable letters. The catholicity of Jackson's taste, the scope of his questing eye were immeasurable. Very rarely did he allow his colleagues from the world of business—"The cash basis of my means of existence"—to enter his home. He delighted in their dumb amazement on seeing his library. But the real library they never saw. "Look!" he said, opening a small door. It led into an inner sanctum lined from floor to ceiling with exquisitely bound books, the first editions of famous presses. "I don't let them in here. They wouldn't know what they were looking at—they'd think I was practising hoodoo on them. They're very suspicious of me already. One of them once found on my office desk a copy of Burton's *Anatomy of Melancholy*. 'Jackson, you're not studying medicine are you?' he asked. And there was an unforgettable occasion when I quoted a poem of Donne's at a board meeting. "Very silly of me," said Jackson, chuckling. "They thought it was an incantation in black magic that would shake the foundations of the textile exhibition we were planning." Despite all, they had great confidence in him for he directed a successful team in a thriving organisation. The editor of the eclectic *To-Day*, the essayist, the bibliophile, never mixed with the editor of ten trade journals. The man who sat at a director's desk in a suite of offices near Covent Garden, dictating to a secretary-typist, appeared to have no connection with the collector of belles-lettres, who edited *To-Day* from a room in Adam Street, Adelphi, in the shadow of Shaw and Barrie.

After the breakthrough at Prince Henry's Room I was soon launched as a speaker. Jackson asked me to address a business conference, on war shipment priorities, and I had invitations from literary societies, Rotary Clubs, a Chamber of Commerce, a Book Exhibition, a Civil Servants' Dinner, and a Bankers' Lunch. It was at one of these functions that I was approached after I had spoken by a Major John Hills, a stranger to me. He was working in one of the Ministries. He invited me to lunch with him, and then told me that I was the kind of young man that his friend Lord Beaverbrook would be interested in. I thought no more of this but a few days later I was surprised to receive from him a letter of introduction to Beaverbrook. I found that my host was Major John Hills, a Member of Parliament for Durham, later Financial Secretary to the Treasury and a Privy Councillor. I thought the matter over. I was happy in my work. What I had heard about Beaverbrook made me somewhat apprehensive of this dynamic gnome. These Fleet Street magnates were apt to be ruthless in their use of people. I had heard a story about the great Lord Northcliffe, the Colossus of Fleet Street. It was perhaps apochryphal but not wholly out of character. One day, going up in the lift with one of his directors, a former war correspondent, Charles Hands, he observed the latter joking with the lift boy, "Charles," he said, as they got out,

"I wish you wouldn't make yourself so familiar with the lift boy." Hands, knowing how swift was the turnover of Northcliffe's favourites, retorted, "Why not? He may be the Managing Director next month!" For myself, I did not want to be swallowed up by Fleet Street. It offered a splendid experience and training in a risky craft, but I wanted to sail my own boat. Independence was my aim. So I did not present Major Hills' letter of introduction, I thanked him for his kindness. I fear he thought I was a young fool who was missing a great chance.

II

In 1917 I wrote a poem called *Futility*. It came from the despair evoked in me by continuous and illimitable slaughter in the bloody death-grapple on the Western Front. The politicians seemed seized with paralysis in a blood-glut that threatened our civilisation. Lord Lansdowne, sickened by it all, made an appeal, in a famous letter, for a return to reason. He was howled down as a traitorous defeatist. Some of our poets from the trenches also made their protest, notably Graves and Sassoon. The latter, expressing his revolt in biting satire against the military brass-hats, was hauled before a court-martial that attempted to find he was insane! The despatches of Philip Gibbs from the battlefields echoed the undertones of despair for the human race. He related to me later how, invited to breakfast by the Prime Minister, Lloyd George, he was determined to say what he and his colleagues thought of those 'bloody minded old men'. "And did you?" I asked him. "No," he confessed. "Do you know, the old boy had tears in his eyes as he asked me questions, he was so deeply upset. It's a juggernaut they've lost control of."

I went to see a friend in hospital, a captain of twenty-eight with part of his face shot away. The bitterness in him surged up. "Where's God if He's all He claims to be, omnipotent, omniscient? Why doesn't He stop it? All the bishops blathering away about 'The supreme sacrifice', the Pope silent in the Vatican, impotent while the Christian nations blow out each other's guts!" The protest was the more surprising because I knew he had been a devout Catholic. Slaughter, slaughter, slaughter, with a hecatomb of the dead at Verdun. The old catch phrases turned sour. 'The war to end war', etc. Young Sassoon voiced the cynicism and bitterness that had followed after the first rapture of Rupert Brooke's sonnets. The incessant flow of the wounded across the Channel came to have a nightmare touch of insanity about it. The casualty lists were approaching the million. Religion and philosophy seemed bankrupt.

One afternoon in October, 1917, I received a visit from a friend, Charles, particularly dear to me. Twenty-one, with a flame-like mind, physically handsome, he had been my tennis partner. Now he suddenly appeared at my lodging in George Street, returning from leave with his family. He had one spare night in London. The next day he would go back to France. We dined, we walked, we talked. Past midnight, he decided not to seek his hostel. He slept on the dining-room divan at my lodging. The next day was Sunday. At six o'clock that evening Charles had to take his troop train from Victoria Station. I had arranged to go to Cookham Dean to lunch with Grant Richards but I telephoned him and explained.

When we had finished breakfast Charles surprised me by saying he would like to go to the morning service at Westminster Abbey. "I'm not 'pi'," he said, seeing my surprise, "but I feel I want to go." So we went. During the singing of one of the Psalms I saw he had tears in his eyes and we held each other's hand. Had he a premonition? I fought against the idea. The service ended, we came out and he was his usual debonnaire self again. He thought it would be nice to have a swim at my club before lunch. We had the long green pool to ourselves. He was a crack diver, swallow-dive, jacknife, etc., and he rocked the high springboard. After lunch we dozed in the club chairs. At four o'clock he wanted tea and toast. "Lots of butter, please!" he said to the steward. Later we took a taxi, collected his kit and went on to Victoria Station. It was like the entrance lobby to Hell. Under the high roof in the misty gloom, in front of the track gates, soldiers, burdened with their kit, were saying Goodbye in reserved desperation to parents, wives and sweethearts. Before shouldering his pack Charles combed his blond hair and stuck his beret jauntily over one ear. "Well, here goes! Mud alley again!" he cried almost gaily, hugged me and went through the gate, lost in the khaki mob. I stood there, senselessly, for ten minutes, crying women around me, until the train went out. I walked down the dark Mall to my club to write letters. I thought how in the splendour of youth they went out at Victoria station, and returned, if they returned, mauled, at Charing Cross. Somehow it didn't make sense, there was something wrong in the plan of the universe. More personally that incident during the Psalm singing had filled me with apprehension.

After supper I walked all the way back to George Street. When I got there my room seemed terribly empty. There were the cigarette ends he had stubbed in the ashtray. Six weeks later I learned from his sister that he had died of wounds in hospital. She enclosed a letter from the padre who had been with him at the end. Charles was the second brother to go in that once happy home.

How are poems generated? At what point is the idea clothed in words? One night, at two o'clock, I was wide awake with the first line ringing in my head. I got up and in three-quarters of an hour *Futility* was written. I sent the poem to Holbrook Jackson who published it in *To-Day*. It appeared in February, 1918, with an editor's note—"In this issue we have deviated from our policy of leaving out the war but no apology is needed for our inclusion of Mr. Roberts's fine poem."*

No one can predict the life of a poem any more than that of an infant. It is a gamble with Fate. Out of a hundred thousand lines only ten may survive, or none. Three-quarters of the works of Shelley, Keats, Byron, Wordsworth, Tennyson and Swinburne are a heavy cargo but with a quarter of it, or less, they reach the port of immortality. Holbrook Jackson's faith in *Futility* naturally pleased me. When the poem appeared later, in my fifth book of verse, *Charing Cross and Other Poems*, John Masefield picked it out. "I have enjoyed reading the poems, especially the poem on Charles which I like very much indeed." Four years later Holbrook Jackson with a generosity so characteristic of him towards young authors, wrote to me—"Ralph Hodgson took tea with me last week and apropos of nothing he said, 'The more I think of Cecil Roberts's *Futility*, the more I am convinced it is a great poem. When London is a desert some survivors will be chanting, "Who cares a damn who died at Salamis?" and in the next war that line will be quoted, not by the pacifists but by the men who go out—ironically.' This is about the third time or more he has spoken along those lines and I have never heard him praise heartily any living bards but Davies, Blundell, de la Mare and, with reservations, Drinkwater. After these he jumps back to Shelley, nodding at the lyrical Tennyson on the way." Extravagant praise, yes, but I could not help feeling warmed by the words of so perfect a craftsman as Hodgson, 'Who uttered nothing base'.

I met him only once, in the street with Holbrook Jackson. He had on leashes a pair of bulldogs, which he loved and bred. The foremost

* Appendix IV.

Philip Gibbs, the Galahad of our Mess. A sketch by Geoffrey de Cholmes

"We were a new species at the War Office. Our rank was hybrid. We carried a brass 'C' on our caps and 'War Correspondent' on our shoulders"

The Great War ends: Mons, 11 a.m., November 11th, 1918. *La Brabançonne* is played in the Grand' Place

Hohenzollern Bridge, Cologne, December 16th, 1918, after Field-Marshal Sir Douglas Haig's farewell to the War Correspondents. *Left to right:* Percival Phillips, H. V. Nevinson, G. de Cholmes, Philip Gibbs, A. Collins, Perry Robinson, Beach Thomas, Cecil Roberts, with souvenir flags in hand

of the 'Georgian' poets, he produced little but all of high quality. He was a passionate lover of animals and ran a campaign to stop the docking of dogs' tails and the clipping of cats' ears. He asked for prayers:

> For tamed and shabby tigers
> And dancing dogs and bears,
> And wretched blind, pit ponies,
> And little hunted hares.

He emigrated to the United States and died there in 1965, aged ninety-three.

The backer of poems takes a greater chance than the backer of horses. *Futility* has never quite died but it has been outpaced by a non-starter. About the time I wrote this poem I wrote also a shorter one called *Prayer for a Pilot*. Imitating Kipling, I had often prefaced my war articles with some verses, and this poem headed one on the Royal Air Force. The *Prayer* leapt the Atlantic and caught the eye of the anthologists. I can find in it no special merit, yet it must have something. Through forty-five years it has trickled in each year a steady ten or fifteen dollars, quotation fee. I call it 'my annuity poem'.*

I have digressed somewhat in order to illustrate the kindness shown to me by Holbrook Jackson in the early years when help is most timely for the budding author. It was to him that I owed my first encounter with George Bernard Shaw, apart from that brief occasion in the pool of my club. Jackson had the idea of forming a kind of Arts League, anticipating the British Council. He took the Aeolian Hall in Bond Street for a meeting to launch his proposal. I was on the list of speakers. It was a lively, amusing evening but it produced no permanent result. The star turn of Jackson's meeting was G. B. Shaw. He did not disappoint. Clad in his advertising kit of knickerbockers, worsted stockings, Norfolk jacket and sandals, his bulbous nose and watery eyes shining under rampant eyebrows, he proceeded to demolish Jackson's proposal, having been enlisted as the chief supporter! When my turn came, I directed my attack on the bearded prophet. I charged him with a traitorous betrayal of our chairman. Judas had betrayed his Master for thirty pieces of silver but here was the Master betraying his best biographer with a mouthful of witticisms. The

* Appendix V.

audience was delighted to see a mouse bite the tail of the cat. Afterwards in the ante-room the great man gave me a sour look. "Who is he? Where did you find him?" he asked Jackson, with a sort of insinuation that I had been found in a rubbish bin. I enquired if he was very annoyed. "Oh, no! After all you kept the limelight on him and that's what he likes. But look out," said Jackson, "he'll keep an arrow in his quiver for you."

My friendship with Jackson lasted until the day of his death, thirty years later, at the age of seventy-four. I was out of England at this time. *The Times* printed an obituary tribute from me. At the funeral service Sir Francis Meynell, long associated with him, pronounced a moving eulogy.

III

In the years preceding the First World War there was a renaissance of poetry in England. Two events marked the spirit of this time, one was the publication in 1912 of the first volume of *Georgian Poetry* edited by Edward Marsh, which had a phenomenal success; the other was a brave enterprise launched by Harold Monro, who, slim, dark, feline, is now remembered only for one of his poems, *Milk for the Cat*.

> The children eat and wriggle and laugh,
> The two old ladies stroke their silk;
> But the cat is grown small and thin with desire,
> Transformed to a creeping lust for milk.

In grubby Devonshire Street, off Holborn, he opened The Poetry Bookshop. It not only sold poetry exclusively but it had a large candle-lit attic for poetry readings. The most original feature of the shop was bedrooms for young poets. Here they could lodge cheaply in a congenial atmosphere. The idea was well intentioned, the result disastrous. Too much egotism was compressed within too small a space, and dogfights ensued, but there were some notable poets lodging there, among them Wilfrid Gibson, Wilfrid Owen and Robert Frost. The hostel had to be closed.

The enterprise attracted much publicity and when the shop opened for business on January 1st, 1913, I inspected it during one of my trips to London. How fair the embarkation, how disastrous the voyage proved for many of those high-spirited young poets!

War, drink, drugs, poverty and mental instability wrought havoc among them. An early sensation was Monro's presentation of a revolutionary thirty-four-year-old Italian poet called Filippo Marinetti. He had created a sensation in Italy and Paris with his verses, his fiery readings, his fierce denunciation of the established gods. Dante was a bore, Carducci a cretin, D'Annunzio a mountebank, etc. The prophet of Futurism, he enlivened his declamation by blowing a trumpet and beating a drum. When, in December, 1913, he gave a recital at the Poetry Bookshop the room was packed to suffocation. The audience was more interesting than the performance. It soon became a near riot with interruptions and catcalls. Everyone enjoyed himself immensely, most of all the perspiring, vociferous Marinetti. But once was enough for Harold Monro, who looked pale and anxious. Subsequent readings were demure. "They've turned from *Asti Spumanti* to Drinkwater," said a wit. Marinetti lived until 1944, completely forgotten, unwept, unhonoured and unsung. Rupert Brooke gave a reading. His voice was so weak that the massive Amy Lowell, from the back, shouted "Speak up!"

The Poetry Bookshop has long disappeared from Devonshire Street, but I still see the ghost of Marinetti the flamboyant futurist when I walk down it.

The shop brought me a pleasant adventure. There, one April day in 1914, I encountered a *grande dame*. She was a handsome woman of about sixty. She was buying books with a lavish hand. "You must be a poet!" she exclaimed. I enjoyed the romantic impeachment with all the eagerness of twenty-one. What had I written? I named two books. She bought them. Luckily they were in stock. Presently she asked for a taxi. I carried out a book parcel for her. "Let us have some tea together," she said in a gracious manner that was a command. She ordered the taximan to drive to Gunter's tea-room in Bond Street. I did not know that it was renowned as a rendezvous where Society drank morning coffee and afternoon tea. Afterwards we walked to the Berkeley Hotel where she took farewell of me. She had the manner of a queen, or such a manner as I thought queens had, having no experience of them. Back in Nottingham, waking in my attic bedroom the next morning, the whole episode seemed a dream. "You must visit me in Cheshire," she said, on parting. Would I hear from her? A week later I received a letter enclosing a return weekend railway ticket. The visit was from Friday to Monday morning. I would be met at Lymm station by her chauffeur. The notepaper was expensive, the envelope crested. "But you don't know the lady!" said my mother, suspiciously smelling the faintly scented envelope. I assured my mother she was elderly, charming, and harmless.

On arrival at my hostess's house after a long drive, I was received by a butler and shown to my room. A note awaited me. It was an apology from my hostess who had to attend a function. She would see me, before dinner, at seven o'clock in the drawing-room. "I hope you have brought your new poems to read to me," she wrote. I had.

My bedroom was luxurious with a canopied Italian bed. The writing table had a bowl of roses. I looked down on to a terrace, with flower beds and a lake beyond. Was there a husband, a family, other guests? The house was very quiet; there was no sign of life. It was six o'clock. I unpacked, lay on a chaise-longue and read. "Madame Récamier, *chez-moi!*" I said to myself. A little before seven there was a tap on the door. A maid entered and informed me that my hostess was in the drawing-room. It was a very long room with tall mirrors and a fire burning in an Adam marble fireplace. I had a pang of dismay. There was a noble-looking white-haired old gentleman dressed in a dinner jacket. I had not thought to bring mine. My hostess introduced me. He looked exactly like a retired colonel in a stage set. He gave me an appraising look. Presently the butler announced dinner. There were only three places set. A maid stood by the sideboard to assist the butler. The dinner was slow, ceremonial, excellent. At the close I was a little apprehensive that I should be left with the Colonel and be found sadly wanting regarding pheasant shooting and salmon fishing. Fortunately, we all went into the drawing-room for coffee. This served, my hostess said, "My husband likes to read the newspapers. Will you fetch your poems, and we will go into that corner and you can read them to me." The corner was actually a large bay window. When I returned with my manuscript she said, smiling, "My husband has no ear for poetry—but he indulges me!" So we talked and read. About ten o'clock the Colonel came over to us and said Goodnight. I made a discovery. My hostess was very well-read, and I was only one of a succession of young poets who had been her guests. She seemed to collect them as some people collect budgerigars. I was surprised by the names in her Visitors' Book.

The next morning when the butler brought a breakfast tray to my room I made a few discreet enquiries. My host was not a colonel. He was a retired Manchester cotton broker. There were two married sons, a daughter and some grandchildren. At eleven o'clock I was sent for by my hostess and we made a tour of the gardens and hothouses. We ended our tour at a large summerhouse looking across the lake and the woodlands. It contained a big soft-cushioned settee and chairs and had a library on shelves with shutters. At noon the 'cotton colonel' joined us. Obviously he adored his wife. He was the first Englishman I had seen kiss his wife's hand. A room beyond the cloakroom revealed his interests. She brought down poets, he brought down pheasants. In the gunroom there were a score of guns, game-baskets, etc. I learned he had a grouse shoot in Scotland.

That afternoon I was taken to a Conservative Garden Fête in the grounds of a large mansion. It poured with rain so we were all packed in a marquee where we listened to an ex-Cabinet Minister denounce Lloyd George as "A rat that gnaws away the bottom of the ship of State". This language was mild compared with that used by Lloyd George in his People's Budget period when he had attacked the House of Lords with inspired scurrility. The speaker received frequent applause when, referring to the Ulster crisis blowing up over Home Rule for Ireland, he avowed, "Ulster will fight and Ulster will be right!" After that there was tea and cakes. It was plain that the County had turned out in force. These were all first-class passengers on the ship of State. They could none of them foresee that this 'rat', within three years, was going to save the ship from foundering, and become the national hero. After dinner, we again spent an evening reading poetry. I had only recently discovered Browning and had worked my way through *The Ring and the Book*. I was delighted to find my hostess was a Browning addict. My host was invisible behind his newspapers.

On Sunday morning we went to church. Neighbours came in for tea, among them a very beautiful girl with snow-white hair and a wonderful complexion. She looked as if she had just come in out of a cold wind, she glowed so rosily. I found she was not English, though she spoke the language beautifully. She was twenty-two, the daughter of a Swedish banker, visiting her English fiancé's parents. Her hair was plaited just as I had seen it on Marguerite in *Faust*. At any moment I should not have been surprised to hear her bursting into the Jewel Song. There was a Bechstein Grand piano and my hostess asked me if I would play something as on the previous evening. I played some Debussy and Chopin. My stock rose considerably with my host. He told me that a former partner's son had studied with Busoni in Berlin. "He must be very good, then," I remarked.

"Nobody knows," replied my host. "Nobody has ever heard him, he always says he's too nervous to play in public. Some of us think it's just an excuse to keep out of the family business and lead a Bohemian life. Very odd, and very expensive," said my host, sadly.

And so Monday morning came. Before I was driven to the station I was given a large bouquet of roses for my mother. It had been a kind of dream, rather like the life I had seen in the cinema, on one of those houseboats in the Vale of Kashmir. Here it was, a beautiful country house, floating serenely through life, with a butler, three parlour maids, a cook, a chauffeur and two gardeners, embalming two elderly kindly persons, one interested in poetry, one in shooting. Back home, I exchanged a few letters with my hostess. Then the curtain of a world war descended. Looking back, I now realise that I experienced in that strange episode a manner of life, gracious, tranquil, deceptively secure, that was soon to vanish in a discordant world.

It was in the Poetry Bookshop that I met in 1917 another extraordinary person. I found myself in lively conversation with a young man of about my own age. He was good-looking, tall, slim and intense. There was something febrile about him, together with a touch of exhibitionism, so that I was not surprised to learn that he had been shell-shocked in France. He was at Trinity College, Oxford, when the war broke out, got a commission in the Royal Field Artillery and within a few weeks of front line service had suffered shell-shock in the autumn of 1915. After five months in hospital he had been invalided out of the service. I learned all this later. During our talk he mentioned his friends, Robert Graves, and Siegfried Sassoon who had recently come into the limelight as young men of promise in England's nest of singing birds. It is remarkable how many notable poets the First World War produced, Rupert Brooke, Francis Ledwidge, Julian Grenfell, Wilfrid Owen, Robert Graves, Siegfried Sassoon, Charles Sorley, Edmund Blunden, etc. The Second World War did not produce a couple of any note, perhaps because a repetition of horror had no inspiring element. The youth of the Second War found it a 'bloody bore' brought on by incompetent politicians. They knew that the landscape of England was dotted with War Memorials—'Their name liveth for evermore' now forgotten in a new cataclysm. "*Dulce et decorum est pro patria mori* once, but not over and over again, old boy!" said a friend of mine with an arm missing. "What price that war to end war!" The bitterness of disillusionment had not eaten into the consciousness of the young in 1914. They had, at the beginning, the spirit of a crusade, but little by little the Sassoons and the Graveses began to have misgivings.

When I asked the vivacious youth in the bookshop his name and what he had written he gave me an aggrieved stare. "I'm Robert Nichols. I'm considered the soldier-poet of the war. Haven't you read *Ardours and Endurances*?" I had not but I was aware of the ecstatic acclaim it had received from the critics. Eddie Marsh had 'pushed' his book. The feline Edmund Gosse, whose claws were feared, had given it his blessing. He had called Ezra Pound 'A preposterous American poetaster and provincial charlatan', Nichols he found 'violent, mercurial and excessive but most attractive in his flaming zeal and pale vehemence'. Gosse gave his work unstinted praise and compared him with Keats and Shelley, and saw in him a physical resemblance to the latter. Nichols was also taken up by Lady Colefax, a powerful patroness of letters. She was a celebrity-snob with a quick eye and dauntless enterprise. One day, observing the crowd eating and drinking at her reception, she said to Arnold Bennett, as they left the room, "Look how they've got their feet in the trough!" Nichols' portrait was drawn by Rothenstein and Augustus John. Eddie Marsh put him in the next volume of *Georgian Poetry*. His book had made him one of the foremost soldier-poets of the year; he appeared to have passed the portal to immortality.

An emotional and histrionic reader of his own verses, Nichols was much in demand in the West End. On his invitation I went to one of these recitals. Unlike most poets he read his poems well. I can still see and hear him reciting his tribute to the British soldier—

> Was there love once? I have forgotten her.
> Was there grief once? Grief yet is mine . . .
> O loved, living, dying, heroic soldier,
> All, all, my joy, my grief, my love, are thine!

Young, handsome, romantic, if he erred it was in being too histrionic, but in these days we were all keyed up. At this reading, in a large drawing-room in Eaton Square, he was fêted afterwards by all the fashionable ladies. Greater men have been undermined by adulation. I did not see Nichols again until our paths crossed in a singular fashion. He was sent on a lecture tour of the U.S.A., sponsored by the British Ministry of Information. When I arrived in New York in

January, 1920, I found he had given offence and was adversely criticised. A rapid talker, volatile, he had cultivated the romantic attitude and become the *enfant gâté* of the wealthy 'culture vultures' whom he often treated with erratic rudeness. He was basically unhappy and nervous.

The Establishment in England had in its gift nominations to Professorships of English in foreign universities. Gosse sponsored Nichols and in 1921 he occupied the Lafcadio Chair of English at Tokio University. In 1924 he went to Hollywood as an adviser to Douglas Fairbanks. He collaborated in a play that had a modest success.

Fame is often a treacherous jade. She throws her searchlight on a person fitfully and then switches to another, leaving the discarded favourite to darkness. This was the fate of Robert Nichols. The years were not kind to him. A second book of verse fell dead. "He is self-centred and *vaniteux*," wrote Wilfrid Owen. One evening in 1926, recorded Arnold Bennett in his Journal, returning to his house, he found "Robert Nichols, the poet, wearing his opal ring, waiting downstairs, full of himself. I was dying to sleep but I had to listen to him. He had got in through a window." His marriage came to shipwreck. He grew increasingly neurotic and bitter. He wandered about from country to country. He had never been disciplined by necessity. On his death, aged only fifty in 1944, he left an inherited fortune of £27,000. Despite temperamental storms he could inspire devotion. A friend of mine who attended him in his last years spoke of him with affection, and a letter he wrote to her a year before his death, on the loss of her son in the Second World War, was such as only could emanate from a sensitive spirit. Robert Nichols is another ghost that walks for me in Devonshire Street.

IV

In those war years, 1914–1918, there was a touch of delirium in the London scene. The capital was crammed with officers and men on leave. The air menace was negligible and the night life of London was never gayer. In 1918 the submarine threat had been conquered. In the Ministry we saw the appalling tonnage losses diminish with the institution of convoys. There was a stalemate on the Western Front but the entry of the American troops in growing numbers began to tilt the balance. In September, 1918, the Diaghilev Ballet reappeared and delighted London, reviving memories of earlier triumphs at Drury Lane when Nijinsky had danced in *L'Après-Midi d'un Faune*. The company performed to packed houses and received a great ovation. It was like the return of the gods from Parnassus.

There had appeared one August day in my lodgings in Upper George Street a dark squirrel-quick creature, a member of the ballet which had just arrived, after some adventures, from Barcelona, where it had known lean times. I occupied a ground-floor back room. My landlady slept in the basement. Reading in bed late at night I heard the doorbell ring twice. I got up and went to the door. A young woman stood there in the dim light, wrapped in a camelhair coat. Hatless, she had large eyes, her black hair pulled tightly over her small head. She spoke in a husky voice with an accent. At first I could not understand what she said, then I learned she was lodging in the house and had forgotten her key. I let her in and watched her go up the stairs. She thanked me with a flashing smile. She was very lithe and young. I went back to my room somewhat unsettled by this vision out of the night. An extraordinary young woman, foreign obviously. A French actress?

In the morning the mystery was solved. My dark, frail little Indian landlady was a kind soul. The front sitting-room had no tenant. There was a communicating double door between it and my bedroom. She put my breakfst in the sitting-room, and we often chatted as I poured the tea. I never learned how she came to be keeping a rooming-house in London, whether the furniture in it was hers, or rented, whether she was the landlady or the housekeeper. She flitted about in her mauve sari, a woman of about fifty, born in Jaipur. Her connections were astonishing. She was a friend of the Indian poet, a Nobel Prize winner, Rabindranath Tagore, then enjoying a great vogue, and had a large autographed photograph of the handsome, bearded old poet. One day a Rolls-Royce car stood in front of the door, with a pair of chauffeurs. A Maharajah was calling on my landlady.

When she brought me my breakfast the next morning I asked about the girl I had let in overnight. It seemed she was Polish, with an Indian mother. "My cousin in Warsaw sent her to me. She is here with the Russian Ballet." Her name was Zadia. Could I see her again, in daylight, I asked? My landlady smiled. Well, she would try to arrange it. And that was how I came to know her and her friends, members of the Diaghilev Ballet. It was a new door that opened on to an astonishing world.

The great autocrat Diaghilev had got together a new company. The war had somewhat shattered the earlier ballet, making grave inroads on his famous dancers. But somehow he had now collected Lopokova, Tchernicheva, Woidzikovsky, rubbery little Idzikovsky with his impish face and Leonide Massine, etc. When I began to meet Zadia's friends, in and out of the rehearsal and dressing-rooms, I soon made a discovery. Her companions were not all Russian, despite appearances and names. Diaghilev had had to cast his net wide to recruit a full company, and many of its members proved to be English under their disguises. They were given Russian names, and somehow they contrived to look Russian after Maestro Cecchetti had dragooned and transformed them. They even affected broken accents. Diaghilev, in time, converted an Irish girl into Ninette de Valois, Alice Marks into Alicia Markova, Vera Clark into Vera Savina, Doreen Miller into Mlle. Pavlovski, Laura Wilson into Mlle. Olkhina, and an Irish boy, Patrick Kay, into Patrikeyev (later Anton Dolin). They were all destined to fame. I had a shock when one day I learned that the entrancing little Mlle. Butsova was not only not Russian but was English and, moreover, born in Nottingham where her father was in business!

I soon became aware of the dominant dancer, the boy who had taken Nijinsky's place as the *premier danseur*. Diaghilev had first seen Leonide Miassine (he dropped an 'i' in his name later) in Moscow in 1913. A youth of seventeen, very handsome, he was playing small character parts and dancing in the *ensembles* at the Bolshoi Theatre. Diaghilev was looking for someone to play the title role in *La Légende de Joseph*, then being composed, Nijinsky having become more and more intractable. With his unfailing flair Diaghilev took the unknown youth in hand. In a short time Massine had made such progress as a dancer under the instruction of Fokine and Cecchetti that he was cast for star roles. He was soon to reveal another talent, for he proved to be a choreographer of genius, under Diaghilev's inspiration.

Fascinated, I watched Massine, slender, very boyish and volatile, at rehearsals and performances. I got to know him and we became friends. He was a somewhat shy person for all his 'attack' on the stage. With his lustrous eyes and black hair he was more southern Italian than Russian, but there were moments when he looked exactly like some Byzantine mosaic portrait found on the walls at Monreale, Ravenna, or Constantinople. He had a splendid though small physique and moved with the grace of a panther. He had not Nijinsky's *elevation* or *mystique* but he was a presence the moment he came out from the wings. He had created a sensation when he first appeared at the Paris Opera House in 1914 in *La Légende de Joseph* though the ballet itself did not appeal greatly to the French, the audience finding the music of Richard Strauss, who had conducted, too bizarre. In London Massine had a great triumph with this ballet which was vociferously received. There came in time from his fertile brain, *The Midnight Sun*, *Las Meninas*, *The Good Humoured Ladies*, *Russian Tales*, and *Parade*, all in three brief years since his discovery.

The new season opened at the Coliseum on September 5th, 1918. Diaghilev was not altogether happy for he had to become part of a vaudeville programme but necessity drove him to accept. London was still under a blackout. At one moment it looked as if the company would not arrive at all. Clemenceau, angry with the Russians over the Treaty of Brest-Litovsk, and their withdrawal from the war, would not give the company transit visas to enable it to journey from Barcelona to London. Happily, King Alfonso, always a good friend of the Ballet, came to the rescue. He instructed his Ambassador in Paris to put pressure on the French Government and the visas were issued. All this had caused a postponement of the opening date. At last the curtain went up at the Coliseum on *The Good Humoured Ladies*, another production of Massine's. It had had a warm reception in Rome, and Paris was enchanted by it. Diaghilev was a little nervous about London. Lopokova, Tchernicheva, Idzikovsky, Woidzikovsky and Massine danced in it. It brought the house down. Unhappily I did not see it. I had only recently met Zadia who was to turn me into a balletomane. But I was soon initiated. It was she who got me into the rehearsals, introduced me to her friends, took me to dingy lodgings where the company lived, in very different style from Diaghilev and some of the principals who lived at the Savoy. She knew the cafés they frequented. It was she who introduced me to Geoffrey Whitworth, of Chatto and Windus, the publishers—"for, since you are an author you must know publishers!" In turn Whitworth took me into Cyril Beaumont's fascinating shop in the Charing Cross Road, which contained a very wide range of books on the Ballet, including his own. It was in his shop that I met Serge Grigoriev, the *régisseur*, Diaghilev's obedient and unfailing friend until the latter's death.

The more I saw of the inside of the Ballet the more I marvelled. If the theatre is illusion, the ballet is the great illusion of illusions. How is it possible, I asked myself again and again, standing in chaos, with everything at sixes and sevens, that such perfection of form, dancing, scenery and music could emerge from it, an alchemy of enchantment. There were moments when I thought I would like to be a member of the company. It would have been a hopeless ambition, I was too late and too tall; above all I was not tough enough, for how tough you had to be! Under the limes it was all flimsy and thistle-down fancy, but by day, behind the scenes, one had to be constituted of wire and whipcord to endure onslaughts of nerves, crises and merciless rehearsal to the verge of physical collapse. Economically considered, the whole thing was nonsense. The girls drew a salary of four pounds a week. From this they had to provide their own shoes and tights. The terms of their contract were punitively rigorous. If a member of the company broke them he was subject to a fine of £25, as in reverse was the Company. As a stipulation this was derisive for the reason that neither of the contracting parties ever had £25 to spare! There were desperate periods when Diaghilev, wildly extravagant in production, was on the verge of bankruptcy and the dancers often went unpaid for long stretches but hung on hopefully. When Diaghilev arrived in London in September, 1918, to open the Coliseum season, he was at the last gasp—except that with him the last gasp was never the last since he was such a magician in the coils of adverse fate. His scanty wardrobe was painfully shabby, the *grand seigneur*, the born aristocrat, was almost out-at-elbows. The fortunes of the Diaghilev Ballet went up and down like a barometer in a typhoon. Only sheer admiration and faith in the Wizard held the desperate assembly of genius and youth together.

To compensate for this gamble with fortune there was always plenty of excitement, breath-taking experiments and triumphs, hair-raising discords and jealousies. Who could believe, sitting in front of the curtain on an opening night, how near to shipwreck from various causes was the spectacle, so smooth, so finely harmonised in all its aspects of music, décor and movement! Sometimes up to the very verge of production the chaos seemed insuperable, then, suddenly, like a jigsaw puzzle, the whole thing resolved itself into a perfect pattern.

The economics of all this were as fragile as an eggshell. There was no money in it for anyone, save a very small astute or lucky percentage of the cast. When Diaghilev died there was not enough money to pay his hotel bill. There was little permanence in the profession. The life of even a *première danseuse* was about as insecure and brief as that of a pugilist. Indeed the simile of the ring was often in my mind as I watched them. It is a profession founded solely on youth, strength and beauty. For most, at forty, their career is ended. What becomes of all these bright, volatile creatures—*où sont les danseurs d'antan*? Their speed and beauty diminished, they cannot go to stud for high prices like racehorses. Forty hours after its founder's death the whole Russian Ballet was not worth purchasing. As a going concern its basis, Diaghilev, had gone. A lucky few got harassing jobs as producers at foreign opera houses; some started dancing schools, often of brief existence. There were sporadic attempts to revive the Russian Ballet.

All this was known, but there was never a lack of eager young recruits, and never a backward look. Bright and brief butterflies of youth's summer, what gaiety, what courage they revealed, and what enormous fun amid all the nerve-racking anxieties they had! Little of all this is known to the audience when the last bars of the overture fade in the darkened house and the curtain slowly rises on the enchanted terrain of the ballet.

Behind that curtain, before it rises, there is another world of enchantment, of a very different order, the work of a conglomeration of gifted men and women. What a sorcerer Diaghilev was! Can there again be such a massing of genius as he conjured up from the worlds of art and music? The very names are a pageant written into the history of the era: Nijinsky, Pavlova, Karsavina, Lopokova, Nijinska, Massine, Braque, Picasso, Bakst, Cocteau, Matisse, Stravinsky, Poulenc, Ravel, De Falla, Respighi, Prokofieff, Strauss, Beecham, Ansermet, Monteux; they are trumpets sounding in that grand march-past of twenty years marshalled by the Russian wizard. And how bold in experiment he was. Answering some adverse criticisms of his innovations, he wrote to *The Times*—"For twenty-five years I have endeavoured to found a new Movement in the theatre. Society will have to recognise that my experiments, which appear dangerous to-day, become indispensable to-morrow."

For me, the scenes behind the curtain were no less exciting than those on which it rose. I have used the simile of the boxing ring. A ballerina descended in her white tutu and stood withdrawn in the wings. Around her were others, fair youths and maidens, in groups like those offered to the devouring Minotaur, or thronging the plain of Troy. Here were Paris, Achilles, Hector, Helen, Andromache. Restive, they danced, stopped, danced, limbering-up like the boxer in his corner of the ring. There was even the tray of resin in which they rubbed their shoes against slipping. This is a business of muscle, sweat and speed, for all the grace that masks the effort. When the ballerina flies off stage into the wings, to a volley of applause, a dresser goes forward with gown and powder puff to mop up the sweat beaded on the make-up of the panting performer. Quick changes have to be made in costume and make-up. Those minutes of the interval that seem so long to the audience involve rapid transformation. There was an astonishing scene after *Cléopâtre* had been performed. A posse of Egyptian youths of the *corps de ballet* rushed into a room where tubs of steaming water awaited them. In a trice they were all naked in it, washing the bronze off their lithe limbs, in readiness for the next ballet. It was like Michelangelo's cartoon of the *Battle of Cascina*, where the naked young soldiers, summoned by the trumpet, hastily scramble from the water to put on their accoutrement. The dressing-rooms, those of the principals apart, were miserably inadequate to the physical needs of the dancers. There was a mêlée of bodies desperately wriggling out of tight costumes gummy with perspiration. The smells of powder, eau-de-cologne and grease-paint, mingled with body odours, before the glare of make-up tables, while, faintly off, strains of the orchestra came from the auditorium. The stage hands rapidly wheeled their properties into place, the lights went on and off, the dancers assembled, casual yet intense, Grigoriev, the *régisseur*, stood by the prompt corner, his eye on everything. There was a woman doing a brief sketch. It was Laura Knight, Diaghilev's friend, who had the run of the house. Some ballerinas had her sketches of them proudly displayed against their mirrors. In a corridor Diaghilev passed me coming from a dressing-room, going back to his box. I only spoke with him a few times, introduced by Massine. I must have been a nameless face, unlike the young Guards officer, one of the Sitwells, a trio much talked about just then, in whose company, as in that of Cyril Beaumont, Diaghilev seemed to find pleasure. But I came to know Lopokova, after her first appearance in London which she conquered with her airy, fairy grace and élan, and Woidzikovsky, Idzikovsky, and, on her return from Russia, Karsavina the unsurpassable, and above all Massine, foremost in that galaxy of youth.

I had missed the opening performances at the Coliseum on September 5th, 1918, but saw *The Good Humoured Ladies*, inspired by Goldoni's comedy and set to the music of Scarlatti, *Cléopâtre*, and other ballets before I left for France. Early in 1919 I was home to witness a series of fresh delights, *Petrushka*, *Les Sylphides*, etc.

Massine was now engrossed with *La Boutique Fantasque*, with Rossini's music. The first performance took place at The Alhambra on June 5th and was an overwhelming success, with Lopokova and Massine receiving a tremendous ovation as the can-can dancers.*

Diaghilev now felt encouraged to produce, on July 22nd, after long preparation, Massine's *The Three Cornered Hat*. The music was by De Falla who came to London to conduct it. I watched him at rehearsals with singular interest. Dark, quiet in manner, courteous to all, his playing of his own score on the piano revealed a consummate pianist. One day I introduced him to Yvonne Arnaud. I had it in mind to arrange a benefit concert for ex-ballet dancers, at which De Falla and Arnaud would play piano duets but before I could do this de Falla had to leave England.

In 1950, while visiting Granada, I was taken to see his former home. It had a long terraced garden overlooking the great plain and the snowy Sierra Nevada. In the grounds there was a memorial bust to the composer. I was told that he never dined before two a.m., and never went to bed—he slept in a chair. He would have died in his beloved Granada retreat but he was driven to desperation by a neighbour who played gramophone records. So music drove out music. He went to Argentina and died there in 1946, aged seventy. He had spent the last thirty years of his life making an exhaustive study of Spanish folk music.

How different was a fellow Spaniard in that production, Picasso. He was chunky, assertive, with a square head and a strong face with a lock of hair falling over his brow. He had a possessive air with the Russian girls; after all, he had married a Russian dancer. His design for the new ballet created a sensation, especially the drop curtain which showed a group of Spaniards in an arena box watching a bull-fight.

There were incessant rumours concerning the preparation of this ballet, true and untrue. At one moment it looked as if it would not be produced. Picasso had bellowed, Diaghilev had stormed, Massine,

* In 1934 Moira Shearer, aged eight, saw *La Boutique Fantasque* at Covent Garden, in de Basil's Ballets Russes. Massine danced the can-can in it. It was the same role in which he had appeared in the original production at the Alhambra Theatre in 1919, with Lopokova. He danced the same part again in this ballet in 1947, this time with Moira Shearer as his partner! In December, 1967, I once again watched him rehearse this ballet in the Opera House in Rome, just as forty-eight years earlier I had watched him rehearse it at the Alhambra, the choreographer on each occasion.

the choreographer and *premier danseur*, had walked out—all over a pair of breeches! The ballet was off, said Zadia, but the next day the ballet was on. To keep the eighteenth-century décor Picasso had given Massine knee-breeches. But Spaniards always danced the *farruca*, an Andalusian folk dance, wearing long trousers. Diaghilev insisted on long trousers. Picasso insisted on knee-breeches. Finally they compromised, to Massine's anger, with him wearing long trousers in the first half and changing to knee-breeches in the second. Very soon it became obvious that *The Three Cornered Hat* would be a great success, with De Falla composing the music, Picasso creating the décor, Massine producing, after intensive study in Spain of the Spanish technique, and dancing with Karsavina.

There was a note of tragedy connected with this production. Diaghilev had discovered in Madrid a young Spaniard, Felix Fernandez, whose brilliant dancing suggested his suitability for roles in the Spanish ballets Diaghilev was planning. He brought the young man to London. Unfortunately, though a brilliant solo dancer, Fernandez was unable to adapt himself to ballet ensemble. This may have preyed on his mind. One day the Company was stunned by the news that Fernandez had been arrested after dancing before the altar of St. Martin's-in-the-Fields and smashing its windows. He was found to be hopelessly insane and taken to an asylum at Epsom where he died twenty-two years later.

There was another loss to this ballet. A bereavement called De Falla back to Spain and he was unable to conduct his score. The Swiss conductor, Ansermet, took over.

I was present at the Alhambra for the first performance of *The Three Cornered Hat* on the unforgettable night of July 22nd, 1919. Massine danced the Miller, with Karsavina as his wife, and Woidzikovsky as the Corregidor. London had never seen and most probably will never see again such a production, with these dancers at the peak of their form. The house thundered, the curtain rose and fell while Karsavina and Massine stood there, holding a large cake wreathed in flowers.

After the performance there were jubilant parties that went on until the early hours of the morning. Diaghilev hated parties, birthdays, anniversaries. He disappeared, despite Lady Cunard's determination to take him off to her own party. That heady night we went to a succession of celebrations. The last was at The Albany, in the apartment of a well-known art critic, P. G. Konody. It was the first

An Impression of Karsavina as the Miller's Wife in *The Three Cornered Hat*. By Dame Laura Knight, R.A.

time I was in that withdrawn Piccadilly cloister, the haunt of Byron, Macaulay and Gladstone. When we emerged into the street dawn was breaking. There was an old hansom-cab coming down Piccadilly which I summoned and in it I took Zadia and her companion home, after which I went on to my new lodgings in Tavistock Square. As I drew down the blind of my room the birds were chirping in the garden below. Oh Youth! Youth! Oh lovely old London in 1919, with a ghastly war finished! It was the period when young Edward, Prince of Wales, had conquered the world with his devastating charm, when the years to come were full of promise.

V

Massine had other triumphs. For six years, until his break with Diaghilev in 1921, he was to reign supreme with eight ballets to his credit—*The Midnight Sun*, *Las Meninas*, *Parade*, *Children's Tales*, *The Good Humoured Ladies*, *La Boutique Fantasque*, *Pulcinella*, and *The Three Cornered Hat*. In fourteen years he was the choreographer of sixteen successful ballets. He was twenty-two at the time of our meeting, famous since his début at eighteen in Paris. I have lived to see him dance with undiminished verve, aged fifty-two, in the role of the crazed cobbler in *The Red Shoes*, with Moira Shearer for partner. I watched its genesis in Monte Carlo, a natural ballet setting. I have seen him produce ballets with unfailing touch in New York, Vienna, Paris, Munich and Rome. When in 1962 he staged a splendid revival of *The Good Humoured Ladies* at Covent Garden *The Times* critic abused it. It is too often a habit of a *nouvelle école* critic to be smart at the expense of the established master. I recalled how, on the production of *Les Noces*, in 1926, the Press was so hostile, calling Diaghilev a charlatan, despite its warm reception at His Majesty's Theatre, that H. G. Wells wrote a protest "against this conspiracy of wilful stupidity that may succeed in driving it out of the programme". I thought, in turn that *The Times* criticism, with its sneer, was an outrage, and wrote and said so. From Massine's retreat in Neuilly-sur-Seine came a postcard:

> To have real friends in life is very rare. It is dear to me, appreciation such as yours. I have revived *The Good Humoured Ladies* for a few persons like you. The generosity and the warmth of your words

have greatly comforted me . . . As for the critics, I do not attach much importance to their ravings and their attitude to Diaghilev by whose inspiration this work was created.

When in 1964 Massine asked me to write a preface to his memoirs, I declined. I was not insensible to the compliment but who was I to stand between him and his public? Only one man could have done this appropriately, and he was dead—Diaghilev. However, in Rome with Massine three years later, I was happy to work with him on his autobiography, *My Life in Ballet.*

Looking back fifty years, what a strange and rewarding sequence that was, opening the door of my London lodgings at two a.m. to an unknown girl who, in turn, opened a magic door for me! And as I watched that night in July, 1919, Karsavina, the Miller's wife, move out from the wings, sheer poetry of movement dissolved in music, I would not have believed, had it been prophesied, that twenty years later a son of hers would be in a play of mine, she having married in St. Petersburg an English diplomat, gifted as a writer and an artist, and of the line of squires of Clifton, Nottingham. They both came to Liverpool to see their son make his stage début.

The tremendous prestige of the Diaghilev Ballet has not faded in fifty years. Time has immortalised the name of its creator.* Often I observed him intently, coming and going at rehearsals, in the wings, or sitting in his box, watching closely, a withdrawn and wordless Colossus. A Russian aristocrat, with a touch of the *grand seigneur*, a soft, pleasing voice, stocky, square-headed, there was a sinister touch in his tastes and habits. He was as imperious as a Sultan, easily offended, and quick in reaction, capricious in his favours and stubborn in his demands. He loved physical beauty and youth, and he moved with a small court of devoted and gifted young men in the background, always a little fearful of the Wizard. Intimacy was not in his gift, but in a few he evoked deep loyalty, and they became slaves to his genius. He had immense courage and faced one disaster after another from which somehow he always emerged. His finances were so chaotic, his extravagances so ungoverned, that often the company went unpaid and hung together out of sheer faith in his genius. After Massine left him in 1921 he launched a wildly expensive version of *The Sleeping Princess* with music by Stravinsky, choreography by

* The French, with infallible flair, have named the space behind the Paris Opera House *Place Diaghilev.*

Bakst. "Look at it," he said, "this is the last relic of the great days of St. Petersburg." Artistically it was a great success, financially a failure, and Stoll of the Alhambra sequestrated the scenery for debts, as had happened before. Nevertheless, like the phoenix, Diaghilev rose from the ashes and went on to fresh conquests, and fresh crises.

I last saw him in July, 1929. The season closed triumphantly, he having presented *The Ball, Le Sacre du Printemps, The Prodigal Son* and *Swan Lake.* It was rumoured that he was ill. He left London and went first to Munich and Salzburg and then on to his beloved Venice, to the Lido. On the morning of August 19th I was walking down the acacia-green avenue that leads from the ferry to the Lido shore when I met the assistant manager of the Grand Hotel des Bains. He stunned me with the news that Diaghilev had died early that morning, having been unconscious for twelve hours. He was fifty-seven. He had been ill in London with a septic stomach ulcer and the doctors had ordered him to rest when the Ballet Season ended. But instead of going at once to his favourite Lido—*Venise Inspiratrice constante de nos apaisements*—he insisted on going to Bayreuth where he wished the seventeen-year-old composer-pianist, Igor Markovitch, his latest protégé, to hear *Tristan and Isolde.* From Bayreuth, suffering, he went to Venice. He had with him there two youths, Serge Lifar and Boris Kochno; one his *premier danseur*, successor to Nijinsky and Massine; the other, his choreographer. Desperately ill, he sent a wire to Misia Sert in Paris, an adventurous *mondaine*, wife of José-Maria Sert, the artist, an old friend.

Diaghilev died penniless. There had been a lamentable scene in his last conscious hours. A priest had been sent for. When he learned that the dying man was Russian he refused to give the last unction to a member of the Greek Orthodox Church. Under violent protest from Misia Sert, now arrived, he consented to give Diaghilev a brief absolution. Why a Greek Orthodox priest was not sent for no one could explain. My informant told me, as we stood in the avenue with all the gay tourists streaming towards the beach, that Lifar and Kochno were now in the death chamber, in a state of hysteria. There was no money to meet the bills, no one seemed to know who belonged to the dead man, who would pay for the funeral. The company was dispersed on holiday. What was to be done? Who would take charge? To me the answer seemed obvious—the City of Venice, of course. It had once given Robert Browning a state funeral down the Grand Canal on the way to Westminster Abbey. Here was an opportunity for a magnificent spectacle, a superb setting in a superb city: they could bury a great European figure like a Doge.

As it transpired his friends came to the rescue. Misia Sert got Baroness Catherine d'Erlanger to cash her cheque, and another friend who had just departed on the Duke of Westminster's yacht insisted, having a presentiment, on the astonished Duke returning to Venice and landing her there. She, too, subscribed towards the funeral. A service was held in the Greek Church of San Giorgio, with its leaning campanile and Carpaccio paintings. It was performed with all the rich ceremony of the Greek Orthodox rite by a handsome bearded archimandrite. The coffin was carried to the *riva* where awaited a stately gilded barge with a gold canopy, a mass of wreaths, and four sashed gondoliers in white. The priest led the procession standing in the front gondola with acolytes holding a great crucifix. The mourners followed in black gondolas. There was a small contingent of the English colony. The procession of boats made its way down the canal and across the lagoon to the island cemetery of San Michele, where Diaghilev now rests amid the cypresses but is still a living legend. He would have approved of the décor of that final curtain. Nor is he forgotten; each year, on the anniversary of his death, fresh flowers are heaped on his grave.

What is singular in this story is that Venice took no notice of his passing. The City sent no representative, and the local newspaper, *Il Gazzettino*, noted the event in only a brief, cool paragraph.

VI

From 1917 on, after coming to London, I lived a life of great pressure, carried onwards by the intoxication of youth ever thrusting forward to new adventures. By day I was a civil servant, by night I was a London correspondent, doing interviews, art, music, dramatic criticism and book reviews. Sandwiched in with this was my own personal work. I came to be more and more in demand for lectures, for speaking at public dinners. In those sixteen months in London, in addition to my administrative duties at the Ministry I wrote and published a novel, three books of verse and one of prose. I was young and intensely ambitious, enjoying the struggle to keep my head above water and make a brave show. I received £156 as Burton Chadwick's assistant, £156 a year as London correspondent of my paper. To this I added another £150 a year with my writing. At twenty-five I was earning some £450 p.a. with income tax almost negligible. I vowed I would save a third of my income towards that goal of £10,000 capital I had set for thirty-five. With £150 put aside annually this left me with some £300 a year on which to live and from this I sent to my mother £52 a year, leaving me under £5 a week. My room cost eighteen shillings. I could have got one for twelve shillings but not with such a good address. I succumbed to the snobbism of the right address. Perhaps it was not as good as I thought. I was not yet aware of the prestige of Chelsea and of the Royal Borough of Kensington, or that it was thought better in those days to be south than north. Rent paid, I had £3 10*s*. a week for food, clothes, fares, and amusements. I got lunch for one and ninepence in a restaurant at the side of Charing Cross Station (Villiers Street had Leicestershire connotations for me). Dinner at the Royal Automobile Club cost three and six, my breakfast a shilling, a total of about £2 a week for food, but I began to be asked out. The saving of food-cost, from a weekend in the country, paid for the fare and the servants' tips. I seldom took a taxi—the meter made me apprehensive, something I could not shake off until well past middle-age. My big expense was for clothes, shoes and shirts. I exercised little economy there, being something of a dress snob and I felt it was a good investment. I got my suits at Scholte, my shirts in Jermyn Street, my waistcoats in the Burlington Arcade. I was elated when I heard someone had said that I was one of the best-dressed young men in London. If they only knew of the cost of that effort! I pressed my suits, and cleaned my shoes, adept from my father's training.* I could give tips to my paragon, Major Brodie. Perhaps I overdid it at times; he did not think it necessary for a very young man to wear gloves, and once, when I was being taken in a taxi by him to Hurlingham, wearing a straw 'boater' with a gay ribbon, he looked at me critically and said, "I feel as if I am riding with the young Beau Brummell."

It was all a very tight squeeze, since I always paid cash down. I fought against getting into a milieu I could not afford and I exercised an iron will over setting aside a third of my income. I felt the pinch when it came to taking out a girl friend. Fortunately Zadia, a bohemian, was not fussy and would cheerfully eat in a chophouse or at a Lyons Corner House. But her eating hours were peculiar. An old beau who used to take out one of her colleagues said to me—"My boy, ballerinas are frustrating creatures. They must not eat before dancing.

* See *The Growing Boy*, Ch. I, III.

After dancing, they are hungry and tired. They eat a large meal and go to sleep on you."

My immediate ambition was set at earning a £1,000 a year. Only very successful authors made that, and such a sum was far over the horizon for me but I stepped resolutely towards it. Then, miraculously, it came. I was ill in bed from overwork when I received a telephone call from my London editor. A week earlier I had collapsed after speaking at a meeting of the To-Day Club at the Caxton Hall. I fainted in the anteroom and was taken home by Holbrook Jackson, my chairman. It was all my own fault. My day was too strenuous. I rose at six, wrote from seven to eight, went to the Ministry at nine, and at six p.m. was in Fleet Street for instructions, tickets, books, etc. If I had theatre reviews I rushed down to Fleet Street after the show to get my copy in for the morning edition. I often read past midnight the books I had to review. Foolishly I economised on food. That one and ninepenny lunch was really not enough. The doctor found nothing seriously wrong. My battery was run down. I must stay in bed a week. My landlady was an angel and brought me meals. Zadia, always rehearsing, rushed in with fruit and flowers. It was useless to fall in love with her for one could have no chance with a water-sprite. Moreover, I could not compete with all the young officers who came and went in cars or taxis, with money in their pockets to burn. I discovered there was a particular boy, a Georgian, with the head of a Crusader, in the corps-de-ballet. "I loff you verih mooch!" she said to me alluringly but I knew it was part of her make-up, and would vanish as easily.

I had been in bed seven days when the telephone call came from my London editor. Was I better? There was something urgent he wanted to talk to me about as soon as I could call. I said that I would come that evening. I dressed and indulged in a taxi. I was both hopeful and apprehensive. They seemed very pleased with my work but I detected a change in the voice of my taciturn London editor. When I got to the office the news was astonishing. Most of the London newspapers had their own special correspondents on the Western Front. Their articles were syndicated for the provincial Press, which had grown restive. It now asked for its own correspondent. The Newspaper Society gained its point with the authorities. It was considering me for the post. The salary would be £1,000, a year, all found. I would be insured for £5,000. There was nothing definite yet but I was the favourite nominee. I accepted the proposition at once. I thought of Winston Churchill.

He was much in my mind these days. A number of persons had told me that I was like him when he was my age, a bit of flattery that I swallowed though I was much taller in stature and smaller in achievement. When at my age he was appointed war correspondent in South Africa for *The Morning Post*, his salary was fixed at £3,000 a year and all expenses paid. But he was already a public character with fighting in Cuba and the Sudan behind him. Moreover, he carried the prestige of the Marlborough line, born at Blenheim Palace, of a father, Lord Randolph, who had been the correspondent of a London newspaper in South East Africa in 1892. So I felt satisfied to receive a third of Churchill's salary.

In a week my appointment was confirmed. I said goodbye to my colleagues at the Ministry. I called on Eddie Marsh, half hoping that he might take me in to see Churchill but his chief was out. I made a brief visit to Nottingham to say farewell to my mother and my good friend William Kiddier. He had just suffered a paralysing blow with the death in action of his only son. The weight of his business now fell upon him, and he had little time for his painting. I was also unhappy about the situation of my mother. At sixty-three she was without a home of her own, living in a small bed-sitting-room in a grey street. As it turned out it had been a mistake to sell up the home and have her move to Liverpool to join me for only a few months. She uttered no word of complaint, stoic by nature, but confessed that she had been to look covetously at the little house in Grove Villas to which we had removed after the sudden death of my father. What seemed to worry her most was sharing a kitchen. It was now almost impossible to find a house: the war had put them at a premium. I insisted on increasing my mother's allowance, making it thirty shillings a week, and urged her to find a little house. "Don't worry, I'll be all right," she said. I returned to London unhappy at all this. I told her about the insurance on my life and that it would come to her if anything happened to me.

VII

I was given sixty pounds for uniform and kit, on which Harry Brodie advised me. I bought an officer's tunic, a Sam Browne belt and riding breeches and boots. There would be no horse to ride but much tramping over shell-bogged land and trenches. I also needed a portable camp bed and a sleeping sack. At the last moment I learned that my despatches would have to be typed in triplicate. I did not own a typewriter. I bought a portable model. I was interviewed at the War Office, given a certificate of credentials and a brass C (for Correspondent) to put on my cap, and another gilt badge (War Correspondent) for my shoulder straps. What was I, an officer or a private? Was I to be saluted or not? I discovered that we were something of an enigma to the troops. The War Office had never been able to make up its mind about us. We were a new species. Our rank was hybrid. Lord Kitchener did not like war correspondents; he was more frightened of the Press than of the Germans. Perhaps the indomitable Winston Churchill had frightened him with his escapades in South Africa. The Brass Hats remembered also that terrible fellow, Howard Russell, the correspondent in the Crimean War. Russell had fearlessly exposed the incompetence of the generals, from Raglan who monstrously traduced him, down. Special correspondents outside military discipline were a menace. Little Philip Gibbs, the most famous of all on the Western front, in the days when they had no official status, had been arrested five times by order of the Secretary of State for War and sent home. Somehow he always got back. Gibbs and his colleagues had not been allowed near a battlefield. When they tried to get to the opening battle at Mons they were held back by British bayonets. All Gibbs could learn about that battle was from a sergeant who told him that we had 'got it in the neck'. Baulked, they were compelled to report by hearsay, suffering crippling restrictions. The War Office could tell the public what it liked in its communiqués, often cooked. Until the time of the Battle of the Somme the correspondents were frustrated and muzzled. The indomitable Gibbs brilliantly extemporised with material collected from the soldiers back from the lines.

In 1916, under protest, there was a change. The war correspondent was officially recognised. He was given a pseudo-officer's uniform, he was housed in a Press Château but he was only allowed to venture abroad in an Army automobile, accompanied, in pairs, by an official guide who had the rank of captain. All they wrote was read by censors resident at the château before it could be released to the despatch riders to take to a cabling centre. When a despatch reached London it went through the War Office sieve before reaching the Press and the sub-editors' tables. They in turn had to work within a list of warnings. It was a wonder the public ever got anything of the truth. In the winter of 1917–18, tardily, a Ministry of Information was created. It added to the confusion and was singularly inept, having a dual control, half-civil, half military. It put out a Loan Exhibition of war photographs, which were enlarged and smeared with bad colour. The man who enlarged and coloured the photographs got a knighthood, the photographers, who had risked their lives, got only the O.B.E.

Little by little men of the calibre of Philip Gibbs (*Daily Telegraph*) Perry Robinson (*The Times*) H. W. Nevinson (*Daily News*) Beach Thomas (*Daily Mail*) and Percival Phillips (*Daily Express*), built up such a reputation with the public that they became powers and claimed more and more freedom. At the time of my advent the status of the war correspondent had been clearly established. Lloyd George invited them to Downing Street for breakfast, to gain confidential reports. Lord Northcliffe was a powerful backer. With the tragic death of Kitchener the wall was breached. In time Philip Gibbs became so trusted by Field Marshal Haig that he was allowed full access to all confidential reports from commanders in the field.

During my preparations I had one bogy haunting me. If my employers, not unreasonably, asked for a medical report it might prove disastrous. Happily, no such demand was made. There remained another disturbing fact. It might be that my chance had come too late. There had been a tremendous change on the Western Front and in the position of the Allies. Austria was reeling, there was an ominous crack on the Balkan Front, the power of the American Army was steadily mounting. On the high seas the Germans had been defeated. There were rumours of mutiny in the German Navy. "It'll perhaps be all over before you get there," said my London editor. I was dismayed by this prospect and then felt ashamed of myself for placing personal ambition before the fact that every day, on all fronts, hundreds of men were being killed, carrying higher and higher the frightful hecatomb of the dead.

CHAPTER SEVEN

Lille, Brussels, Copenhagen

I

I CROSSED THE Channel in a troopship in the darkness of an October evening, together with a colleague, the veteran H. W. Nevinson, returning from leave. So here I was again two years later in the track of the Dover Patrol. While we crossed in darkness, the boat crammed with Tommies, a rumour ran through the ship like a powder trail. The war had ended. The Germans had capitulated. "We'll all be going home, boys. Jerry's bust!" shouted a sergeant and the troops burst into singing, "It's a long, long way to Tipperary." But landing at Calais we learned the rumour was false. A staff car met us for the first stage of our journey. Lille had fallen. The Press Headquarters had been moved forward into the relieved city. When we arrived the next morning its inhabitants were in a state of delirium after almost four years of ruthless oppression. What we were told in Lille surpassed all that had been surmised. In 1916 began the deportation of women and girls. Those between fifteen and forty were rounded up at five in the morning and torn from their families. They were sent into a silence that was never broken for their crazed relations. Underfed, housed in barns with men and boys, without a change of linen, they were put to forced labour in the fields. Eight thousand young women were exiled at Easter, 1916. Two weeks later twelve thousand men and boys from Lille joined them. The city itself was gutted. Bicycles, lead piping, copper kettles, silver spoons, nothing metallic escaped the Germans. Our headquarters, a large private house, had not one metal handle left on the doors. The gas brackets had gone, as also the stair rods and window catches. The lead piping was missing from the lavatories and kitchen sinks. The factories had been systematically gutted under expert directions. No machinery worked. The rubber on the wheels of baby carriages had been taken. I saw a factory from which four dynamos had been requisitioned. To obtain them the concrete bases had been dynamited. There was not a driving belt left. The ground floor was crowded with boxed machinery, labelled, which the retreating Germans had had no time to remove.

An England never invaded could have no conception of this systematic looting. In Lille there was no ringing of church bells to hail the entry of the British, smothered in flowers and kissed by the inhabitants, for all the bells had gone. A *curé* showed me where the pipes of the church organ had been wrenched away. There was a singular exhibit on a sideboard in our Headquarters. It was an elaborate coffee urn. It bore a tag on it. If you cherished a particular object there was a fixed tariff. You paid and the article was tagged and free from requisitioning.

We arrived at the Press Headquarters in time for lunch. We assembled in a large sitting-room with a fire. I now met my colleagues. Their names were well known from their articles but one above all interested me, Philip Gibbs, the most famous of the group. He had a tremendous public in England and the United States. His vivid sensitive despatches had made his name a household word. When he entered the room I was surprised to see how small he was and how frail he looked. The frailty was deceptive. He was pliant-steel. He looked young, about thirty-five until you examined his face. His hair was tinged with grey, with a tendency to curl. The face was finely sculptured with chiselled nose and cheekbones, the thin mouth small and tightly closed. It was a handsome head, that of a medieval knight. But these features alone did not constitute Philip Gibbs. It was the expression built up with the lines of his face that proclaimed his personality. His skin was colourless, almost parchment-like in its taut transparency, its pallor heightened by contrast with grey-green eyes which at times seemed to slumber but on occasions, when moods of indignation or sympathy stirred him, suddenly became luminous with the fire of emotion behind them. One felt at once that this man had suffered every line he had written. I came to know him more intimately later but nothing reduced the sharpness of that first impression. His human charity, his almost feminine tenderness, his restless revolt against the insensate brutality of warfare, the ungrudging tribute to the foe's heroism, the almost holy love of his countrymen in their revelation of stoic courage, all these qualities stamped his character. Of no writer could it have been said with more truth *le style c'est l'homme.*

I did not know then, as he advanced towards me, shook my hand and spoke to me in a voice whose deep tones were always so surprising in so frail a figure, that I was destined to become a lifelong friend until he died, forty-four years later, aged eighty-five, my affection and admiration never diminished. There are very few men to whom I would apply the term Christian. My agnostic spirit finds them diamond rare in the dross of humanity. Nor was I alone in my conception of his character. Many years later in Madrid I found myself seated next to a lady who was the sister of the famous ecclesiast-statesman, the late Cardinal Merry del Val, with whom Gibbs had once had a memorable interview. I mentioned this. "My brother vividly remembered him," she said. "He felt he had a character as beautiful as his head. And I thought so too when I met him."

Gibbs was the son of a civil servant who had been born in Windsor Castle, his grandfather being a Queen's Messenger and variously employed at Court. His Aunt Kate was able, thereby, to claim that she had spanked the Kaiser Wilhelm when, a naughty little boy, he was visiting his grandmother, Queen Victoria. The grandchildren of the Queen's Messenger seem to have been born writers. Philip's sister, Helen, a nun who left her convent, became a novelist, as did Philip's elder brother, Cosmo Hamilton Gibbs, his youngest brother, Arthur Hamilton Gibbs, and his only son, Anthony. His cousin, Mary Hamilton Gibbs wrote a *Life* of Ramsay Macdonald who called her 'The most intelligent woman in London'.

When I first met Philip Gibbs, he was aged forty-one and already had a remarkable career behind him. The literary editor of the *Daily Mail* at twenty-one, a skilled interviewer, a linguist, fearless, he had written the best novel of Fleet Street life in *The Street of Adventure*, which had a resounding success. He was the first English journalist to be accorded a special audience with the Pope, Benedict XV, after the First World War. He risked his career when he denounced as an imposter the American explorer, Dr. Cook, who, in 1909, sent word from a ship in the Arctic that he had reached the North Pole. The statement electrified the world. Gibbs, a jump ahead of his colleagues, chartered a boat, intercepted Cook's vessel and on the journey to Denmark got Cook's story from him. Gibbs decided he was a fraud. Cook had a triumphant reception in Copenhagen. The Crown Prince of Denmark presided at a banquet given in his honour by the University. Gibbs cabled his denunciatory despatch. The directors of his newspaper held a special session debating whether they dare publish it. They did. An angry Copenhagen mob demonstrated outside Gibb's hotel. Subsequently, Dr. Cook's faked notebooks were rejected by the Royal Geographical Society. He was discredited later by Copenhagen University, and branded an imposter.

Gibbs, an idealist, was ever on the side of the angels. I often clashed with him in subsequent years and treated him to cold drenchings of fact. Disappointed again and again by human folly, ever raising a voice of hope, as heard in his phenomenally successful post-war novel, *The Middle of the Road*, he never lost his optimism for the human race. With his beautiful head he was Sir Galahad, the spirit shining through him. On his eightieth birthday I impishly wrote some verses on a greeting card—

> Whatever man plans for his future,
> Whatever result may hap,
> You believe in poor *homo sapiens*,
> With emphasis strong on the sap.*

Back came a letter—"Alas, my dear Cecil, you have been right, but I was born incorrigibly optimistic and will die so."

All this was in the future, after I met Gibbs at the War Correspondents' Mess in Lille, overawed by those veterans of the battlefields. He took me under his wing. I was angry when someone called him a sentimentalist. He never wrote of war as though it was a glorious football match. The Great War was no Roman holiday for him. He took risks and daily made a rendezvous with Death, and knew most intimately the patient courage of the unlettered men, as well as that of the sensitive, intelligent soldier and philosopher who lived the life of a rat but kept his soul intact. His despatches were read in the clubs of Piccadilly, the kitchens of Lancashire and the lone shanties of Canada. In the earlier years they stirred the American public, secure behind its three-thousand mile Atlantic sea barrier, when it sat in a ringside seat, falsely safe behind a policy that isolated it from war-riven Europe.

There were others in that group of war correspondents with memorable qualities. There was H. W. Nevinson, a veteran in his sixties, white-haired, ruddy faced, with a Colonel Cody goatee. He

* The Australopithecine line of fossil-men began at least three million years ago and led directly to *Homo Sapiens* who, despite various gospels of 'salvation' has been in trouble ever since.

hated war yet was proud to have a chest bright with decorations from other campaigns. He had survived two Balkan wars and had been shut up in the siege of Ladysmith during the South African war. Speaking of his Hampstead house one early dawn as our car threaded its way through the ruins of Armentières, he said, "I built it with the blood of the Boers," as if he had paid for it with blood money. He had been in the Dardanelles campaign and wrote a near-classic about it. Ever a combatant journalist, he fought passionately with the Pankhursts for Votes for Women. At one time he was literary editor of the *Daily Chronicle* and numbered Shaw among his reviewers. Once the Bearded Prophet threatened the paper with all the powers of the Society of Authors on the matter of a fee. "I am directed to inform you that the Editor will see you damned before he gives you more than five pounds for the review," wrote Nevinson. "Inform the editor that I will see him, you and the whole of the *Chronicle* staff boiled in Hell before I will do it for that money," retorted Shaw. Nevinson won and Shaw wrote it. He could be caustic as well as firm. Once when a colleague failed to keep an engagement he wrote—"I hope you are dead, for nothing but death could excuse your absence." One of his colleagues in our mess was *The Times* correspondent, Perry Robinson. They had been at Oxford together. Able but pompous, Robinson could never forget the importance of *The Times.* At Verviers, during our advance, seeking quarters in an hotel, Nevinson came to me along the corridor, red in the face, tears in his eyes. Robinson had seized the best bedroom and rudely pushed him out. "But why didn't you push *him* out?" I asked. "I couldn't. It's his birthday!" explained Nevinson.

Aggressiveness was not in the character of one gentle soul in our midst, not a correspondent but one of our resident censors. This was Captain C. E. Montague, a man turned fifty who had been a leader writer on *The Manchester Guardian* and who had married his chief's daughter. His father had been an Irish Roman Catholic priest who withdrew from Orders in order to marry. Shy, reticent and almost morbidly timid before authority, Montague was forty-six when the war broke out, grey-haired and a pacifist. He dyed his hair in order to enlist as a private. He was wounded and mentioned in despatches three times and rose to be a Captain. In after years, at a complimentary dinner on his retirement from the *Guardian,* Nevinson, in a speech of tribute, said—"We have heard of men whose hair has gone white through fear but he is the only man whose hair turned black through courage." In the mess Montague seldom spoke. I often wondered what he thought about us in his scholarly mind. Once he surprised me by saying, "You are one of the clearest despatch writers I've met—and give the least trouble. You're in Gibbs's class." Coming from Montague it was a great compliment. When I told Gibbs this he said, "Ah, but just what is my class with Montague? Anyhow it's something to have evoked any comment from silent C.E."

By far the most picturesque figure at the War Correspondents Château was the man in charge of it, the Hon. Neville Lytton, a brother of the Earl of Lytton and grandson of the author of *The Last Days of Pompeii*. Tall, handsome, of fine physique, he never quite succeeded in looking like a soldier. He was more like a faun out of the wood. Given the opportunity, I was certain we should find horns in his dark curly hair. At dawn I could hear coming from his room the low, plaintive music of his flute which seemed to be calling to Pan and all his nymphs. A marvellous raconteur, French seemed to be his first language, and since he had a passion for all things French he was always over at their Correspondents' Headquarters and brought back wonderful tales and gossip. It was he who reported the famous *mot* of Maréchal Joffre. After reviewing some Scottish troops Joffre was asked his opinion of the kilt. "Pour la guerre, non! Pour l'amour, bon!" he responded.

Lytton was a fine artist. I was already aware of his portrait of Francis Thompson in the *Collected Poems*. He had studied in Paris, exhibited at the Salon, and had further identified himself with France by marrying, in 1924, as his second wife, a Frenchwoman, being divorced from the first wife, the Baroness Wentworth (echoes of Lord Byron and his daughter Ada) by whom he had a son. He was also an athlete and in three successive years had won the Paris Cup as International Tennis Champion. Lytton was destined to succeed his brother as the third earl, but at this time there seemed not the slightest likelihood of his succession. His handsome and gifted brother, Victor, three years his senior, at one time Governor of Bengal and Viceroy of India, had two boys, Anthony, Viscount Knebworth, killed in a flying accident in 1933 and John, killed at Alamein in 1942.

Neville Lytton was now forty-two. He had a slightly Mephistophelian countenance. I could see him in *Faust*, serenading Marguerite under her garden window. The bohemian flautist-artist was sometimes supplanted by the *grand seigneur* with touches of arrogance that

The author, aged 24. Portrait by Denholm Davis

America. Will you let me know if you are a practised speaker? If not, you had better begin with a few lessons in voice production, as that will save you a lot of fatigue. Practise especially a great variety of manner, "get it across with plenty of pep", as you will presently learn to call it.

If you can intersperse your talk with songs & dances they will like you all the better. I mean this seriously. Let your way be:-

This, rather than

This.

Yours very truly.
John Masefield

John Masefield's letter of advice for my American lecture tour might be accounted for by the fact that he had been 'born in the purple'. His father Lord Lytton was Viceroy of India when his son Neville was born during a ball that was in progress at Government House, Calcutta. When he came to the table where he presided he expected the correspondents to rise. Some did. Those who did not got a cold look. "After all, he's only a decorated concierge," growled Nevinson, refusing to rise, "and when he's late he should apologise." Sir William Orpen, the painter, also refused to rise. "He scowled at me and I scowled back." I always rose, being the baby of the mess and impressed by the literary traditions associated with his name. Also, he was a gifted artist as well as a great personality. I was in grace from the day when I asked him if he could play Ravel's *Pavane pour une infante défunte*. He knew Ravel and anything French touched his heart. When Lytton wished to charm he was irresistible. After the war he wrote a book *The Press and the General Staff*. In it he said—"At first the soldier's idea of a newspaper man was that he was a badly bred, ill-mannered, uneducated fellow who revelled in indiscretions. It is entirely to the credit of the correspondents that before the end of the war the soldier came to look upon them with affection, confidence and admiration."

Each morning, sometimes before dawn, we set off for the trenches to reach the front line, at this time always being advanced after long stagnation. We were paired off, two correspondents being conducted by an officer, in an open Vauxhall touring car. The censors awaited our return in the late afternoon. We rushed to our rooms, typed our despatches and passed them to our resident censors. They were then taken by despatch riders to the cabling office at St. Omer. Thus our copy, vetted again by the home censor, reached the newspaper offices in the early evening, for the morning's papers.

When an offensive opened in the Lille salient on October 14th it became obvious that the Germans were pulling out. On that day, the fall of Lille being imminent the German commandant had assembled the inhabitants at four a.m. Adventurous refugees from Lille, Tourcoing and Roubaix rushed homewards, trapped between two fires, so anxious were they for liberty. The inhabitants, assembled in the Grand Place, were told, "You may leave in the direction of your friends, the enemy." There was some cunning in this. The flood of refugees towards our lines seriously impeded the advance of our men and transport.

On October 18th we were drawing near to Maubeuge and Mons.

The fighting around Le Quesnoy was still desperate. Lille seethed with rumours. We had a great collector of these in Russell, who represented *Reuters*. He found he got much fuller reports by remaining at home in the war correspondent's headquarters, picking up local gossip and cross-examining us on our return. He was tired after four strenuous years and was longing to be relieved of his job. In return he kept us abreast of local news. He had just heard the Kaiser had committed suicide after shooting the Crown Prince, that Hindenburg had been hanged by the Berlin mob. He did not believe any of this though he had been told it by a French correspondent who had been told it by a staff officer of Maréchal Foch. "Wishful thinking, my boy. You'll see all of them live to a comfortable and respectable old age."

The Germans quitting Lille left one good legacy. When they had captured it a new theatre was being built. They completed it with Teutonic thoroughness. They staged grand opera for their troops, *Lohengrin*, etc. Many of the sets were comic or gross. The Australians were as notorious for fierceness as the kilted soldiers, *Damen von Hölle*. There was a special Australian drop scene. A naked Aboriginal with a club, furiously smoking, stood in the centre. To his right there was a kangaroo, cub in pouch, to his left a steaming cauldron being stirred by a savage with a thighbone. The naked foot of a man being boiled for consumption protruded. Thus the cannibalistic nature of the Australians was portrayed. The Germans staged four plays a week and Shakespeare was in the bill. *Was Ihr Wollt* (*As you like it*). The cost of seeing this in a French theatre acted by a German company was three and a half marks for a stall, down to one mark. The audience was brought from the trenches by organised buses coming in from miles around. These theatre parties were collected from Cambrai, Roubaix, Valenciennes and from as far as Ostend. A soldier could leave the trenches at noon, see an evening performance of Shakespeare or Wagner in the theatre at Lille, and be back in the trenches by early morning. Fate often wears a sardonic smile. The first thing shown to the Tommies who packed the theatre where the Germans had sat was the film of General Allenby entering Jerusalem.

The opening days of November clearly foretold the end. Le Quesnoy at last surrendered. The town had walled fortifications and a double line of moats. The fighting under the fortifications had a medieval character. The New Zealanders brought up scaling ladders and attempted to mount the walls as in the days of old. They came under deadly machine-gun fire and the moat was strewn with their bodies. The town was then encircled and it was only when the German commandant found they were cut off and the New Zealanders were fixing their bayonets that he surrendered with a thousand men.

We heard the lasts shots of the war at Maubeuge on November 9th. Nevinson and I had motored out to the fortress. The Germans still occupied the town. At noon our men broke through. We were warned that three Germans were stationed by a covering machine-gun up the road. We halted. Half an hour later it was found that they were all dead and we went on. The town had been evacuated. It was a frightful scene of bodies and discarded transport. I mounted to the top of one of the walls where I could overlook the surrounding country. In the waning light of the November afternoon the plain around was grimly desolate. Splintered trees and shattered houses bore witness to the lapsed tide of war. Over all lay the silence of death except for an odd shell that moaned over us, a useless last gesture of anger. The horizon was filled with clouds of smoke from burning dumps. In the dark we regained our car and turned homewards, passing pathetic little groups of returning refugees, all their belongings piled up on the handcarts they pushed. "La guerre est finie, m'sieur?" they cried, and somehow found heart to wave to us. These refugees streaming back became a serious problem for they clogged the roads and hindered the forward movements of our troops, but in vain we tried to check them; back they went to roofless hovels, with no food, no heat, no light—but they were home again.

On Sunday we were in liberated Tournai. On Monday, just before breakfast, Major Lytton came in with great news. The armistice had been signed. Orders were issued for the cease-fire at eleven o'clock. We set out at once for Mons. We reached the suburbs at ten o'clock. At one point the body of a young German soldier lying across the road blocked our passage. The chauffeur got out to pull him aside but not before we had seen something as moving as it was strange. He lay face upwards, one hand stretched out to the sky as if in a despairing appeal against his fate in this last hour when peace was so near. He was recently dead. Someone had had the decency to cover his face with a handkerchief through which the blood had soaked. Cheering women and men surrounded our car indifferent to that young corpse with its tumbled blond hair. There had been hard fighting around the town. The streets held many dead Germans. Children who had witnessed the fighting from the windows gave us excellent descriptions.

We could hardly get into the town, being surrounded by a mass of cheering citizens. There was a noise of drums, bugles, marching men. The church bells endeavoured to play *Tipperary* from the steeples, convinced that it was the British national anthem. They disliked *God Save the King*, suspicious that it was a German tune.

We abandoned our car and fought our way through to the Grand' Place. On the steps of the Hotel de Ville the Mayor and the councillors, in frock coats and top hats, were lined up for the official entry of the troops. We took our place with them and looked down on the 7th Brigade of the 3rd Division of the Canadian Corps lining the Place and hemming back the crowd. We waited; the minute hand of the town clock was drawing near to the momentous hour of eleven. Precisely at the hour, breaking a deep silence, a bugle rang out the Cease Fire. A squadron of aeroplanes overhead released a shower of white Very lights and the next moment the town burst into a long roar of cheering. There was another bugle call and at the distant corner of the Place the Canadian Black Watch marched in, their kilts swinging behind the skirl of the pipers' band. They marched into position for the crowning ceremony, the entry of the Commanding General on horseback. He rode in, dismounted, was greeted by the Mayor and presented to the councillors. He mounted again, and gave the order to salute. At this moment massed bands struck up *La Brabançonne* and the whole thronged Place, from roofs to pavements, rang with the lusty singing of the national hymn of liberty, all the pent-up emotion of four hard years vibrating in the massed voices.

A week later we were in Brussels. Outside Waterloo Gibbs nearly lost his life. On the slippery icebound road his car came into violent collision with a lorry. It was wholly wrecked. The chauffeur had a broken leg. Following behind, I found Gibbs on the ground unconscious. I had once claimed, laughingly, that I had saved his life. He was an inveterate smoker and one night in Lille he fell asleep and set his bed on fire. Awake, and smelling burning, I traced it to his room. I was just in time to pull him out of bed and bat down his flaming pyjamas. This collision was an even more serious affair. We got him, suffering much pain, into Brussels. Our hotel accommodation proved wretched. As elsewhere, the Germans had taken away the water pipes, lamp brackets, blankets and radiators. There was no running water. I undressed Gibbs and examined him. There was a bad contusion and sprained muscles of the right shoulder. I tore up a bedsheet, bound him up and then sought for a doctor. But Brussels was in a state of hysteria awaiting the return of the King and the Government. All the doctors seemed to be out celebrating. Gibbs was intermittently delirious, running a high fever. I gave him a sedative and had a camp bed moved into his room so that I could be on hand all night. It was ten o'clock the next day before we got a doctor. There was no fracture but it would be a week before he could move. In the evening, somewhat better but still with a temperature, on being told that he must stay in bed several days, he said firmly, "Nonsense. To-morrow the King enters. Do you imagine I'm going to miss that—it's one of the great events of the war!" None of us could dissuade him.

That night I slept in my own room. Before leaving him I stealthily took away his clothes and shoes, and locked them up. The next morning I found him out of bed wrapped in a blanket. "Someone's stolen my clothes!" he cried. I told him that I had taken them. He was not to go out of his room. "You devil!" he said, "Bring them here at once!" We argued. "You can't put them on," I said, "and none of us will help you, and the doctor will not let you out. Two of us are going to write to-day's despatch for you. You can sign it if you like. Now get back into bed." He was still in much pain and, defeated, obeyed sullenly. But at four o'clock that day he got to the Hotel de Ville.

II

In the late afternoon of November 22nd I stood with my colleagues in the great hall of the Hotel de Ville. Outside there was a seething multitude crammed in the Grand' Place. Around us in the Salle Gothique were Ministers of State, Aldermen, Councillors, judges, officers, all the representatives of the capital. The crowded hall was unlit, the last light of day filtering through the stained glass. The King was returning from exile. Three State chairs awaited him, his Queen, and the young Crown Prince. Near these chairs, in his official dress, stood the famous Burgomaster Max who had defied the Germans until they had carried him off to prison in Germany. He talked with the U.S. Ambassador, Brand Whitlock, his name known through his valiant effort to rescue Nurse Cavell from execution for assisting in the escape of our soldiers. Major Lytton was there with his brother Lord Lytton and his lovely wife. We waited. The Escalier d'Honneur up which the King and Queen would come was lined with halbardiers in their medieval costumes. At the head of the staircase stood a choir of girls all in white, holding madonna lilies.

From outside came a murmur, then a prolonged roar. We knew that the cortège of the King had arrived. As they entered, to mount the stairs, the choir sang a song of welcome and strewed the lilies for the ascending royalties. There followed a pause in which we heard an usher cry "Le Roi!" The King walked on into the centre of the hall. He waited until a band had ceased playing the National Anthem. With him and the Queen stood a figure of singular grace in a scarlet robe, Cardinal Mercier, another champion of the Belgian people in their hours of trial. An address was presented by the Burgomaster and answered in a speech of great simplicity. Presentations were then made, many advancing in tears. Finally, King Albert moved out to the balcony overlooking the Grand' Place, accompanied by the Queen and thc young Prince. Night had fallen. From across the Place, in the Maison du Roi, where Charles V had once lodged, the beam of a searchlight isolated the King as he stood waving to the dense black mass below that acclaimed him deliriously. Never again would one see such a scene, the King above, the vociferous crowd below, the façades of the magnificent old guild houses in one of the most beautiful squares in Europe, glimmering in their Gothic beauty beneath the drapings of banners and pennants. The crowd took up the singing of *La Brabançonne.* They sung it one, twice, thrice, ending in a tumult of cheering until the King withdrew, the window closed, the noise was shut out.

III

Three days after the official entry into Brussels we began our advance towards the German frontier which was to be crossed on December 1st. Our route lay along the Mons-Namur-Aix-la-Chapelle line. The French had already reached the Rhine in their sector, the Americans were advancing through Luxembourg. We found the road blocked with derelict transport, frost, floods and refugees.

In Namur I was awakened early the next morning by voices mournfully chanting. From my hotel window opposite the railway station, where the refugees, sleeping and squatting on the steps, waiting for trains, looked like black crows in the snow, I saw a strange tragic sight. Russia, torn by revolution and betrayed at Brest-Litovsk, now belonged to neither side. The Germans, vacating Namur had left behind a hospital full of sick Russian prisoners. Below me, chanting, in the grey dawn, in a snowstorm, a sad procession passed. The Russians were burying some of their comrades. A barrow bore the coffins. Behind it, bearded, bareheaded in his robes, walked a Russian Orthodox priest, preceded by a soldier bearing a crucifix. The straggling mourners shuffled over the snow-covered road, some of them limped, some were on crutches. They chanted a sad, beautiful dirge. Many of them would never see their homes again. Ill-clad, sick, hungry, disowned, they passed disregarded by all.

In the afternoon I sought out the Russian hospital, carrying as many cigarettes and cakes as I could find. It proved to be not a hospital but an empty factory. It bore, written roughly on a placard, a memorial notice to some Belgian workmen who had been among fifty hostages shot two months earlier by the Germans, including a seventy-year-old man who had died singing *La Brabançonne*. The three floors of the factory were furnished with iron bedsteads but were devoid of any other kind of furniture, except for a few chairs. Water, gas and electric light were cut off. The place was an icehouse, and the prisoners lay in the gloom. There was a stench of putrifying flesh on every floor. There were no nurses, only a few shuffling orderlies attended the sick. There were only two doctors, Russians, one with an amputated leg. The Red Cross had not yet found the hospital, or perhaps was too busy with the Belgians. A soldier who spoke some French (he had been stage door-keeper at the Mariinsky Theatre in St. Petersburg and talked of Nijinsky, whom he had known as a pupil there) told me that none of them had received any mail for five months and no pay. They knew little beyond rumours of what was happening in Russia. I distributed the cigarettes and cakes, utterly inadequate for over a hundred wounded soldiers. What would become of them? No one had an answer. It was a heart-breaking experience. No one remembered the service the Russians had rendered the Allied cause, those millions of bodies in the Eastern marshes where they had held the Germans at bay.

When we arrived in Spa there was the curious sight of German and English batmen lining up for milk and cakes outside a dairy shop. The German Armistice mission and part of the German staff, left behind to superintend the surrender of the war material, occupied the Hotel Britannique. Here the last Grand Council had been held and the Kaiser had signed his abdication before seeking refuge in Holland. I saw the long council table in the ballroom, and a cot bed in which Hindenburg had slept.

Beyond Verviers we took the road towards Malmédy, the German frontier village. We halted early on the morning of December 1st at a little stone bridge over the Rothwasser. This was the boundary, the threshold of Germany whose door was to open to our occupying troops at nine o'clock. Our cavalry waited, the horses champing their bits, the foot soldiers, steel-helmeted, stamping to keep warm. A cavalry patrol with pennants fluttering awaited the word to advance. Five minutes to nine, four, three, two, one—and our car went over the bridge with the patrol as the barrier lifted. A sergeant of the Dragoons cantered after us. "You are the first over!" he called, joyfully saluting, his red face beaming. We were on German soil, the occupying army. Here was the first visible sign of complete victory.

The countryside was very quiet. With its snow-laden fir forests it was like a German Christmas card. Not a soul could be seen. The road into Germany was unguarded and deserted. When we came to Malmédy there was a strange absence of life but we felt we were being watched from behind a hundred curtains. Nevinson and I called on the Governor of this Prussian *Kreis*. He received us formally in a large room, standing beneath portraits of the Kaiser and of Hindenburg. It was a dramatic moment. We were the victorious enemy. Nevinson, who had been to a German University after Oxford, spoke fluent German. The Landrat expressed one fear. It was nearing Christmas. The children had toy pistols with which they fired caps. He hoped our soldiers would not mistake them for weapons. As we talked there was the clatter over the cobbled square of our entering cavalry. We turned and looked. I saw the Landrat's hand grip the top of the desk before him. His head bowed almost imperceptibly, and when he wished us Good-day his voice broke.*

Fifteen miles distant behind Malmédy, dark and silent under defeat, Belgian Verviers was ablaze all night with singing and dancing in the streets, our Tommies whisked round in the arms of buxom Belgians. When we dined that evening our napkin rings had the names of

* Despite all the talk of self-determination, Malmédy, five-sixths German-speaking, was transferred to Belgium in 1919. In the Second World War, by an error of the American Air Force, it was severely bombed, with a heavy loss of lives including those of American troops holding the town. So it was more fortunate in defeat in 1918 than in victory in 1945.

German officers on them. A girl in the hotel who had been to bed with them had had her hair shorn off. One of our men rescued her from assault and took her off, probably supplanting the Germans. My washstand drawers were papered with a recent copy of the *Kölnische Zeitung*, and in one of them I found a letter beginning—My darling Otto, I am sending you these gloves which Lottie has knitted . . ." Where was Otto now ? Wearing them on the march home, or dead ? Outside, there was a sound of revelry by night, as Byron wrote of another Belgian town, and a rosy glare in the Grand' Place long after midnight. It had not ceased when I went to bed. The good people of Verviers danced until dawn crept over the hills and paled the light of the lamps.

IV

We pushed on to the Rhine, going through country which had no signs of the grim devastation behind us. At Düren we were received with something like joy by the German Burgomaster. He feared a revolution fomented by the local Socialists. We put a stop to the tyranny of the Workmen's and Soldiers' Council. Something of the same fear was in Cologne. We received repeated messages from the young Burgomaster there, beseeching us to come quickly. The mob was wholly out of hand. Looting and shooting had begun. We sent in by train two companies of machine-gunners. Everywhere the Germans wanted us to occupy their towns, not the Belgians or the French. In Aix-la-Chapelle the Belgian commandant played a grim joke on the town. He produced the severe edicts of the German Governor who had occupied Brussels, and pasted over them, "This now applies to you." I was embarrassed by Germans who, seeing us in uniform, had to raise their hats and step into the gutter as we passed, the German order during the occupation.

We were received demurely in Cologne. The populace was cowed. There had been rioting led by the socialists, and the sailors from Kiel dockyards. All fraternisation with the Germans was forbidden but sex-starved soldiers have no nationality. I accompanied on a tour of the back streets the Town Major's assistant. Our posse rounded up over eighty of our men in the brothels. Some of them bolted without their trousers and jackets. They turned up later ludicrously clad, vowing the Germans had stripped them of their clothes!

My comfortable room in the Domhof Hotel looked on to the Platz. We were well fed. The cafés were all full, their windows bright with confectionery. Prices in shops were high but the trade was brisk. All was well if you had the money, it seemed. Nevinson brought in harrowing stories of famished children. I ate uneasily. The blockade, still unlifted, was pressing hardly on the poor. Nevinson wrote an angry letter of protest to Lloyd George, but he greatly exaggerated the situation.

We went to call on the Burgomaster, Dr. Konrad Adenauer, at the Rathaus. We were courteously received. I was surprised to find how young he was. He had been Burgomaster for a year, brought in when disorder threatened. His insistent plea was for food for a hungry city. When next I saw him, forty-five years later, at his villa at Cadenabbia on Lake Como, he had just relinquished the Chancellorship of the German Republic. He was still alert and active at eighty-seven.

Our troops behaved well and soon their good nature evoked a response. The men in billets had their washing done for them by the *hausfrauen*. Children, Christmas approaching, soon learned from whom came sweets and dolls. I heard a kilted Jock, followed by a band of admiring children, two of whom he led by the hand, exclaim to another Jock—"Before we know where we are the bastards will be loving us!"

V

On December 13th our forces occupied the bridgeheads across the Rhine. Our sentries patrolled the Hohenzollern Bridge. We made excursions along the west bank as far as Coblenz, in the sector occupied by the American army. On December 16th our official duties came to an end. I was glad of this, being eager for Christmas at home. Moreover, I was very tired. In mid-November Reuter's correspondent, ill, asked me if I would take over for him. I agreed. This entailed double despatches. Over everything there was now a feeling of anti-climax. Our services had come to an end. Thank God there was no more need for war correspondents.

On the cold, rainy morning of December 16th, 1918, we were lined up at half-past nine under the shadow of Kaiser Wilhelm I's statue on the Hohenzollern Bridge, the grey Rhine flowing below us. It rained steadily. A cavalry detachment approached, escorting the car of the Commander-in-Chief. When it stopped, grey-haired, handsome Field

Marshal Sir Douglas Haig stepped out. We were in three groups, the British, the Allied and the Neutral correspondents. Haig went down the line shaking the hand of each of us. He made a brief speech. "I know that you have displayed untiring vigour, energy and contempt of danger in following the troops in all their offensive actions," he said. Then came a memorable sentence: "For my part I sincerely hope that in our time of victory we may not lose our heads, as the Germans lost theirs after 1870, with the result that we are here." His short speech finished, he presented to each of us a Union Jack, roughly attached to a staff, a small hurriedly-made souvenir—"Like the one I carry on my car." We all saluted, he retired to his car. Our official duties were closed.

The war correspondents to the Allied Press, to whom Haig had also given the little flags on sticks, were indignantly disappointed. One of them felt quite sure that Marshal Haig would give him the Order of the Bath! Some of them got suitable decorations after waiting two years. (Illustration, p. 209.)

VI

In the attempt to get home Gibbs and I foolishly dismissed our automobiles and chauffeurs. We thought it would be quicker to go by train than over the war devastated land. All went well until we got to Aix-la-Chapelle. After that the rail service was in chaos. There was no train schedule, the rails had been torn up, engines broke down, carriages were stripped of windows and cushions. Our carriage had even the footboards missing and we could see the railbed passing under our feet. The train started and stopped, it crawled at four miles an hour. Outside Namur it came to a full stop. We sat in a cold dark carriage from nine p.m. until seven a.m. without food. The journey to Boulogne that we thought would take thirty hours took four days. We crossed to England in a dark wintry evening, the boat packed with soldiers.

How curious was that aftermath of the war! We all really thought we had gone through 'the war to end war', as the slogan ran. The statesmen began to gather for the Versailles Peace Conference. On the evening of November 11th, the first Armistice Day, after our entry into Mons, Gibbs had written—"The war belongs to the past. There will be no flash of gun-fire in the sky tonight. The fires of hell have been put out, and I have written my last despatch as a war correspondent. Thank God!"

On the last page of *The World Crisis*, Winston Churchill's history of the First World War, he wrote—"Is this the end? Is it to be merely a chapter in a cruel and senseless story? Will a new generation in their turn be immolated to square the black accounts of Teuton and of Gaul? Will our children bleed and gasp again in desolated lands?" Alas, we know now the answer was 'Yes'. And in December, 1939, Philip Gibbs, now aged sixty-two, was back again as a war correspondent on the Western Front until May 1940, when the Germans began to engulf France.

VII

Immediately on my return to England I went to Nottingham to see my mother. She was still in her miserable little room, so I stayed with my old friends the Laings, with morning prayers, the ex-groom-chauffeur, the maids lined up to present their alarm clocks for winding. This corner of England seemed untouched. Lloyd George was going to hang the Kaiser and make England 'a land fit for heroes to live in'. The gold sovereign had disappeared forever. The country was sunk in debt and bitter against America for having made so much money out of the war.

After a week I returned to London and in January, 1919, began civil life again. I had to find a new lodging. My landlady informed me that she was giving up the house. Zadia, adorable yet evanescent as ever, had moved and was in rooms with a girl friend. I found a new lodging in a residential club in Tavistock Square. I had a pleasant room, with a french window opening on to a balcony that overlooked the Square, with large trees and a garden to which I had access. My room cost thirty shillings a week with breakfast.

My own future now had to be recast. I had to plan again. Once more I burned my boats. I had no desire to return to Liverpool, having tasted life in a capital, with all its manifold contacts. I agreed to carry on as the half-time London correspondent of *The Liverpool Post*. I had in mind to write the novel that had been dormant in my mind for so long. I would take another risk, but this time I was better fortified. I had saved some £800. An American magazine had taken four of my articles on the March to the Rhine, and Reuter's had given me a generous honorarium for the despatches I had written when their representative returned home after Lille. But there was a serious fall in my income. The wonder-stipend of a thousand pounds a year as war correspondent had disappeared. The Ministry of Munitions was gone, with the secretaryship to Burton Chadwick. I had now only the £156 a year from my paper. Yet I was not in any way apprehensive. The confidence of youth sustained me.

One day in February I met a former Ministry colleague, a civil servant. When he asked what I was doing, I replied, jocularly, like thousands of others, "I'm out of work!" I had just turned down the idea of taking myself to Oxford. He had a suggestion. He offered me a position as an Examining Officer to the Civil Liabilities Commission at a salary of £300 p.a. This body had been created to enable ex-Service men to establish themselves in their lost businesses and crafts. It would make small grants of money. It expected to complete its work in eighteen months. Actually it took five years.

I resigned after ten months. The task was too harrowing. The operating rule was to grant as little as possible to the applicants. There was reason in this. When a Government starts giving away money two things inevitably happen. It becomes a target for scroungers and then, to protect itself, it compiles rules that often cripple its good intentions. Day after day, month after month, we waded through stories of hardship, ruin and folly. There were applicants who had lost businesses and incomes of one or two thousand pounds a year. The maximum grant was one hundred and fifty pounds, and often this could not be given because the case did not fit the rules. The Commission sent out over the country Examiners, mostly barristers, who interviewed the claimants. The cases mounted to a damning indictment of the unintelligent and sometimes brutal policy pursued by the recruiting and tribunal boards. Fully twenty per cent of the cases were those of men who should never have been taken into the Forces, and who, in them, were never anything but a liability. Men supporting families and running successful businesses had been set to do batmen's and charwomen's work, being unfit for active service, while their businesses fell into ruin. The travelling Examiners were often enraged when we cut down the sum they had rightly recommended. We were compelled to do some cheeseparing. I was repeatedly warned against the liberality of my confirmations.

This work brought me one good bonus. One of my colleagues was

Beresford Chancellor, a man of means, a scholar and a well-known writer on the topography and history of London. I was the weekend guest of his beautiful wife and himself in their country home at Wargrave-on-Thames, and later in their town house in Onslow Gardens. At Wargrave there was a river creek below their garden. One evening I saw a boy dive into the creek. He did not reappear. I waited and waited and concluded that he must have swum away under water. There were no clothes in sight on the bank. It was dusk. At dinner that evening I mentioned the boy and his mysterious disappearance. I saw a startled look on my host's face, shared by his wife. Later, in the library, he drew me aside and asked if I could describe the boy. In the dusk he had not been clearly visible but I gave a suggestion of his age. "That is very odd," remarked my host. "We had a tragedy here some time ago. Our gardener's son was drowned one evening bathing in that creek. His body was found the next day. You must be psychic." It was a profitable ghost for me. A few months later I wrote a short story based on the incident and an American magazine paid me £200 for it.

I had two other sources of income that year. I edited a World Map, and also supplied the notes for a de-luxe edition of Raemaeker's famous war cartoons. My total income for 1919 was £700 but it was hard work with Fleet Street, the Commission, some lectures, and odd articles, and it was precarious, leaving me little time for my own writing.

One day I received a letter from my mother. She had succeeded in finding a house and could escape from her miserable lodging. "I don't think you will approve, it is in a very mean street but houses now are impossible to come by at any cost. But it will be my own, at least. It consists of one room and a scullery downstairs, and two bedrooms upstairs. The rent is 5*s.* a week. I'll furnish it from the Fund and what we have stored." That Fund, so dear to my mother since the death of my father! There were thirty pounds left of the fifty-six after almost ten years! Later, she informed me, triumphantly, that she was in the house and had furnished it for twenty pounds. She had taken furniture out of store but there was no room for the family portraits. The coat-of-arms, the family Ju-Ju, was hanging this time in a place of honour, a tribute to my father's memory, perhaps in mitigation of the scarcely veiled derision with which my mother had treated it as a valueless object. "I am At Home every Friday. Yesterday I had a tea party. Mrs. Horsley and the vicar came. The neighbours were all agog. They had heard Mrs. Horsley recite, so I asked them in. She was very *grande dame* and it has given me social standing!"

A few weeks later I visited my mother. My unfortunate and gallant married brother had suffered another operation. He was a shadow of the handsome gay young man who had sung "Speak, speak, speak to me, Thora". When I arrived and saw the long mean street I hid my dismay but my mother was happy, which was all that mattered. It was her very own and she had achieved a miracle with twenty pounds. Moreover, it was not far distant from her beloved Grove Villas, and her friends. Her neighbours were quiet working-class people. One drove a tram, the other was a labourer at the gas works. "I reign here like Queen Victoria. They couldn't be nicer and there are no squalling babies," said my mother. She was now sixty-four, retaining her peach-blossom complexion and her long, beautiful hair. She seemed very cheerful but I suspect she must have been lonely. Around this time she had a passion for reading books on theology. She complained she had exhausted the Public Library, and the vicar's. I left after this first visit feeling happier about her.

VIII

In August I took two weeks' leave from the Commission to go with a party of journalists on a visit to Denmark, arranged by the Danish Foreign Office. There was a political motive behind this invitation. Until 1864 the Duchy of Schleswig had been Danish and to it King Christian I, in 1460, had added the German Duchy of Holstein. Prussia and Austria refused to recognise this incorporation when Christian IX ascended the throne. In 1864 they declared war on Denmark. At the point of the sword they achieved the unconditional surrender of Schleswig and Holstein. The Danes of Schleswig never ceased to protest. Now, the World War ended, the map of Europe was being redrawn. The Danes sought revision. Very wisely their Government made no claim to Holstein which had always been German in character nor did it press a claim, despite local clamour, to the more southern part of Schleswig where German influence greatly predominated. This was, therefore, divided into three zones. The southern zone was ceded to Germany, but the middle and northern ones were to have a plebiscite. The strong Danish majority in the north zone left the issue there in no doubt, but the middle zone was a field of the fiercest contention. In this zone was situated the prosperous town of

Flensburg. Obviously Germany would spare no effort to secure the retention of a territory just north of the Kiel Canal and their chief naval base. Unfortunately, a blunder in the changed version of the Peace Treaty added to the anxiety of the Danes. They had asked, very reasonably, that not only the north and middle zones should be evacuated by the German authorities before the plebiscite was held but also, to secure a vacuum, that the southern zone, held by Germany with Danish consent, should be evacuated to a depth of ten kilometres to avoid undue influence and imported German voters during the plebiscite. This had been provided for in the first version of the Peace Treaty but to the consternation of the Danes the provision was omitted from the final version owing to a typist's error.

Our visit was made just prior to the plebiscite. It was prophesied that as a result of this typist's error the middle zone would be lost to Denmark, a prophecy that proved correct, for the voting was 75% German to 25% Danish votes. Most Danes thought it better so, to avoid dissension.

A private steam-yacht sent by the Danes to Newcastle took us to Denmark. For a fortnight our tour was marked by receptions, banquets and brass bands until we nearly fainted with fatigue. The Danes had been menaced by the Germans during the war and had been compelled to hide their sympathy with the Allies. They were now determined to leave us in no doubt about their pro-British feelings.

This time I was not the baby in the group of British journalists. There was a handsome young man, a year my junior, Francis Meynell. The name carried a reminder of the family that had befriended poor Francis Thompson, the drug-addicted poet of *The Hound of Heaven* and other memorable poems. It was (Sir) Francis Meynell who, almost thirty years later, would pay a farewell tribute to a fellow typographer, our friend Holbrook Jackson.

We came into Danish waters off Skagen, a village on the tip of Jutland, where a narrow strip of land separates the waters of the Skagerrak from those of the Kattegat. We must have sailed near the scene of the Battle of Jutland fought three years earlier. After that battle bodies of sailors, German and English, had been washed up on the long sandy shore of Jutland. This stretch of coast bore a great resemblance to the sand-dunes and beaches of the English east coast, known to me from my boyhood holidays at Skegness.

Skagen with its red tiles and whitewashed cottages, its miles of silver sand running out to the spit of land where the two seas met, had long been a favourite haunt of Danish painters and poets. There under a stone cairn lay their national poet, Holger Drachmann. How lost and eerie this stretch of sea-land was! The Raabjerg Miler, a great mountain of glittering sand ever changing shape under the wind, threatens and lays waste the adjacent land. One climbed and climbed in quest of its shifting summit to look down on the two seas, blue and green on either side of the finger of land. Out of this desert of sand rose an old church tower, a lone memorial to a village that once knew a hardy race of North Sea fishermen. Well might Hans Andersen call this place 'The Pompeii of the North'.

Inevitably we were taken to the Castle of Kronborg at Elsinore to walk the battery where tradition alleged that Hamlet had seen his father's ghost. The site certainly is dramatic, and there is 'a nipping and an eager air', as one looks out over the Sound crowded with shipping voyaging between the North Sea and the Baltic. Over this water had come Shakespeare's Fortinbras, 'from the Polack wars', to look on the dead Hamlet and bury the prince who had named him his successor.

Tourists have to be catered for now that tourism has become a national industry, so that wherever Shakespeare set a scene and drew a plot there are English tourists to be satisfied. In Venice they are shown the palace of Desdemona, in Verona the tomb of Juliet, obliging frauds. The Danes are a kindly race and they are not going to spoil the pleasure of Shakespeare enthusiasts by telling them that the Kronborg was built one thousand years after Hamlet, who had lived in a quite different part of the country. On the terrace behind the Château at Marienlyst we were shown 'the grave of Hamlet', a stone cairn in a circle of trees. Nearby, obligingly, the Danes had utilised a brook. It is now called 'Ophelia's Brook'. Here she is supposed to have drowned herself, a considerable feat in water only a few inches deep.

Inland from Copenhagen we saw the Castle of Frederiksborg, which might have been the castle of The Sleeping Beauty. It is romantically situated upon three islands, in a lake like a mirror, its high walls reflected therein, and surrounded by deep woods. Mullioned windows, towers, spires, galleries and loggias form a labyrinthine design. Inside we saw the banqueting hall and the Knight's Hall with its great black marble fireplace, musician's gallery, columns, coffered ceiling and tapestries, creating wonder at the pomp with which kinglets and princelings surrounded themselves with fairytale splendour. It proved too magnificent for later kings who dwelt, in retreat, at the nearby palace of Fredensborg, where we walked down terraces leading to the lake through the famous Garden of Adam and Eve, ending with a long vista of woodlands and a sheet of blue water. Here King Christian IX, 'the grandfather of Europe' as he was called, held those family gatherings that called his children from many of the thrones of Europe. I saw the ghosts of two small sisters on those lawns, Dagmar and Alexandra, later Empress of Russia and Queen of England.

In beautiful water-haunted Copenhagen we were fêted to a point of exhaustion. There was a special ballet performance at the Opera House. We found it strange that by a long tradition the audience never applauds at the fall of the curtain but goes out in a church-like silence.* We were sumptuously dined at The Shooting Club on such a summer night of stars as I shall never forget. We were received by the King and Queen in the Royal Palace and given an official welcome at the Folketing, the Parliament, and attended another gala dinner in the lamplit Tivoli Gardens. Towards dawn we got back to our rooms banked with flowers. When our yacht took us away from the capital on a tour of the islands we gave a grateful sigh. We were promised the quiet simplicity of Stubbekjöbing on the island of Falster. When we arrived the next noon the whole of its inhabitants seemed to have assembled on the quayside. Alas and alas! The local band on the quay played the whole three droning verses of our National Anthem, so that we stood bareheaded in a chilling air. Our skipper, berthing the yacht, collided with the quay. We were due to make only a short call, but now, fast in, we could not quickly get out again. There seemed the prospect that we should have a reposeful night there but we did not know Stubbekjöbing. When it learned we were stuck for the night it organised in a few hours a public reception, a dinner and a dance. Firstly, we were hurried off to the garden party and a public tea, which had been planned for our visit. The tea ended at six o'clock. A banquet began at eight o'clock after an hour of schnapps and skaals. We rose from the table around midnight, after which the dance began.

The next morning we were on our way. At Odense there is the

* This rule was still observed when I was present at a ballet performance forty-three years later, but in 1966 the custom was abandoned, and Copenhagen audiences now applaud, which seems more human and grateful.

shrine of St. Knud but the true shrine is a little corner cottage where Hans Christian Andersen was born. The birthplace of the cobbler's son is kept exactly as it was in his day. In it are preserved the top-hat he wore and the large umbrella, and, of course, some manuscripts, and the long rope with which he travelled, having a great fear of fire in the night at his inn.

At Ribe, a town of the Middle Ages, where the houses lean together over the cobbled streets, we looked out on the land filched by the Prussians in 1864, for it stood on the edge of the frontier. Here we found the inhabitants in great excitement over the impending plebiscite. The old town, once a place of great prosperity, had an important harbour on the west coast of Jutland but the sea had receded and left Ribe inland, dreaming of past glory. It seemed strange to find the inhabitants of this dead town stirred by modern politics. A few Danish soldiers in their bright blue uniforms strolled along the street, the ducks waddled down to the water through lush meadows, and the storks stood in their nests on the chimneys. It was a place where Time had gone to sleep.

Amid all this kindness and hospitality the deepest impression was made by something unrehearsed that we saw one Sunday evening as our yacht sailed from Kolding to Copenhagen. We rounded the southern end of the island of Samsö, with the sun setting behind our ship in wonderful glory. There were heavy rain clouds above a dark sea rifted with crimson. A white radiance rimmed the horizon, with a high cloud silhouetted in golden fire. In front of the ship rose a vast double rainbow of a singular intensity against the cool sky, the reflection in the water making a complete circle of prismatic colour. I watched it fade in the incoming night while the land darkened under the crimson sky. And there on the cliffs of the vanishing island, at its southern extremities, flashed the sapphire beams of two lighthouses spearing the darkness.

We were sent home to England in a new ship, loaded with souvenirs. I was given, together with a large blue bowl of butter and a case of cheese, two beautiful pieces of Copenhagen china, after visiting the famous factory. One was a tiger, the other a hippopotamus modelled by the Princess Waldemar, a gifted sculptress. Forty-eight years later in Monte Carlo, lunching at Baron Eugene de Rothschild's, a fellow guest was Princess Margrethe of Denmark. I mentioned my visit to Copenhagen in 1919, and that I was given a hippopotamus modelled by Princess Waldemar. "Does it have its mouth open or closed?"

asked the Princess. "Open," I replied, "my mother used to hang her rings on its tusks at night." "Ah," said Princess Margrethe, "I know that model. My mother was Princess Waldemar, and she made one hippopotamus with its mouth open and one with it closed."

CHAPTER EIGHT

John Masefield's Advice

I

SOON AFTER MY return from the Danish visit I went to Nottingham to see my mother. I was glad to find her so happy and content in her little house. I was looked upon with some wonder by the neighbours on each side after what seemed to them a Hans Andersen fairy tale. I presented some of the Danish cheese and butter to them. The tiger and the hippopotamus on the mantelshelf were much admired. I went to see William Kiddier and gentle Denholm Davis, who made me a present of the pencil portrait he had drawn of me when I was twenty-four, and exhibited at the Walker Art Gallery in Liverpool and the Nottingham Art Gallery, a portrait with a gossamer quality.

I divided my time between staying with my mother and with the Laings. It was like going from Sparta to Sybaris. After a week I returned to London. Zadia and her friends were in a state of excitement, ecstasy and exhaustion. The Russian Ballet was reopening at the Empire, following its triumphant summer season at the Alhambra. In the rehearsal room there was tremendous activity and on the stage great confusion, or so it seemed to me as I watched from the dark cavern of the house. The orchestra played and stopped, played and stopped for a trial ensemble. When next I was present at a ballet rehearsal forty years had gone by and I sat in the dark Opera House in Rome, again Leonide Massine's guest, watching him produce the *Snow Maiden*. Now, on the night of September 29th, 1919, out of all the apparent disorder of the rehearsals a perfectly rhythmical form had evolved, a synthesis of music, movement and colour.

On November 1st there was an unforgettable performance of *La Boutique Fantasque*, *Cléopâtre* and *Les Sylphides*, in honour of the Shah of Persia who was visiting London. And once I saw there King Alfonso. He was a faithful supporter of Diaghilev. For him they gave performances of *Les Sylphides*, *Schéhérazade*, and *The Three Cornered Hat*, the all-Spanish ballet.

I did much dramatic criticism in that year. The most memorable event was a production at the Lyric Theatre of *Romeo and Juliet*. Doris Keane, who had had a tremendous success with Edward Sheldon's play *Romance* in 1914, decided to appear as Juliet in Shakespeare's play, with her husband as Romeo. The play was most lavishly staged and the house was packed. An additional attraction was that Ellen Terry had been induced to come out of retirement at seventy-one to play the Nurse. The cast was well chosen. The first night promised to be a great event. The curtain rose upon an excited audience. For a time all went well until it became painfully clear that the role of Juliet was beyond the reach of Doris Keane. Romeo was equally ineffective. When the curtain rose on Scene III, 'A Room in Capulet's house' and Juliet's mother entered with the Nurse, Ellen Terry only got as far as her first line—"Now by my maidenhood, at twelve years old . . ." when a tremendous ovation held up the play. She wore a large picture hat tied under her chin. She was still lovely but prematurely aged. She bowed and bowed. Presently the play proceeded. But alas, when a few minutes later she came to the long monologue beginning—

> Even or odd, of all days in the year,
> Come Lammas-eve at night shall she be fourteen

she began to falter, memory betraying her, and came to a stop. There was a painful silence. She began again but the lines would not come. She tried. She stopped. Then a member of the company prompted her. She took the cue smiling bravely and stumbled on, somehow reaching the end. It was moving and pathetic.

There was one triumph that evening. Leon Quartermaine as Mercutio delivered the Queen Mab passage—"O, then, I see Queen Mab hath been with you." The voice, the verve, the perfectly timed words with their music and fire captured the audience, and until his exit in the fatal brawl—"A plague on both your houses, they have made worm's meat of me"—the evening was his. Very modestly he was out of the house when the final curtain fell. But neither he, nor the presence of Ellen Terry could save the play and after a brief run it was withdrawn. At the fall of the curtain, with the air of doom over it, how gracefully Ellen Terry came forward, her arms linked in those of Doris Keane and Basil Sidney, and said with infinite charm—"I do hope you will love these young people as much as I do."

On that memorable night, in a stall in front of me, there was a small boy wearing an Eton collar. He seemed very excited and applauded Ellen Terry vigorously. In the interval I spoke to the lady accompanying him. "Oh yes, you see Ellen Terry's his great-aunt." So the little boy was John Gielgud. Referring to that evening, forty-eight years later, John said, "Yes, it was me and the lady was my mother."

I saw Leon Quartermaine once again. I regret that I saw him only twice in his long theatrical career. *The Times*, writing of him on his ninetieth birthday in 1966, said that his Mercutio, and Buckingham in *Henry VIII*, rank as 'collector's pieces'. But I would add to this collection my second memorable experience of him, in the role of Ishak the Poet in James Elroy Flecker's *Hassan*. I sat in His Majesty's Theatre entranced by his performance in that exquisitely beautiful play. I felt sorrow for Flecker, some eight years dead, who had never known the magic of his creation, consummately revealed by a great actor.

II

In the spring of 1919, Philip Gibbs came back from the United States after a triumphant lecture tour. Known from coast to coast by his despatches, he had packed houses. Only the Irish element sounded a discordant note. It had been a very profitable tour. I visited him on his return and he said to me, after telling me about the tour, "My boy, you've got to make one!" I demurred at this proposal but he was insistent. "With your platform gift you'll have a great success." I pointed out that no one had invited me to go and that I was quite unknown in the United States. "Don't worry about that. I've told a lecture agent about you, and he'd like to come to London and hear you."

When I went to see Gibbs he was living in a large Georgian mansion at Stamford Hill. It had a two and a half acre garden. He was married, with one son, then at Oxford, the apple of his eye. Gibbs, a little fellow, had married a very tall girl. It was a marriage that started happily at twenty-one and continued so until death took his wife some forty years later. A devout Catholic, she had bought the mansion at Stamford Hill to run as a home for delinquent Catholic boys. "It takes all my pennies," said Gibbs, cheerfully. She was a little frightening at first sight, an intellectual who, starting from scratch, took a degree in science at London University at the age of fifty-six. Always capable, a planner, her serene manner hid a warm heart. She regarded Philip and myself as wayward children, to be guarded from the penalties our enthusiasms evoked.

Their house was always open to me. I should write 'houses' for she was a restless woman with a passion for moving. They lived in seven houses in the next fifteen years. There was a period when we were near neighbours, the Gibbses living in Cliveden Place, I nearby, in Eaton Terrace. This was the time of the comedy of the overcoats, a sure proof to Alice that we were a pair of irresponsible boys. I had noticed that my dark double-breasted overcoat had become rather short in the sleeves, and that somehow a hole had been burnt in it. I decided to give it away to an errand boy who came to the house. One day he returned with the overcoat. "My mother thinks I should bring it back, sir. She says it's not yours. It has the name 'Philip Gibbs' inside." I realised then that I must have taken it from Gibbs's house in mistake for my own. It explained the shortness of the sleeves, and the hole in the front, for Philip was a great cigarette smoker. I went over with the overcoat to Cliveden Place and explained to his wife. She looked at me with a cool eye. "Yes, it's Philip's coat. But the one you left looked so shabby that I thought it time for him to have a new one, so I gave it to the gardener's boy at our cottage." We decided to let things remain as they were, and the errand boy had Sir Philip's overcoat back.

In June I received a letter from the lecture agent in New York saying that he would like to arrange a lecture tour and would I suggest two subjects: it was better to have alternative titles. But he would like to hear me speak first, and proposed to be in London in July. I wrote back that I was interested in his proposal and I would try to arrange that he should hear me speak. This presented something of a difficulty, as I had no speaking engagements just then, but the ever helpful Holbrook Jackson at once saw a way out. "I'm a friend of the chairman of the London Rotary Club. They have a lunch at the Holborn Restaurant each month. I'll get him to invite you as a guest-speaker, and you can take your lecture agent there."

The agent arrived, and heard me. He was quite enthusiastic. "Yes, I think I can book you. You've certainly got it," he said as we left the luncheon. It? The word in those days of the Dolly Sisters and Mae West had a sexual inference. The agent explained. "I mean audience-appeal. You have it or you haven't." He warned me that it would not be easy to 'sell' me. I was not famous or notorious. So he departed and I wondered if he would change his mind while crossing the Atlantic. I learned that he had booked Sir Oliver Lodge, who had created a sensation with his book about spirits that smoked cigars and drank whiskys and sodas in their next existence. Bereaved parents with sons who had 'passed over' in the war made a gullible audience.

Before the agent left I produced a trump card. At one of Grant Richards's weekends at Cookham Dean I had met an American publisher. I put together my four volumes of verse to make one volume entitled *Collected Poems*, with American publication in view. It was to be my last venture in poetry for almost twenty-five years. I could not afford to keep company with my unremunerative Muse any longer. For this proposed collection I was fortunate enough to obtain a preface written by John Masefield, whose fame was great in the United States, which knew him personally. When I showed the publisher this he took the book at once. It was an amusing preface, touched with Masefield's generosity of spirit. He wrote:

> "If I may say so without offence Mr. Roberts is a little like the Mysterious Stranger in a novel. One says of him (as the Count says in the novel), He knows more of the French King than any man I have ever met; yet who is he? In conversation with him I understood him to say he is about fifty-four years old. In conversation with a friend of his I was told that he is twenty-five years old. For my own part I should have said that he is somewhere between those ages; yet it is difficult to be sure. When I think of the Mr. Roberts of real life, a very well-informed liberal-minded experienced journalist and war correspondent, who has seen much and many of the naval, military and political doings and persons of the last five years, I say with Mr. Justice Shallow—"He is old, he cannot choose but be old". When I think of the poems, I felt he must be young, not young enough perhaps to be carried away, or destroyed by the recent great events, but young enough to see them clearly, to respond to them, and to realise that the tragedy of them has been the tragedy of the young, the blasting of the young for the benefit and at the bidding of the old."

I had kept in touch with John Masefield since that happy encounter in 1918 in the train from Oxford. Upon my return from the Western Front I went to his house at Boar's Hill to see him. I was always welcomed by the family. There was a small theatre in his garden, the gift of American friends, Florence and Thomas Lamont, where he staged small plays. At the bottom of that garden I saw a half-naked tousle-headed youth wheeling two babies in a barrow. He did not look like a gardener's boy, so I enquired who he was. "Oh, that's a young poet living in my cottage, married to Nancy Nicholson, the painter's daughter—Robert Graves. Those are his children." The little boy, David, grew up, to be killed fighting in Burma, the little girl, Jenny, married the Rome correspondent of an English paper and died too young. There was another little boy in the garden, Masefield's only son, also doomed in the Second World War. I did not see Graves again until forty-eight years later when on June 20th, 1967, I attended the memorial service in Westminster Abbey for Masefield. Leonine, white-headed, he pronounced the eulogy for the Poet Laureate, our lifelong friend. From him I learned of the fate of those two babies in the wheelbarrow.

Early in 1919, at Masefield's I encountered John Drinkwater, just leaving. Our friendship started there. "You come from Nottingham," he said. "Did you know I lived there for three years working in an insurance office?" He told me that when he left school, aged sixteen, he went to Nottingham to work for the Northern Insurance Company. Its office was immediately under the old *Nottingham Journal* premises. Our experiences had been very similar in that city. We were both office boys at eight shillings a week; we both copied letters into a tissue-leaved letterbook, by damping the sheets and using a press, and we both had charge of the stamp-book. "I was very poor there and often short of food," said Drinkwater. "I used to buy rotten fruit in the Market Place to augment my threepenny lunch." Like me, he hated his office and felt a prisoner. He had no literary ambitions then, and knew nothing of Milton or Wordsworth. He wrote his first poem when he was eighteen. "I went in for amateur theatricals there and made my first appearance on the stage—and that led me to the Birmingham Repertory Theatre."

After three years Drinkwater was moved to a Birmingham branch and left Nottingham with no regrets. Now he was famous as one of the 'Georgian' poets and as a dramatist having written the highly successful play *Abraham Lincoln*. We had one more point of contact—he went to Oxford High School where one of the masters was B. O. Corbett, of my Shardlow Hall schoolmastering days. "B.O. has always remained for me the greatest outside-left who ever kicked a football," said Drinkwater. My next meeting with Drinkwater was in New York, where he had attended the American production of his play.

When I informed my lecture agent that my visit to America would coincide with the publication of *Collected Poems*, with Masefield's introduction, he had no more doubt. I was to go at the beginning of January for a three months' tour and give readings from my poems as well as lecture on aspects of the war and its personalities. As it chanced there would be two other Englishmen giving readings of their poems just then, Siegfried Sassoon and Drinkwater, they with a reputation, I with none. W. B. Yeats would also be there.

The approaching visit to America opened up another prospect. I was not happy about my position. I had turned down the chance to be converted into a permanent civil servant, just as five years earlier I had refused a 'safe' position as a local government officer. I was determined not to be diverted from a literary career. I had seemed to be on my way at Liverpool. Then the Ministry of Munitions had opened a path to London, irresistible to any ambitious young fellow. Now here I was, in the somewhat precarious position of a freelance. Fleet Street was overcrowded with journalists returned from the war, and journalism was not the street of adventure in which I wished to stay. I had already begun work on a novel but my immediate resources were too slender for the gamble. On returning from the Western Front I had decided to take a degree at Oxford, which I could now finance. Ever ambitious, I had my eye on the Presidency of the Union, with the Bar and politics in the offing, urged to this by an ex-President and barrister.

The preliminaries arranged, I went to Oxford for an interview with the Master of Balliol, to whom I had an introduction. If I had not taken a train that arrived one hour too early the course of my life might have been very different. 'There is a destiny that shapes our ends.' Having one hour to dispose of, I went into a café near Carfax. Presently four undergraduates entered and took an adjacent table. They were nice boys but as I listened to them I realised in what different worlds we lived. Between my age and theirs there had been a World War. Between our minds there was a whole lifetime. I was prematurely aged. As Masefield wrote, I was somewhere between twenty-five and fifty-four. These blithe youths with their schoolroom prattle and ignorance of life, my companions for the next three years? Clearly we belonged to different generations, different worlds, the pre-war and the post-war. It would never work. I paid my bill and went out sadly. When later I told the Master of my reversed decision he agreed with me. "You have made yourself a career. You are where most of these boys would like to be one day." I left Oxford, somewhat sorrowful but wiser. What I had missed I had missed. I was not the kind that could put back the clock. Some years later, a lecture guest at a Pembroke College club, I looked on the quick, eager young faces before me, envying them the zest of youth in such an atmosphere of intellectual excitement. It was strange to reflect that to them I was an enviable 'somebody'. They sir'd me and treated me with deference.

The American adventure offered a new prospect. It was a land of opportunity for young men with bright swords. Stories of rapid and phenomenal success came out of the United States. The condition of flux, of enterprise, of quick money, was there. Gibbs had returned after a tour of three months with five thousand pounds and profitable commissions from editors. Churchill, a young man of twenty-six in 1900, netted £1,000 in seven weeks. Mark Twain had presided at his first lecture. I had not their fame but I had a good story, a command of the platform and some ability with my pen. I began to think of America as an El Dorado where I might stay. This old European world was tired and cluttered with debts, taxes, and feuds. The 'brain-drain' of a later epoch had begun.

And then Fate played an astonishing card. Just before I departed for New York I was asked by a Fleet Street colleague, who wanted to go somewhere else, to 'cover' for his paper a public dinner at which Sir George Riddell, Lloyd George's Press officer and a newspaper owner, was being given his portrait painted by Orpen. "It's at the Savoy so it'll be a good dinner. You needn't stay to the end, only a couple of paragraphs," he said.

At the dinner I found myself sitting next to Sir Charles Starmer of Darlington, a name unknown to me. On our making acquaintance he asked if I was Cecil Roberts the war correspondent whose articles he had read. He then asked me what I was doing. I said I was going on a lecture tour to America, and might remain there. Within an hour he had offered me the editorship of any of his fifteen newspapers in the Provinces. He mentioned *The Nottingham Journal* among them. I tried not to show my astonishment, "*The Journal*!" I exclaimed.

Four years earlier I had been an 'unpaid pupil' there. I asked what salary he offered for editing the paper. "Would £750 for a start satisfy you?" I said it would but that I could not begin until after I had returned from my lecture tour, in April. He agreed to that. I then suggested that he might commission a series of articles on my impressions of the U.S.A. He thought that a good idea. We settled for ten articles for £100. I told him I was attracted to Nottingham as I had been born there.

Getting my hat in the cloakroom I reflected on (1) the value of living in London at the centre of things; (2) the 'flukes' of daily life; (3) the amazement in *The Nottingham Journal* office when, formerly an 'unpaid pupil', I came back an editor, aged twenty-seven; (4) the fact that I would be reunited with my mother and able to give her the easy life she merited; (5) what nonsense it was to teach children that hard work was always rewarded. By sitting next to a newspaper owner at a public dinner I had short-circuited by some twenty years the remote chance of an editor's chair; (6) the fact that in a provincial city I could save. I was a long way off the capital sum of £10,000 at thirty-five that I had set as a target on that evening in my bedroom, eleven years ago, when, on the sudden death of my father, my mother and I seemed faced with destitution. The audacious vow I had then made was not likely to be fulfilled but by 1920, at the age of 27, I had reached a salary of £750 a year, and I could feel that I had gone some way towards realising the independence I sought.

When I informed John Masefield of the impending lecture tour he wrote me a letter of advice, illustrated. He warned me against the constitutional gravity of the English lecturer. "Practise especially a great variety of manner, get it across with plenty of 'pep', as you will presently learn to call it. If you can intersperse your talk with songs and dances they will like you all the better. I mean this seriously." To illustrate his meaning he drew two inimitable sketches, one of a man doing a fantastic dance, the other of an orator with an extended arm in the grand manner. There was much truth, I found, in his counsel. (Illustration, p. 241.)

III

My lecture agent in New York wrote to say that he had booked twenty lectures which would only cover my passage and hotel expenses. My arrangement with him was that he paid all travelling expenses and that we divided the net sum, if any. He charged a lecture fee of $100 to $150. He left it to me, such being the circumstances, whether I should undertake the tour. I did not hesitate for a moment. It was a great adventure; and now my return ground was assured. When I got to America I discovered that the lecture fee should have been doubled if one was entertained for one had to work hard as an exhibited guest, performing the social graces. Often they wanted a little speech at a lunch or dinner party. You spoke not sang for your supper. My agent hoped that on my advent, after interviews, etc., there might be additional bookings. He was nervous about the margin but I was not dismayed—indeed I was elated at the prospect of seeing a new world even if I did not earn a dollar.

I booked my passage to sail from Liverpool towards the end of December. A former colleague at the Ministry of Munitions, an Englishman who had been educated at Columbia University, and had now returned to his home in New York, arranged accommodation for me at the Columbia University Club; and in his unfailing kindness Holbrook Jackson organised a farewell dinner for me. It was done with his flair for organisation. The menu card, beautifully designed, bore the emblem of a winged Eros, charioted and drawing his bow. The hand of the gourmet was revealed in the menu itself, all for seven and sixpence! Huitres Natives, Hors d'Oeuvre Spéciaux, Bisque écrévisses, Sole Clarence, Côte de Pré-salé Alsacienne, Pommes Annette, Céleri-rave à la Möelle, Faison en Casserole, Pommes Colbrettes, Salade Mâche, Asperges Sauce Mousseuse, Pêche Glacée Melba, Gaufrettes, Café.

The dinner was held on December 19th, 1919, in the Duke's Salon at the Holborn Restaurant. There was a company of fifty. The chairman was my old chief Burton Chadwick, who proposed the toast to me which Jackson seconded. 'The Younger Generation' was proposed by Philip Gibbs and replied to by Alec Waugh, aged twenty-one, already famous with his first novel, *The Loom of Youth*, and home from a war prisoners' camp in Germany. The gathering was composed of friends woven into the tapestry of my life, William Kiddier, Denholm Davis, Harry Brodie, Charles Prescott, Keighley Snowden, Paul Bewsher, etc. It was a case of 'Youth on the prow, and Pleasure at the helm'. Forty-seven years later, when I was lunching with Alec, he asked me if I had a copy of the menu card of that dinner. "It was a wonderful evening. Good food, good speeches, when we were all young and hopeful." He wished he had a copy of the menu. I found one and gave it to him. It had a melancholy note in July, 1966. We were now a pair of old gentlemen, happily lively enough at seventy-four and sixty-eight respectively. Of that blithe company of fifty in 1919 only five were left.

I went home to spend a few days with my mother in her little house before sailing. It was sad I could not spend Christmas with her. I had been warned, since I should arrive in New York in the depth of winter, that I must be provided with goloshes ('rubbers' in U.S.A.) to keep my feet dry in freezing slush. In a mood of elation and great extravagance I provided myself with something else. I bought for twenty pounds a sable-lined overcoat with a deep astrakhan collar, intent on an impressive and warm entry into the New World. It was secondhand and reputed to have been the property of a derelict Russian Grand Duke. He must have been a very tall man, for it nearly buried me. When two years later I had it cut and reclothed I got a fur stole out of it for my mother. My elder brother was amused and critical as usual. He surveyed me in the splendour of my fur coat and said—"Where's the Circus?"

My mother hid her excitement at my good fortune under her habitual stoic calm but I could see that the prospect of my returning to Nottingham and living with her made that Christmas a very special one. In turn, William Kiddier, though sad with the loss of his only son, gave a little dinner for me. Then, on a dark December afternoon of 1919 I boarded the Atlantic liner at Liverpool and we glided down the Mersey to the open sea, New York bound. From the rail I watched the twin towers of the Royal Liver building fade from sight. Next came the line of lights on the Egremont Promenade along which I had so often walked from my lodging to my office in the days when I was lonely and apprehensive about my future. Could it be that only four years had passed between that first nervous embarkation and this, carrying me to a New World? I was now twenty-seven, with Time in hand, ambitious and hopeful.

Our liner crossed the Mersey Bar, unmenaced now. I watched England fade into the darkness behind us. Arthur Hugh Clough's poem, with its first and last lines, came to mind as I turned to go below:

Say not the struggle naught availeth . . .
But westward look, the land is bright.

The end of the second volume of this Autobiography.

Appendix I

JAMES ELROY FLECKER
1884–1915

In Memoriam

Weave for his brow the laurel wreath, he lies
Forever dumb, the lips that sang so well
Are locked in silence 'neath the alien skies,
And all the tales are told that he shall tell.

Ah, mourn a little, for his life was sweet,
And silence is too solemn after song,
He has gone hence ere men had time to greet
One who but seldom sang nor tarried long.

So sweet and light his singing, scarcely heard,
Only the silence touched our ears with sense
Of something void, as when a fluting bird
No more breaks on the valley's somnolence.

He has gone hence, —ah, whither who shall say?
Perchance he treads the trackless paths of Night,
Long wearied in the Caravan of Day,
Perchance he seeks the Gardens of Delight.

And thro' dim-shaded valleys journeys on,
A moon-led pilgrim seeking for the Thing
Which dreamers spake of in the days long gone,
And poets sang of in a Grecian Spring.

It may be he has found those mounts of snow
All flushed with rose, those glades of endless sleep,
And knows the truths which many sought to know,
And wonders now why men grow sick and weep,

Why some are sad, as he was sad in days
When Beauty was too beautiful and frail,
When a dear voice was sweet beyond all praise,
Rising at night-time from a starlit vale.

O nevermore for him the sunset fades,
Nor ocean lifts her waters to the moon,
No more his feet shall wander in the glades,
His soul with mystic rapture deep aswoon;

For him no caravans with sound of bells
Move from the Syrian cities shadow-dim,
Nor long-lashed maidens dream by palm-girt wells,
Their phantom world is all unknown to him.

He holds a wider converse with the stars,
And roams unfettered through the jewelled night,
His song flows in the wind 'mid nenuphars
Swaying and rustling in the dawning light.

Weave for his brow the laurel, for his name
What brighter memory than those sweet songs
Sung in a too-brief life that knew not fame,
Yet gave this wealth which now to Time belongs.

Appendix II

THE DOVER PATROL

We are the grey destroyers,
  The hornets of the Fleet;
The tall ships, our employers,
  Disdain our lonely beat;
Through night and day we prowl about,
Take one turn in and one turn out,
  Not very far from Dover;
Through every hour of the twenty-four
We hang about the Huns' back door—
Lord! what a life for a young sea rover!

We make no claim to beauty,
  The big guns know us not;
We never dress for duty—
  One suit is all we've got.
We oil ourselves, for speed's our role,
We'd race aught floating to the Pole
  And back again to Dover;
Yet every hour of the twenty-four
We bar the dismal Huns' back door—
Lord! what a life for a young sea rover!

We barter with the chances
  That snatch our living breath,
For danger so entrances—
  We run full speed to death;
"The Lords of the Admiralty regret
That H.M.S.—"—and then forget
  The T.B.D. from Dover,
Yet every hour of the twenty-four
Somebody watches the Huns' back door—
Lord! what an end for a young sea rover!

Dover 1916

Appendix III

SPRINGTIME IN COOKHAM DEAN

How marvellous and fair a thing
It is to see an English Spring,
He cannot know, who has not seen
The cherry trees at Cookham Dean,
Who has not seen the blossoms lie
Like snowdrifts 'gainst a cloudless sky
And found the beauty of the way
Through lanes bedecked with petalled may.
It is a rare, a holy sight,
To see the hill with blossoms white,
To feel the air about one flowing
With the silent rapture growing
In the hidden heart of things
That yearn, that flower, put forth wings,
And show their splendours one by one
Beneath the all-rejoicing sun.

Perhaps the joy of all the earth
Moved through us on that day of mirth
When in the morning air we trod
Hills sacred to the river god
And heard behind us as we ran
The laughter of a hidden Pan,
Who dropped his flute because he heard
The artless cadence of a bird;
And we, who love the southern sky,
One moment ceased to wonder why
A poet in his exile cried
To see an English Spring, and sighed
Because a chaffinch on the bough
Sings and shakes the blossom now.

For who would sigh for southern skies
Who once had seen the paradise
Of this new Eden where the flowers
Drench the woods with odorous showers,
And give delight till the sense sickens
With the rapture April quickens?
This heaven where petals fall as stars,
This paradise where beauty bars
Its dew-refreshed, embowered portals
Against the clamouring of mortals,
And from green altars in dim shrines
Calls to the riven soul that pines
For leafy solitude, and prayer
That murmurs through the branches there.

When Spring in her ascension fills
The chalice of the sacred hills
With blossom like the driven snow
And longing takes the heart, then go
On pilgrimage to Cookham Dean,
And through dim aisles of shadowed green
Dappled with the light that trembles
Round each tree, till it resembles
A maiden letting fall her hair
In cataracts of gold—draw near
The secret that brings Englishmen,
Faithful through exile, home again;
And watch the miracle of dawn,
And hear the lark, with wings upborne
Into the cloudless empyrean,
Pour his lucent, quenchless paean,
And feel the awakened senses start
In wonder at the artless art
Of orchards all in blossom showing
Against the blue of heaven glowing
Through great depths of luminous light;
Then from the windy, woodland height,
Through dim ravines where tall trees wait
For day's decline to gild their state,
And touch them with caressing fingers
Of the sun-god whose smile lingers
Upon their limbs, by paths that wind
Into the valley, go—and find
The village by the water's edge

And listen to the wind-stirred sedge
That by the churchyard whispers—go
And tread the woodland paths I know,
For whosoever has not seen
The cherry trees at Cookham Dean,
Who has not roamed its hills and found
Delight in that enchanted ground,
He cannot know, he cannot tell,
Where Spring performs her miracle.

Appendix IV

FUTILITY

They send me, Charles, long letters on your death,
Full of fair phrases culled from poetry
That do not blind me—let them save their breath;
The nectared lies of immortality,
The sounding rhetoric, the pompous phrase,
The talk of 'supreme sacrifice', the 'great
Reward'—what are these 'gainst your withered days,
Your dear lost face, the squalor of your fate?
That you were brave, I know, but still you clung
To life that meant so much; they say you cried
In that last hour, feeling you were so young,
And desperately fought for life, and died.
These letters, Charles, they mock me with their lies,
Their borrowed phrases that belittle life
And love and laughter—I can see your eyes
As once they glowed, your body like a knife
Tempered and flashing in a summer sea,
Or hear your voice enraptured over books,
Or in the bathroom singing merrily
At early morn, and days in river nooks
And tennis sets—these memories all seem
Like ghosts that haunt your room now you are gone,
And make me think your end is but a dream,
How can it be the end—at twenty-one?
But when I read these letters then I know
You will not come again, nor does their praise
Lighten the heaviness of this great blow:
I cannot kiss your brow, nor see the place
Where they have left you; as they write of 'fame',
Your 'splendid gift', my only thought is this—
What will they care ten years hence for your name,
Who cares a damn who died at Salamis?

Appendix V

PRAYER FOR A PILOT

Lord of Sea and Earth and Air,
Listen to a Pilot's prayer—
Send him wind that's steady and strong,
Grant that his engine sings the song
Of flawless tone, by which he knows
It shall not fail him where he goes;
Landing, gliding, in curve, half-roll—
Grant him, O Lord, a full control,
That he may learn in heights of Heaven
The rapture altitude has given,
That he shall know the joy they feel
Who ride Thy realms on Birds of Steel.

Index